Learn Microsoft Powe

Build customized business applications without
writing any code

Matthew Weston

BIRMINGHAM - MUMBAI

Learn Microsoft PowerApps

Commissioning Editor: Kunal Chaudhari
Acquisition Editor: Shriram Shekhar
Content Development Editor: Ruvika Rao
Senior Editor: Rohit Singh
Technical Editor: Pradeep Sahu
Copy Editor: Safis Editing
Project Coordinator: Francy Puthiry
Proofreader: Safis Editing
Indexer: Pratik Shirodkar
Production Designer: Aparna Bhagat

First published: November 2019

Production reference: 1291119

Published by Packt Publishing Ltd.
Livery Place
35 Livery Street
Birmingham
B3 2PB, UK.

ISBN 978-1-78980-582-6

www.packt.com

For my wife, Laura, and my sons, Eddie and Reggie, who are the inspiration for everything that I do.

For Mom and Dad, without whose support growing up, I may never have had these opportunities.

- Matthew Weston

Subscribe to our online digital library for full access to over 7,000 books and videos, as well as industry leading tools to help you plan your personal development and advance your career. For more information, please visit our website.

Why subscribe?

- Spend less time learning and more time coding with practical eBooks and Videos from over 4,000 industry professionals

- Improve your learning with Skill Plans built especially for you

- Get a free eBook or video every month

- Fully searchable for easy access to vital information

- Copy and paste, print, and bookmark content

Did you know that Packt offers eBook versions of every book published, with PDF and ePub files available? You can upgrade to the eBook version at www.packt.com and as a print book customer, you are entitled to a discount on the eBook copy. Get in touch with us at customercare@packtpub.com for more details.

At www.packt.com, you can also read a collection of free technical articles, sign up for a range of free newsletters, and receive exclusive discounts and offers on Packt books and eBooks.

Contributors

About the author

Matthew Weston is an Office 365 and SharePoint consultant based in the Midlands in the United Kingdom. Matthew is a passionate evangelist of Microsoft technology, blogging and presenting about Office 365 and SharePoint at every opportunity. He has been creating and developing with PowerApps since it became generally available at the end of 2016. Usually, Matthew can be seen presenting within the community about PowerApps and Flow at SharePoint Saturdays, PowerApps and Flow User Groups, and Office 365 and SharePoint User Groups. Matthew is a **Microsoft Certified Trainer** (**MCT**) and a **Microsoft Certified Solutions Expert** (**MCSE**) in Productivity.

I would like to thank Laura, my wife, for supporting me throughout the writing of this book. She has kept me focused and free of distraction. She was as important to the creation of this book as I was.

I would also like to mention the CDE, Ruvika Rao, who has been a great source of information for a first-time author, providing guidance and lots of constructive feedback. I would like to thank Shriram Shekhar for giving me this opportunity.

About the reviewers

Danilo Capuano is a Microsoft Dynamics 365 CE Technical Manager and Microsoft Certified Trainer with over 13 years' experience in IT, having been involved in all phases of ALM. Currently, Danilo works for AGIC Technology, a Microsoft Gold partner, in the role of Microsoft Dynamics 365 CE Technical Delivery Manager and Naples Delivery Center Head. He is involved in the CRM service line and manages and leads both technical resources and projects' technical phases, dealing with everything from Microsoft DevOps methodology to delivering innovative solutions that help the customer's digital transformation.

Sandeep Kumar is an enterprise solutions architect with over 20 years of IT experience working in large corporations. He has worked as a software engineer, systems analyst, database administrator, solutions architect, manager, and IT consultant. He has designed and developed many enterprise solutions in banking, hi-tech, and government domains. His skills and expertise include CRM (Dynamics 365), BW/BI (Cognos and Microsoft BI), SharePoint, Oracle, Java, Angular, PowerApps, Azure, SQL Server, microservices, TOGAF, DevOps, CI/CD, Linux, Unix, application, and web servers. He has various certifications including Microsoft and Scrum Master.

He also enjoys driving his Mustang GT convertible, doing yoga, reading books, and listening to music.

> *I would like to thank my wife, Shefali, and my kids, Aisha and Ishan, for their constant support, without whom this wouldn't have been accomplished.*
>
> *Special thanks to my parents and my brother, Pradeep, for their super support and guidance.*

Packt is searching for authors like you

If you're interested in becoming an author for Packt, please visit `authors.packtpub.com` and apply today. We have worked with thousands of developers and tech professionals, just like you, to help them share their insight with the global tech community. You can make a general application, apply for a specific hot topic that we are recruiting an author for, or submit your own idea.

Table of Contents

Section 4: Working with Model-Driven Apps

Preface

I would like to take this opportunity to welcome you and thank you for choosing this book. With *Learn Microsoft PowerApps*, you will learn how to build functional canvas apps and model-driven apps using the Microsoft PowerApps application. Throughout the book, you will not only learn about its components and what they do but also put them into practice by incrementally building an app through a number of labs.

The book itself endeavors to introduce new topics in each chapter, gradually introducing more and more of PowerApps' functionality to help you understand how you can continually improve your apps to build something that is just as powerful as a custom-built application.

The book is structured into four sections:

1. The first four chapters deal with the fundamentals of PowerApps, such as how to use the studio, how to publish, and how to create a basic app. This book is intended to be used by a number of different audiences; however, it assumes no prior understanding of what PowerApps is and how it works. Therefore, we will talk through how to set yourself up in terms of licensing, look at how you can install the apps, and then cover how to start to create basic apps.

2. The next four chapters build upon the basic understanding of PowerApps gained in section 1 and begin to address how to build functionality. These are the main chapters, where you will start to see your app take shape as we introduce the controls and look at how they can be used to achieve different effects within our apps. We'll also look at data and connectors to begin to build dynamic content into our apps.

3. Next, we'll begin to add a layer of complexity to our apps by diving into some of the more advanced functionality that you can use within PowerApps, including the ability to use GPS and barcodes to allow your users to do more with their app, especially when the app is being used on a mobile device. Within this section, we will also look at some of the more complex tasks, such as being able to provide offline capabilities as well as introducing security.

4. Finally, we'll look at model-driven apps. This is addressed separately as, commonly, canvas apps and model-driven apps have very different audiences and require development in drastically different ways.

Throughout the book, we will be building an app that relates to a fictional company called Griffton IT Solutions, and we will be using PowerApps to build an asset management app. In each chapter, we will build more and more functionality into the app to leverage each topic that we discuss and to allow you to put the techniques into practice. All of the files that are used within the labs can either be created manually or can be downloaded from the GitHub repository: `https://github.com/PacktPublishing/Learn-Microsoft-PowerApps`.

Updates to PowerApps

PowerApps is subject to frequent updates from Microsoft. As a result of this, there may be times when the illustrations or explanations within this book appear out of date. This is purely a consequence of working within an evergreen platform, so please don't let this stop you from following through and building the examples. While the interfaces may change, the techniques and thought processes that we introduce in the book are likely to remain the same regardless of what else comes along in the world of PowerApps.

We hope that you enjoy the book and find it useful, and we wish you the very best in creating some rich, powerful, and enjoyable PowerApps.

Who this book is for

This book is intended for anyone who has an interest in developing PowerApps. Whether you are a developer or a business user, this book will provide you with the key information needed to develop solutions to your business problems.

What this book covers

Chapter 1, *Introducing PowerApps*, gives a high-level overview of what PowerApps is, how it is licensed, and the development environment.

Chapter 2, *Creating Your First Canvas PowerApp*, is where we take our first steps in creating our first canvas app. We will explore the types of canvas app that we can create, looking at the use cases and also the various options that we have available to us.

Chapter 3, *Creating Apps from SharePoint*, takes a look at the close relationship between SharePoint Online and PowerApps and how the two technologies work closely together. We will also look at how to create apps from SharePoint as well as how to create a list form.

Chapter 4, *Publishing and Leveraging PowerApps*, looks at how we can take our app and leverage it across a number of platforms. We will explore how we can use our apps on mobile devices, SharePoint, and Microsoft Teams.

Chapter 5, *Exploring Controls*, focuses on the various controls that we can add into our apps to build a rich interactive user interface. We will also look at use cases for the controls as well as some of the key properties to be aware of.

Chapter 6, *Exploring Formulas*, discusses how we can write logic within PowerApps. We will explore the formula bar and look at how we can use formulas to interact with various data types such as text, dates, boolean values, and more.

Chapter 7, *Working with Data*, investigates how we can store and interact with data within our PowerApps, focusing on the functionality provided by collections and variables as well as introducing forms.

Chapter 8, *Introducing Connectors*, covers the way that we can connect our apps to services, both services within Office 365 and services provided by other suppliers. We will also look at the difference between standard and premium connectors, as well as creating our own custom connectors.

Chapter 9, *Using GPS in PowerApps*, looks at how we can start to use key functionality afforded to us by mobile devices to track location data and use it within our app.

Chapter 10, *Working with Images and Barcodes*, looks again at utilizing the functionality of the mobile device, this time using the camera to capture images and data from barcodes.

Chapter 11, *Securing Your PowerApps*, explores how various elements of security can be applied and what the impact is on the app itself. We will start from the data source and then consider how we can apply security to the various screens within the app itself.

Chapter 12, *Working Offline*, allows us to explore how we can provide our app the capability to still function even when we lose a connection to the data source.

Chapter 13, *Using Power Automate with PowerApps*, introduces another element of the Power Platform, Power Automate, which we can use to offload heavy processing tasks.

Chapter 14, *Using Azure with PowerApps*, allows us to begin to integrate services provided by Microsoft Azure into our PowerApps by exploring some of the commonly used services and the connectors that allow us to utilize them.

Chapter 15, *Introducing Model-Driven Apps*, sees us open the door to the Common Data Service, the built-in database that can be used to store data directly within the Power Platform. We will investigate entities, views, and how to build entity relationships.

Chapter 16, *Creating Model-Driven Apps*, builds on the Common Data Service to create a model-driven app that allows us to directly interact with the database and provide interfaces for the user.

Chapter 17, *Exploring Environments within Our Tenancy*, allows us to look at environments and understand how they can be used to assist with governance around PowerApps.

To get the most out of this book

In order to get the most out of this book, it is recommended that you have a basic understanding of Office 365 as we will be interacting with various elements of it as we develop our apps. It is assumed that you have a basic knowledge of the following:

- SharePoint Online
- Microsoft Teams

If you have ever written formulas using Microsoft Excel, the thought processes that you used to achieve that will help you to more closely follow the creation of formulas within PowerApps.

Download the example code files

You can download the example code files for this book from your account at www.packt.com. If you purchased this book elsewhere, you can visit www.packtpub.com/support and register to have the files emailed directly to you.

You can download the code files by following these steps:

1. Log in or register at www.packt.com.
2. Select the **Support** tab.
3. Click on **Code Downloads**.
4. Enter the name of the book in the **Search** box and follow the onscreen instructions.

Once the file is downloaded, please make sure that you unzip or extract the folder using the latest version of:

- WinRAR/7-Zip for Windows
- Zipeg/iZip/UnRarX for Mac
- 7-Zip/PeaZip for Linux

The code bundle for the book is also hosted on GitHub at `https://github.com/PacktPublishing/Learn-Microsoft-PowerApps`. In case there's an update to the code, it will be updated on the existing GitHub repository.

We also have other code bundles from our rich catalog of books and videos available at `https://github.com/PacktPublishing/`. Check them out!

Download the color images

We also provide a PDF file that has color images of the screenshots/diagrams used in this book. You can download it here: `https://static.packt-cdn.com/downloads/9781789805826_ColorImages.pdf`.

Code in Action

To see the code being executed, please visit the following link: `http://bit.ly/2OKRdRZ`.

Conventions used

There are a number of text conventions used throughout this book.

`CodeInText`: Indicates code words in text, database table names, folder names, filenames, file extensions, pathnames, dummy URLs, user input, and Twitter handles. Here is an example: "Understanding conditional logic and how you can define branches using `If` and `Switch` statements."

A block of code is set as follows:

```
StartsWith("Griffton IT Assets","Griffton")
EndsWith("Griffton IT Assets","ts")
```

When we wish to draw your attention to a particular part of a code block, the relevant lines or items are set in bold:

```
Navigate(Welcome,ScreenTransition.Cover)
```

Bold: Indicates a new term, an important word, or words that you see onscreen. For example, words in menus or dialog boxes appear in the text like this. Here is an example: "This type of logic is known as a **condition**."

Warnings or important notes appear like this.

Tips and tricks appear like this.

Get in touch

Feedback from our readers is always welcome.

General feedback: If you have questions about any aspect of this book, mention the book title in the subject of your message and email us at customercare@packtpub.com.

Errata: Although we have taken every care to ensure the accuracy of our content, mistakes do happen. If you have found a mistake in this book, we would be grateful if you would report this to us. Please visit www.packtpub.com/support/errata, selecting your book, clicking on the Errata Submission Form link, and entering the details.

Piracy: If you come across any illegal copies of our works in any form on the Internet, we would be grateful if you would provide us with the location address or website name. Please contact us at copyright@packt.com with a link to the material.

If you are interested in becoming an author: If there is a topic that you have expertise in and you are interested in either writing or contributing to a book, please visit authors.packtpub.com.

Reviews

Please leave a review. Once you have read and used this book, why not leave a review on the site that you purchased it from? Potential readers can then see and use your unbiased opinion to make purchase decisions, we at Packt can understand what you think about our products, and our authors can see your feedback on their book. Thank you!

For more information about Packt, please visit packt.com.

Section 1: Getting Started with PowerApps

This section includes the first four chapters of this book and is designed to help you to understand the absolute basics of PowerApps. It will help you first of all to gain an understanding of the technology and then to start taking your first steps in PowerApp development and the use of PowerApps.

Chapter 1, *Introducing PowerApps*, doesn't go into any technical depth with regards to creating PowerApps, but really looks at what PowerApps is as a product, introducing the development environment and some of the considerations that surround the product such as licensing.

The second chapter will begin our journey with PowerApps by creating our first canvas app. This will focus on how you can create apps specifically for tablet and mobile devices, and how you can start to modify the basic app settings to start giving the app its identity. We will also take the first steps in building the app that we will continually build throughout this book.

In the third chapter, we will look at the close relationship between PowerApps and SharePoint and how this technology is starting to transform SharePoint user interfaces. It will show you how you can quickly and easily create an app directly from SharePoint, as well as create forms to improve the way in which users interact with lists.

The final chapter in this section will look at ways in which you can leverage the app once it has been developed. We will look at the ways in which you can access it through the browser or a mobile device, as well as how the apps can be integrated within other areas of Office 365.

This chapter includes the following chapters:

- Chapter 1, *Introducing PowerApps*
- Chapter 2, *Creating Your First Canvas PowerApp*
- Chapter 3, *Creating Apps from SharePoint*
- Chapter 4, *Publishing and Leveraging PowerApps*

Introducing PowerApps

1

In this chapter, we will look at some of the basic concepts of PowerApps at a high level, and look at where we can access the various aspects that add depth to our PowerApps. We will also look at some of the out of the box apps that are provided by PowerApps, in order to give you some good examples of what is easily achievable.

We will also look at the licensing around PowerApps so that you understand how they are charged for, as well as the levels of functionality available with each type of license. This is so you can plan for any specific licenses which you may need during the development of your apps.

Finally, we will look at the development environment, specifically the PowerApps portal and the studio, as part of the learning process is just finding out where information and components are located.

In this chapter, we will cover the following topics:

- Understanding PowerApps
- Understanding PowerApps licensing
- Understanding the types of app
- The start screen
- What are templates?
- Using PowerApps Studio

By the end of this chapter, you will have an understanding of the fundamentals of PowerApps and what is possible within it. You will start your PowerApps journey by discovering what apps are included and how you can get started.

Technical requirements

In order to follow this and all the subsequent chapters in this book, you will need to have access to Microsoft PowerApps. As we will be exploring both standard and premium features, I would recommend that you sign up for a PowerApps Community Plan at https://powerapps.microsoft.com/en-us/communityplan/.

Understanding PowerApps

PowerApps is an ever-growing part of the Microsoft Office 365 ecosystem, where developers and business users alike are empowered to create apps. In the past, for this to be achieved with SharePoint, you would have to use products such as InfoPath, where you could combine custom logic with a number of visual components to extend the user experience:

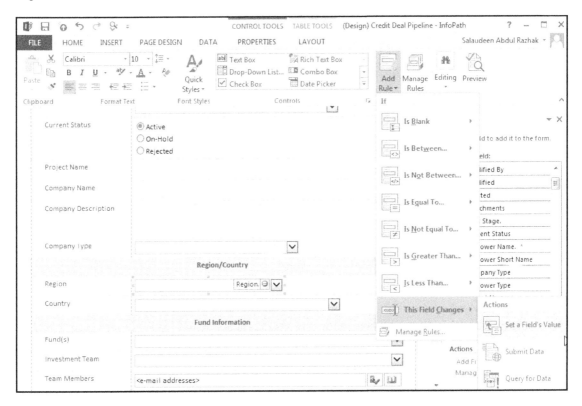

Figure 1.1: InfoPath as an editing application

PowerApps are created using visual tools that are provided through the browser and remove the dependency on needing additional applications to be installed on the desktop. However, this also builds into the Microsoft vision of mobility, where a user can work on their app anywhere in the world, at any time, from any device.

PowerApps aren't written with code; instead, they are created with formulas, similar to Microsoft Excel, a tool that the majority of the modern workforce are familiar with. For example, if we wanted to combine or concatenate strings in Excel, we would use the following formula:

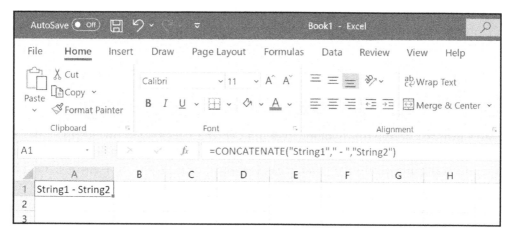

Figure 1.2: Formulas in Microsoft Excel

If we compare this to doing the same within PowerApps, you will see the similarities between the two products:

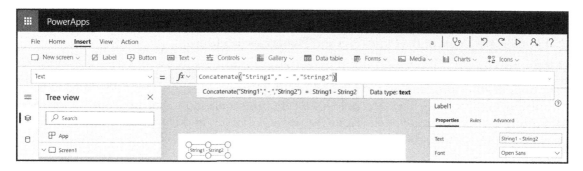

Figure 1.3: Formulas in Microsoft PowerApps

With this familiar approach to building logic, you don't need to be a developer to start creating solutions to business problems. For developers, PowerApps can be enriched using custom-developed functionality that can be deployed to and called from Azure, meaning that PowerApps is a tool that everyone on the IT spectrum can take advantage of.

From personal experience, I find PowerApps to be an excellent prototyping tool. Due to the drag and drop nature of its design, I can quickly and easily place components on a screen to establish a basic look and feel for an app while also connecting to some of the more rudimentary data sources, such as an Excel spreadsheet or a SharePoint list.

Before we dive into how we create apps, we should explore PowerApps' licensing options, since their cost will be a huge influence on the design decisions you make when creating apps.

Understanding PowerApps licensing

There are a number of options available when it comes to licensing PowerApps. Like all of Microsoft's products, there are differing levels of license available, which will govern what functionality you can use or what connectors you have available to you. As of 1st October 2019, PowerApps licensing has undergone quite a radical change, and the following sections will explain what the key licensing aspects are.

Seeded apps

PowerApps is not included with the home versions of Office 365; however, it is included with most of the business licenses and all of the enterprise licenses. This means that the majority of Office 365 users will have the ability to create and use PowerApps to enhance, extend, and customize their Office applications. This is now what is known as seeded apps; that is, they are a part of the Office 365 and Dynamics 365 licenses.

Since they are a part of the Office 365 and Dynamics 365 packages, they do not cost you or your organization anything on top of your existing license. The only thing you need to be aware of is that you only have access to a subset of the connectors that are available on the Microsoft Power Platform. For example, Azure, SQL Server, and Dynamics connectors are considered premium, and therefore not available at this license level.

Per-user plans

Per-user plans allow you to pay for a license for a single user, which allows them to access the full capabilities of PowerApps and Flow. The capabilities that are included in this plan were previously split between PowerApps Plan 1 and PowerApps Plan 2. However, in a more simplified model, the per-user plan encapsulates all of the functionality that the old plans offered.

The types of functionality that this plan unlocks for you include the ability to use the data gateway, which allows you to connect to on-premises data sources. It also gives you access to all of the premium connectors, as well as the ability to create custom connectors. We will explore connectors in more detail in Chapter 8, *Introducing Connectors*.

Upgraded licensing gives you access to the management and administration areas of PowerApps, including the ability to use the **Common Data Service (CDS)** (introduced in Chapter 15, *Introducing Model-Driven Apps*) and the ability to fully utilize environments (introduced in Chapter 17, *Exploring Environments within Our Tenancy*).

 It is worth noting that if your app uses premium functionality, both the PowerApp Creator and the PowerApp User will need to have a relevant license assigned to them. For example, if we were using a premium connector, both the creator and the user would require a per user plan.

Per-user plans cost $40 per user, per month, and allows those users to run unlimited apps. If an organization doesn't want to license every user, there is an alternative, which is the per-app plan.

Per-app plan

The per-app plan is the newest type of licensing to be introduced by Microsoft and has been a response to the community suggesting that paying for a per-user plan for all users, when we only have one or two apps, is too expensive. Therefore, the per-app plan allows you to license just a single app for all the users who are part of your organization. The advantage of this approach is that you are still able to unlock the full capability of PowerApps for all the creators and users who are working with this app.

The cost of the per-app plan is $10 per user, per app, per month. It should be understood that, in the context of this license, an app allows you to create two apps, which can either be two canvas apps, two model-driven apps, or a mix of the two.

Community Plan

If you want to really explore the capabilities of PowerApps without the license costs, you can create a free development environment using the **PowerApps Community Plan**. This is an environment that gives you complete access to the full capabilities of PowerApps; however, only a single user can use this plan, which means you can't share the apps with anyone else:

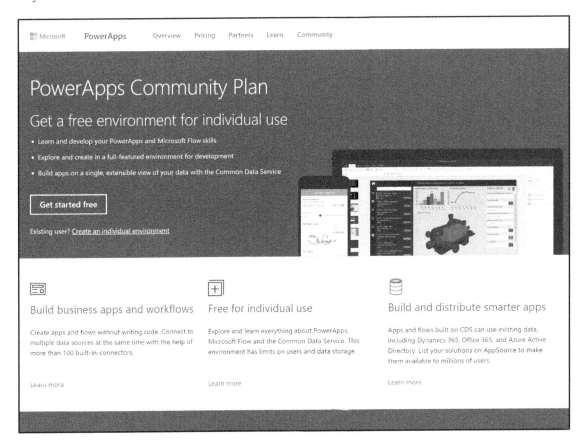

Figure 1.4: PowerApps Community Plan home screen

To sign up for this plan, navigate to `https://powerapps.microsoft.com/en-us/communityplan/` and click on **Get started free**. You will need to enter your work email address, that is, your Office 365 email address, so that the demo environment can be associated with you:

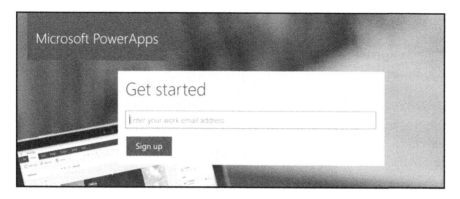

Figure 1.5: PowerApps Community Plan sign up screen

Once you have completed the signup process, a new environment will be created for you, generally with your name associated with it, for example, Matthew Weston's environment, where you can start to create and test your PowerApps.

 This will be a good place for you to build the app that we will create as we proceed through the labs, since some of the elements that we'll require are features that are provided by the per user or per app (premium) plans.

Now that we have looked at how much it's going to cost us to create an app, let's have a look at what we can actually create.

Understanding the types of apps

When creating a PowerApp, there are two distinct types of app, both of which have very different applications. Before you start creating apps, you should have a clear understanding of what these two types are and what benefits they bring. This will allow you to make the right selection and therefore create a great app that will add value to your organization. Both types of app are designed to be codeless and therefore within the realm of the ability of IT professionals and power users; however, developers can add a lot of value by developing code and calling it in various ways.

The two types of app are as follows:

- **Canvas apps**
- **Model-driven apps**

Both apps allow you to easily build apps and share access to the CDS:

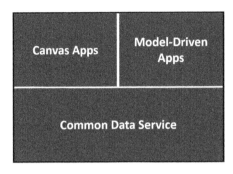

Figure 1.6: Logical hierarchy for the types of app

Understanding what the different types of app are will help you to make the correct decision when you are developing. Let's start by looking at canvas apps.

Canvas apps

Canvas apps are the mainstay of apps that are developed using PowerApps. They allow you to develop lightweight apps that are specifically intended for mobile devices, as well as apps that are being developed for tablet and desktop use:

Figure 1.7: An example of a canvas app that has been generated from the Site inspection template

Creating canvas apps is simple – it follows the drag and drop methodology so that you can add components and position them onto the page, which gives the developer complete control of the layout. Combine this with the ability to create logic by using Excel-like functions and expressions, and you now have the ability to interact with data in a way that allows PowerApps developers of all skill levels to build functional apps.

Model-driven apps

Model-driven apps are used to build apps in Dynamics 365. This functionality was launched in mid-2018 and it introduced a new way of creating immersive apps to improve interaction with Microsoft Dynamics.

Model-driven apps differ slightly from canvas apps in terms of the development approach. With canvas apps being user experience-driven, model-driven apps are driven from the underlying data, as shown in the following screenshot. In contrast to canvas apps, the layouts in a model-driven app are determined based on the components that you decide to use on the screen:

Figure 1.8: An example model-driven app

Model-driven apps share the same principles as canvas apps in that they allow you to create powerful apps without resorting to code; however, the thought process is much different and starts with the underlying data. We will investigate model-driven apps in more detail in Chapter 16, *Creating Model-Driven Apps*.

The start screen

To start your PowerApps journey, we need to navigate to the start screen. Office 365 has shown that Microsoft is being much more consistent in terms of its user experience development throughout the whole ecosystem. Therefore, like other applications, PowerApps is either available from the Office 365 portal page (portal.office.com) or from the app launcher, which is located at the top left corner of the Office 365 portal, as shown in the following screenshot:

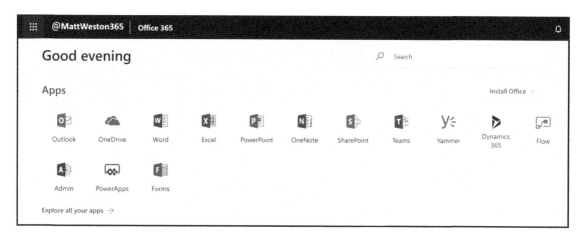

Figure 1.9: The Office 365 home page

Regardless of the navigation approach you take, you will find yourself on the PowerApps welcome screen, which will provide you with a wealth of options so that you can start developing.

The Home screen

The home screen is the first page that you will be presented with and provides you with a number of navigation options, including the ability to create new apps, open recent apps, and any apps that have been developed by someone else and shared with you:

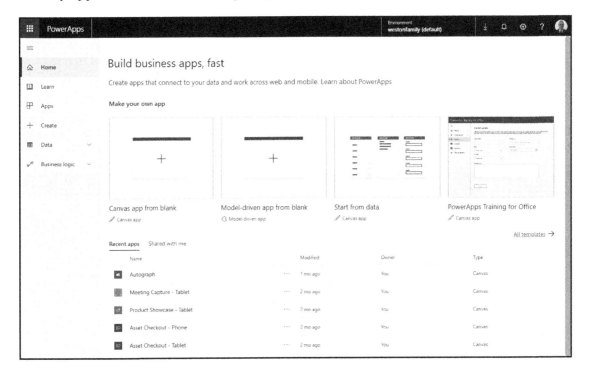

Figure 1.10: The PowerApps home screen

The screen is divided into two key areas:

- **The main screen**: This is the primary working area and will allow you to create a number of apps, which we will explore later.
- **The left-hand navigation**: This will allow us to access a number of resources that will aid us when we start building our own apps.

If you are new to PowerApps, then there will be a number of resources available to you, all of which are available from the learning resources screen.

The Learning Resources screen

Adoption is now at the forefront of the Microsoft agenda; therefore, Microsoft is providing a swathe of learning materials to help users of all abilities to create PowerApps. They have a number of guided learning lessons that provide basic computer-based training so that users can create both a basic canvas app and a basic model-driven app.

This is further enhanced by the Microsoft Docs site, which is dedicated to PowerApps, to provide additional knowledge in textual format. Both of these elements will allow you to take your first steps; however, the Microsoft PowerApps Community is the most valuable resource on here. Just like the Microsoft Tech Community (`https://techcommunity.microsoft.com/`), this is the home of a number of PowerApps experts who are willing to help and share their knowledge with other PowerApps developers.

The final part of this screen that provides a lot of value is the **What's new** section, which will provide you with announcements and updates, as and when Microsoft releases them. This includes technology advances, conference announcements, and general adoption notices:

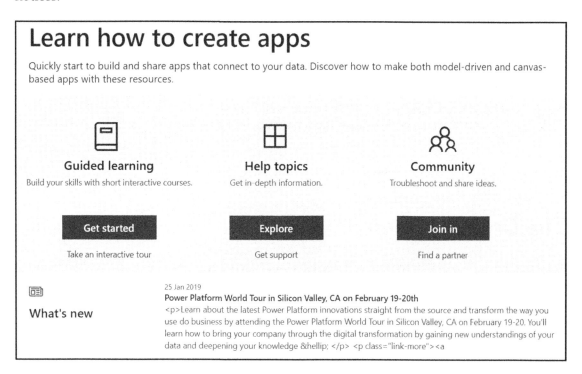

Figure 1.11: PowerApps support resources

Now that we have familiarized ourselves with the learning resources, let's have a look at the apps screen.

The Apps screen

The apps screen works in the same way as many other Microsoft applications, where you are presented with a number of ways of quickly accessing the PowerApps that you have been developing or can access. The list of apps is split into various categories in order to help you locate the app you are looking for. These categories are as follows:

- **Recent apps**: These are apps that you have worked on recently, with the most recently modified being displayed first. It also tells you who the owner of the app is, that is, you or someone else within your organization, as well as the type of the app.
- **Shared with me**: This category shows you all of the apps that either you or someone else within your organization has explicitly granted you access to via sharing. Effectively, this is a list of apps that you can use within your environment, including ones that you have developed yourself.
- **Apps I can edit**: Apps that you can edit are those that have either been created by you or where you have been nominated as a co-owner of another app that has been developed by someone else. The co-owner's rights allow you to use, edit, and share the app, but does not allow you to delete it or change the owner.
- **Org apps**: Org apps are apps that are shared with the entire organization. This means that everyone within the tenancy who has a PowerApps license can use the app.

Now, all you need to know is how you can create new apps.

The Create screen

The creation screen is where you will decide what type of app you are going to create and how you are going to create it. You will have the option to create a canvas app (as either a mobile or a tablet app), a blank model-driven app, a model-driven app from your data, or use one of the many templates that are available to you as a starting point:

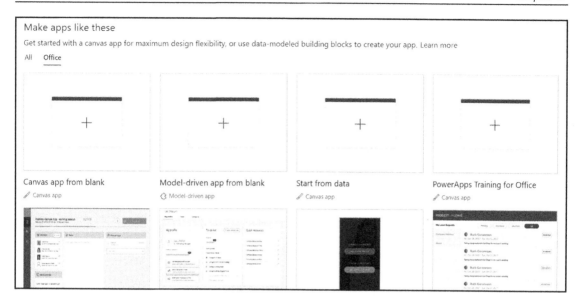

Figure 1.12: App creation screen

We will investigate the creation of apps in more detail in `Chapter 2`, *Creating Your First Canvas PowerApp*. The next area you need to familiarize yourself with is the data menus.

The Data menu

The data section of the menu allows you to access various functionality related to source data that can be used within your PowerApp. Data sources are established through connectors, of which over 250 are available, and more are constantly being added. This also includes any connections that have currently been established and are in use, as well as the data layers, which are leveraged within the CDS.

Entities

Entities effectively allow you to model data within the CDS database. An entity defines the information that is related to a specific type of record. For example, an account entity may have an account number, a sort code, and an account name. This data can then be used within PowerApps and Flow if we refer to the entity. Microsoft provides a number of entities at the point in which you provision your CDS database to cover many basic examples, such as contacts, emails, tasks, and so on.

Each entity is comprised of several fields, each of which has a display name, an internal name, a data type, and some basic user settings so that you can govern how each field is used. Once you have these fields, you can add relationships to them so that you can enforce one-to-one, one-to-many, and many-to-many relationships with other entities.

Business rules can be applied so that you can build logic and validation routines without the user having to write any code. When selecting business rules, you will be redirected to the appropriate PowerApps screen, which relies on Dynamics 365:

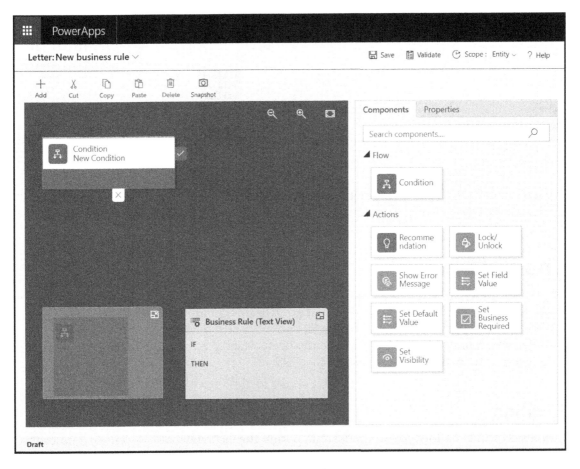

Figure 1.13: Business rule creation screen

The final area within data is related to Option sets, which we can use within our entities.

Option sets

Option sets, formerly known as pick lists, are fields that have a defined set of options available to them. Similar to Managed Metadata terms in SharePoint, they are designed to promote data consistency across the platform. Just like all the other aspects of CDS, Microsoft provides a number of system-generated **Option sets** that you can use in your own apps or which you can follow as examples. One such example is **Fiscal Period**, which has a set of options available, such as **Quarter 1**, **Quarter 2**, and so on:

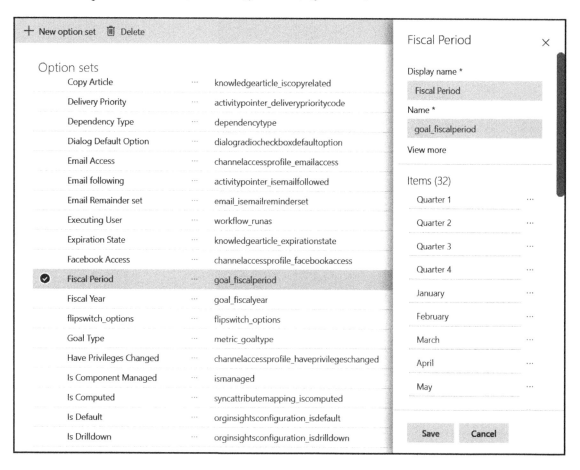

Figure 1.14: The Option sets creation screen

Now that we have looked at the data menu, we can look at the next key area, which is related to our data connections.

Connections

The connections screen is one of the most useful screens you will come across as an administrator because you can easily identify and troubleshoot any issues that may occur with your connections. You'll be able to see what systems are connected, when the connections were created, and their general health. If this screen shows an issue, then you will be able to fix it without having to log in and use PowerApp:

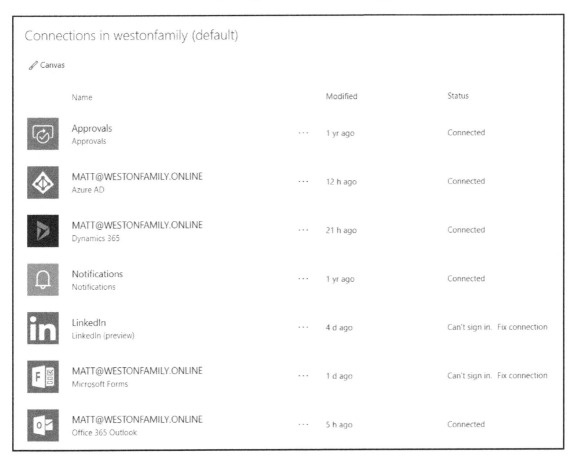

Figure 1.15: The connections list

We will investigate connectors in more detail in `Chapter 8`, *Introducing Connectors*. Apart from looking at in-built connectors, we can also look at any connectors that we have built.

Custom connectors

There are hundreds of connectors that you can use within your PowerApps; however, there will be times where you'll need to integrate with a system that either doesn't have a native or third-party connector, which is usually something that you have developed yourself, or a third-party API that you would like to connect to, for example, OpenWeatherAPI.

Custom connectors allow you to connect to REST web services so that you can interact with data. We will look at how to do this in `Chapter 8`, *Introducing Connectors*. Any custom connectors that have been created within your tenancy will be listed here.

Gateways

A data gateway is a way of quickly and securely passing data from your on-premises data sources to your PowerApps. This allows you to leverage a number of different data sources, such as SharePoint, SQL Server, or even Oracle databases. The gateway can be downloaded directly from this part of the welcome screen.

To take advantage of the data gateway, you need to have a per user or per app license.

Business logic

When we talk about business logic in Office 365, we're talking about Microsoft Power Automate. Power Automate is intended to be the workflow that will replace legacy SharePoint Designer workflows. Business logic will expand and allow you to open Power Automate from the left-hand navigation bar. We will explore Microsoft Power Automate in `Chapter 13`, *Using Power Automate with PowerApps*.

What are templates?

Microsoft provides an expanding gallery of templates that you can use to get your PowerApps journey started. Each template is more than just a scaffold of an app – they are fully functional PowerApps that integrate with various aspects of your Office 365 tenancy to provide immediate functionality. In this section, we will look at two of my favorite apps, but it is recommended that you review the functionality that's contained in the others as there are lessons that can be drawn from all of them.

Leave request app

The leave request app is a good example of a generated PowerApp that can quickly add value to organizations that don't rely on an already established system so that you can manage leave requests. It creates a number of screens that show you how you can use various controls and methods of navigation to achieve quite a common business use case.

This PowerApp creates two connections: one to Outlook in order to save and retrieve leave information in your Outlook calendar and another to the Microsoft Graph in the shape of Office 365 users. This allows the PowerApp to determine the line manager of the user requesting leave so that it can send emails.

The tablet version looks as follows:

Figure 1.16: Leave request app in tablet format

The mobile version looks as follows:

Figure 1.17: Leave request app in phone format

As well as having templates that are based around individual activities, we also have templates that are based around business functions.

Help desk app

The help desk app is another PowerApp that is commonly used by organizations to quickly add value since it captures service requests from a mobile device. This PowerApp is a great showcase regarding how you can store and modify data that's stored within a data collection, which we'll explore later in this book. It also uses connections that go back to the O365 user profile to draw data on the user who has logged in, such as their username and email address:

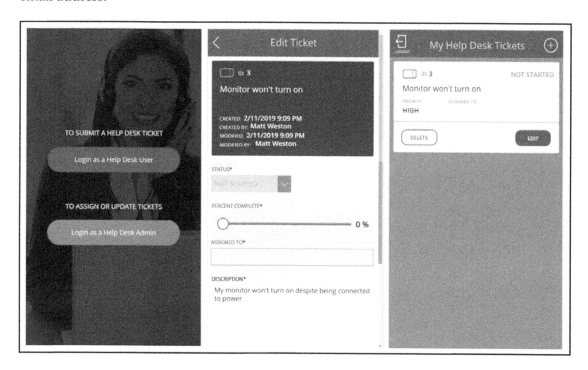

Figure 1.18: The Help desk app, a phone app focused on managing support tickets

Now that we have looked at creating some basic apps, we should familiarize ourselves with the actual development environment so that we're ready to start creating powerful apps of our own.

Using PowerApps Studio

PowerApps Studio is your primary developer tool for creating, updating, testing, and deploying canvas apps. In this section, we will explore PowerApps Studio, which is where you will take your app ideas from their conception and deliver them. It is important that you know your way around the studio so that your development time is spent creating the app rather than looking for options and controls. Understanding your development environment will vastly improve your development experience and will also allow you to greatly expand the functionality that's available within your app.

By the end of this section, you will know about the key areas of the PowerApps Studio, including the primary menu area and the formula bar. You will also learn how to view your screens, use the canvas, and find and review the properties of your PowerApp.

PowerApps Studio is completely browser-driven and is supported by all modern browsers, unlike other developer tools. Everything you do is, by default, saved to your Office 365 subscription, so you don't need to concern yourself with maintaining code in a code repository.

PowerApps Studio will launch when you start creating your app or if you open an existing app in edit mode. This screen consists of the following properties:

- Menus
- Formula bar
- Screens
- Canvas
- Properties

These are shown in the following screenshot:

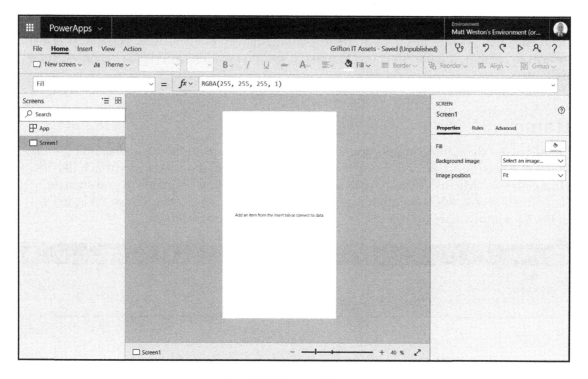

Figure 1.19: The PowerApps Studio screen

Most of the key activities we can perform are located on the Studio menus, so let's familiarize ourselves with what they are.

PowerApps Studio menus

The menus within the PowerApps Studio are designed to have the same look and feel as the menus that you use throughout the rest of the Microsoft Office suite. These menus use groups to combine similar functions to make your app creation experience as consistent as possible.

Home

Home is your default menu selection; this will present you with the basic formatting tools that you'll need to create your PowerApp. The Home's look and feel is very much like the **Home** menu in Microsoft Word, with basic formatting options available to you such as font-weight, bold, italics and underlines, alignment, and so on. You will also find the options for applying borders and background fill options on this menu:

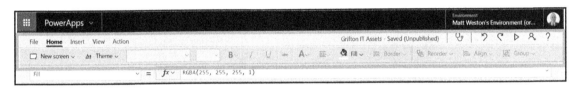

Figure 1.20: PowerApps Menu bar

The first element of the menu is the **New screen**. Screens are the key components of canvas apps and allow you to add controls and separate out content. When **New Screen** is clicked, a dropdown menu of template screens will open, thus allowing you to select what you would like the starting position to be. This is quite common across all Microsoft products within Office 365: you are not always expected to create content from a blank canvas, and there are often predefined starting points that you can take advantage of. While creating a screen from a template, you will have a number of controls that have already been provisioned to the screen, and those that interact with data will have dummy data provided:

Figure 1.21: The New screen layout options

There are a number of preset designs, known as themes, that you can apply globally to your app. These can be selected from the **Theme** dropdown menu:

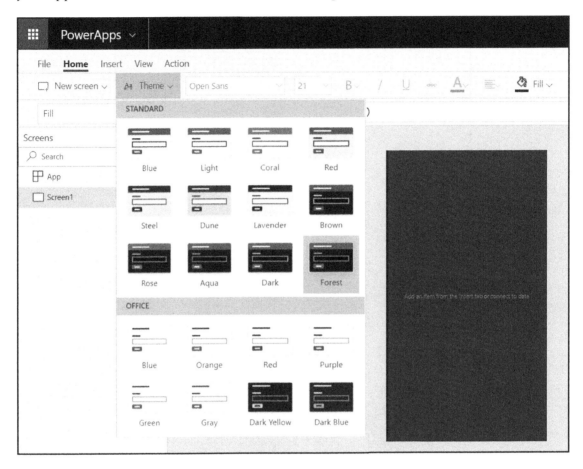

Figure 1.22: The built-in theme options

One of the key components on the **Home** menu is its ability to reorder and group controls. As you start to construct your app – specifically, when you start to try and build your user experience – you will combine multiple components to create an effect, exactly like you would within Microsoft PowerPoint. For example, you could place a shape as a background and then place a text box over the top. Reordering allows you to move the components forward and backward on the canvas, which you will use once you start layering.

Grouping allows you to select several controls on the screen and combine them into a control group. When control is part of a group, you can move the group onto the screen by dragging it so that you don't need to carry out each control individually. You can also apply styles to the group to give your app a common look and feel, and also apply logic to the entire group so that, as we stated previously, you don't have to modify each control individually.

Now, we'll talk about the **Insert** menu.

Insert

The **Insert** menu allows us to start populating our app with controls so that we can add functionality. There is a wide range of controls available to you, all of which we will investigate throughout this book, ranging from basic shape and text controls to more complex Power BI or camera controls:

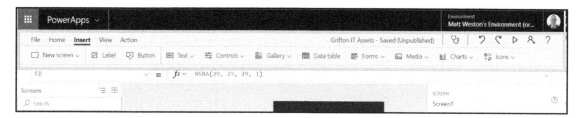

Figure 1.23: The options that are available from the Insert menu

Again, the **New screen** appears on this menu; however, there are far more controls to choose from now. The most common types of control to place on the screen are labels and buttons; therefore, they appear as standalone items on the menu. The other controls that are available within PowerApps are grouped into categories:

- **Text**: Controls within this category deal with the creation and display of textual data, whether that is a standard text input field, rich text, or a pen input, which allows you to add written input to your app.
- **Controls**: These are your interaction controls and allow you to capture inputs or drive actions based on user interaction, for example, sliders and date pickers. There are some additional controls within this menu that allow you to go beyond your normal user interactions, such as Power BI tile, which allows you to embed Power BI into your app.

- **Gallery**: This allows you to display data easily, using repeatable areas. There are three key layouts – vertical, horizontal, and flexible – that allow you to specify how your data is going to be presented.
- **Data table**: This is a single control that allows you to output your data into your app in a tabular format.
- **Forms**: Forms allow you to easily connect to a data source and then build a form so that you can interact with it. They can be created as display forms, where the data will be presented using labels so that they are read-only, or as edit forms, where the data will be placed into text boxes and other relevant controls to allow users to modify the data.
- **Media**: The controls within **Media** allow you to add a little more depth to your styling by allowing you to add images, video, and audio to your app. There are other controls here that allow you to take advantage of the mobile technology that your app will be running on, such as using the camera to take photos or scan codes or using the microphone to capture audio content.
- **Charts**: These allow you to build very basic representations of your data by displaying a column, line, or pie chart within your app.
- **Icons**: These allow you to place a number of basic shapes or pictures within your app to improve its overall look and feel. The most common iconography options are available here, including save, trash, forward, and back, along with some basic geometric shapes.

Next, we have the **View** menu.

View

The **View** menu is one that some people find quite misleading to start off with as it doesn't contain options for changing the view of your app. What it actually does is provide an overall view of what is happening within your app, beyond the controls that you can see on your screen:

Figure 1.24: The options that are available from the View menu

The options that are available on the **View** menu are as follows:

- **Data sources**: This will open up a new blade on the screen that will show you the **Data sources** and connections that have been established within your app, and will also give you the ability to create additional connections. We will explore this more in `Chapter 8`, *Introducing Connectors*.
- **Media**: This will show you all of the media assets that you currently have saved within your PowerApp, and will break it down by images, videos, or audio. As you start building your app, it is worth checking back here from time to time as it will show you how much of the allocated space you have used. At the time of writing this book, there is a limit of 200 MB on media assets stored within the app itself. Should you need more than that, you can store the assets externally and simply reference them.
- **Collections**: These are local cache data objects that you can create, modify, and use throughout the life of your app. This screen is particularly useful when you start to hydrate your collections as you will be able to see a subset of the data that is being stored within your collection. We will investigate this more in `Chapter 7`, *Working with Data*.
- **Variables**: These are temporary stores of data of a defined type that can be used throughout your PowerApp. Just like collections, you will be presented with a screen that shows any variables that have been created and what data is stored within them.
- **Advanced**: This button is simply a shortcut to the advanced options of whichever control you selected at the time of clicking it.

Finally, we have the **Action** menu.

Action

Actions are key within your app as you will need to build elements of interactivity to allow your users to do what they need to do:

Figure 1.25: The options that are available on the Action menu

The primary action that your users will carry out within an app is navigating; therefore, the first option on the menu is **Navigate**.

Note that this control will only be enabled if you have a control selected on your canvas.

The key items that are located on this menu are as follows:

- **Navigate**: There are two key pieces of information that you need to provide for navigation: a target and a transition. Transitions are the effects that are applied to the screen change; for example, they could fade from the first screen to the next.
- **Collect**: This allows you to populate a collection without having to write the formula manually. We will investigate this action in more detail in Chapter 9, *Using GPS in PowerApps*.
- **Remove**: This is the counteraction to **Collect**: you place the formula in order to remove content from a collection. Again, we will investigate this action in more detail in Chapter 9, *Using GPS in PowerApps*.
- **OnVisible**: This part of the **Action** menu will change depending on the object that you have selected on the canvas. This happens because the actions menu will display the common events for that control. Events occur when a user does something; for example, if a user presses a button, it will fire an **OnSelect** event.

Screens will have an **OnVisible** action, which means that, when they are created and displayed, you can execute a formula; for example, when a screen loads, it will set a number of text fields so that they have some default content. Other controls, such as the text box, will have an **OnSelect** or **OnChange** action button on the menu which, when clicked, will open the formula bar for the correct event.

- **Flows**: The final part of this menu is **Flows**, which will allow us to build your business process or workflows using Microsoft Power Automate. This can be used to reference a Flow that already exists or to create a new Flow for this PowerApp. We will investigate **Flows** in Chapter 17, *Exploring Environments within Our Tenancy*.

Now that we have looked at the menu and learned how we can add new items to our PowerApp, let's look at the formula bar, which is where we can tell the app what to do.

PowerApps formula bar

The formula bar is the key development area and allows you to build logic and actions for the components that you place on the screen. Its look, feel, and behavior is very similar to Microsoft Excel, where logic is built using formulas. We will explore formulas in more detail in Chapter 6, *Exploring Formulas*:

Figure 1.26: The PowerApps formula bar

Microsoft has produced an extensive guide to the formulas within PowerApps. This can be found on the Microsoft Docs site at https://docs.microsoft.com/en-us/powerapps/maker/canvas-apps/formula-reference.

When we create content with our app, we need to be able to navigate it. This functionality is provided by the **Screens** browser.

Screens browser

The **Screens** list on the left-hand side of PowerApps Studio is a very important part of your app development experience. It doesn't just show the screens that you have created – it also shows you a hierarchical view of all of the controls that you have added to your screens:

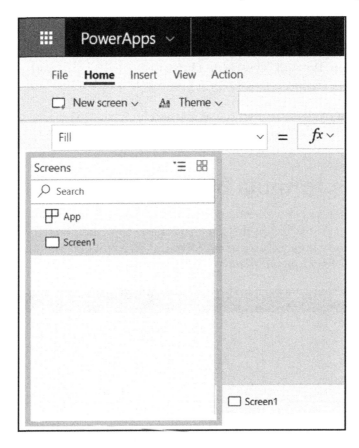

Figure 1.27: The Screens browser

While screens are important, there is one other item listed in the screen's browser that is extremely important.

App

The **App** selection option in the screens list corresponds to the app as a whole. The options that are available to you on this object are extremely limited, but it does give you access to the **OnStart** event. This is a really useful event as you can carry out particular actions when the app is loaded for the first time without the need for any interaction from the user.

This is commonly used to hydrate local caches of data so that the PowerApp is ready to serve data when it's finished loading. It can also be used to populate a cache so that it can be used for offline working. It is worth noting that this **OnStart** event will only run when the app is launched from the browser or from a mobile device; it will not fire when you're using preview mode in the studio.

 You can run an **OnStart** event manually and at any time by clicking on the ellipsis next to **App** and selecting **Run OnStart**.

Now that we have looked at **App**, let's look at the actual screen list.

Screen list

There are two options available for your screens, depending on your navigation preferences:

- The default one is the tree view, which will show the screen and will then nest any control groups and individual controls beneath it, allowing you to expand and collapse it to make readability as easy as possible
- The other one is the thumbnail view, which is very similar to the slide navigation in Microsoft PowerPoint, where you are presented with a visual representation of your screen

When you are in a tree view, screens and components will have an ellipsis (. . .) next to them, which allows you to perform a number of actions without having to interact with the control and without having to locate it on the canvas itself. Some of the key actions that you can undertake are as follows:

- **Rename**: Change the name of the screen or control
- **Copy and Paste**: Copy the selected control to the clipboard and then paste it again

- **Reorder**: Change the order of the controls in the same way as we discussed when we looked at the **Home** menu
- **Align**: Align the control on the canvas (this will only appear when selecting the menu for a control, not a screen)
- **Delete**: Remove the selected object
- **Duplicate screen**: Create an exact replica of your selected screen

Now that we have found out where we can view our screens, let's focus on where most of the work will take place.

The PowerApps canvas

The PowerApps canvas is your main working area and allows you to build your app by placing components on the screen using the insert menu. From here, you can drag and drop them around the screen:

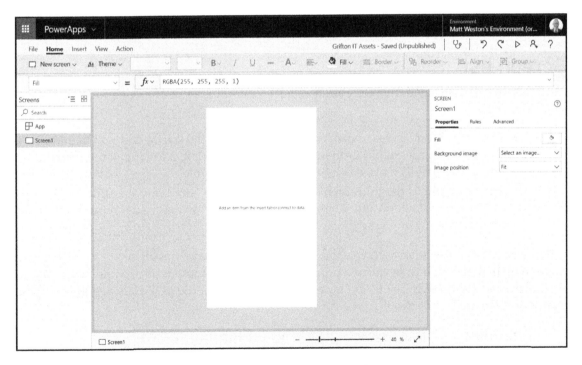

Figure 1.28: The PowerApps canvas in phone mode

Any components that are added to the page can be selected so that you can interact with them. For example, if you place a rectangle icon onto the screen, you will notice that it has a number of handles surrounding it, which means that you can resize the component by holding down the mouse button and then dragging. You can also move it around the screen and place it exactly where you want that control to appear.

To start building our app, we are going to use the rectangle as the header for the app. Let's drag the icon to the top left corner of the screen and then expand it so that it spans the full width of the screen:

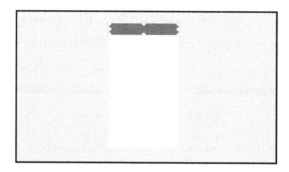

Figure 1.29: Control interaction points, which allow you to move and resize the icon

Unlike other developer tools, you are unable to place a control outside the boundary of the screen, which means that if you use a component, it will be displayed on your screen unless you change its visibility to hidden.

Breadcrumb

Now that we have a component on the screen, you will notice that a breadcrumb at the bottom of the screen has started to build. This will show you the component hierarchy that you are currently interacting with:

Figure 1.30: The breadcrumb

In the case of our rectangle, the only parent for that control is **Screen1**; however, when we investigate **Forms** and **Gallery** controls later in this book, you will see this expand further as we can nest controls inside a form or a gallery.

Zoom

As you start to add more controls to the screen, it is particularly useful to zoom in and isolate specific parts of the screen or zoom out to be able to view the canvas in its entirety. Zoom is located at the bottom right of the canvas window and can be modified by using the slider control or by using the increase (**+**) and decrease (**-**) buttons at either end of it:

Figure 1.31: Zooming in and out with the zoom control

When using your zoom control, you can quickly return to the best possible fit by clicking on the best fit for window button, which is located to the far right of the zoom and represented by the diagonal arrows.

Looking at the properties area

The properties area, which can be found on the far right of the screen, is your toolbox for each component that you place on the screen. This will allow you to quickly browse and modify the various properties associated with the control that you have selected:

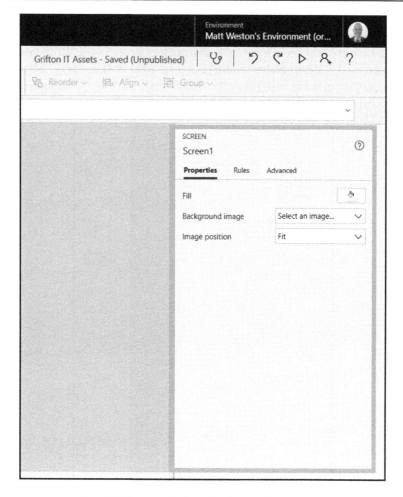

Figure 1.32: The properties for Screen1 being displayed in the properties area

The properties panel will group these options into three distinct areas, as follows:

- **Properties**
- **Rules**
- **Advanced**

Let's look at each of them in detail.

Properties

When you select a control on the canvas, the **Properties** group will show you the common properties that you will need in order to start customizing it. If we take our rectangle as an example, the properties display will relate to the fill color, border, and positioning. If we were to compare this to a label control, we would also see text color as a property:

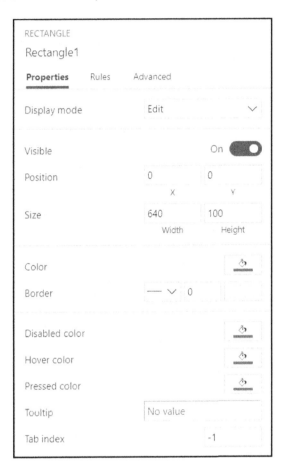

Figure 1.33: The properties of a rectangle showing the different parts of the control that you can change

Properties, however, don't need to be static. They can have **Rules** associated with them so that they're more dynamic.

Advanced

While the properties group will show you the common properties that you can set, the **Advanced** tab will show you all of the properties for your selected control. It also gives you the ability to search for a property and type your formula or value straight into the property:

Figure 1.34: The Advanced properties tab

The key difference to be aware of when working with **Advanced** is that you don't have the same graphical representation that you do on the **Properties** tab. For example, the **Fill** is represented as the red, green, blue, and alpha values, which means you can't select a color from a color palette.

Summary

In this chapter, we looked at the various types of apps that can be created using Microsoft PowerApps and the differences between the canvas apps and the model-driven apps. We explored the ways in which we can get started, whether that's by using a blank app or by using one of the excellent templates that are provided by PowerApps.

As we explored the left-hand side menu, we came across connectors, data models in the form of entities, and Microsoft Power Automate, which is our business logic platform. We can combine all of these to create a powerful app without having to write any code.

We also looked at the key elements of PowerApps Studio, which is the key development tool on your PowerApps journey. We looked at various menus and how they can be used to apply basic styling and configuration to our app and components. We investigated the insert menu and the types of controls that can be added through those menus, which range from screens to media controls.

Then, we looked at the makeup of the main development area, including the screens list, which contains not only your screens but also any components that have been added to that screen. From here, we have the ability to undertake basic actions on those components, such as reordering, copying, and duplicating.

Finally, we started to delve into the realms of formulas and functionality through the formula bar and the properties pane. We can apply conditional logic using rules and see all of the available properties by selecting the **Advanced** tab.

In the next chapter, we'll create our first canvas app.

Questions

1. What are the two types of apps that we can build?
2. What is the name of the underlying database?
3. What is used to bridge PowerApps and Flow to other systems?
4. What technology can be used to access on-premises data sources?
5. Which type of app gives you full control over the layout of your components?
6. What can be used to control the potential values of a data field?
7. Who do I need to share the app with to make my app an org app?
8. If I want to use the data gateway, which license do I need to buy?
9. Which submenu should I use to insert a pen input control?
10. What two views can we use on the screens list?
11. Which menu should I select if I want to create a connection to Flow?
12. Where would I go to check my data sources?
13. What would I use to create conditional logic for a control?

Further reading

- *What is PowerApps?* by Microsoft: `https://docs.microsoft.com/en-us/powerapps/powerapps-overview`
- Formula reference for PowerApps: `https://docs.microsoft.com/en-us/powerapps/maker/canvas-apps/formula-reference`

2
Creating Your First Canvas PowerApp

In this chapter, we will look at how to create our first PowerApp by creating a canvas app. Canvas apps are generally what people think of when they think of PowerApps and are where most app development takes place. Canvas apps have the smallest learning curve in terms of grasping the basics, so this is the ideal place to start your PowerApps journey.

We will also look into the basic settings of our app so that you can start changing its settings and ensure you have the right app for the type of functionality that you want to present. By doing this, you will also be able to ensure that your app has the right identity for your users so that it can be identifiable and therefore used.

In this chapter, we will cover the following topics:

- Creating a mobile app
- Creating a tablet app
- Changing the app settings
- Lab 1

You will also gain insight into how you can find out what is coming to PowerApps next and actually start testing some of the new components as they get released through the Microsoft application life cycle.

As we progress through this book, we will build an app that will allow us to practice some useful techniques and implement elements of the functionality that will be discussed in each chapter. Each chapter will contain a lab that will give you step by step instructions on how to create our asset management app. Copies of each app can be found in this book's GitHub repository (`https://github.com/PacktPublishing/Learn-Microsoft-PowerApps`).

Technical requirements

To follow the steps in this chapter, you need to have access to PowerApps, either through an Office 365 subscription or a PowerApps plan such as the Community Plan, as described in `Chapter 1`, *Introducing PowerApps*.

Creating a mobile app

The mobile rendition of PowerApps is likely to be the most common type of app you will create. It is extremely important for your users to be able to access and interact with data, regardless of where they are in the world. This is made possible through the use of a mobile device.

Often, when you create PowerApps, you will start from scratch. Templates are useful if you want to look at working examples and how to work within the scenarios that Microsoft provides out of the box, but as soon as you start building more bespoke apps, it will become much easier to start from scratch.

Creating a blank app is exactly what it sounds like – you will have a completely blank canvas to start from. However, one screen will always be created by default:

1. To create a new blank phone app, access PowerApps by going to `https://web.` `powerapps.com`. Alternatively, navigate to the Office 365 portal (`portal.office.com`) and select **PowerApps**:

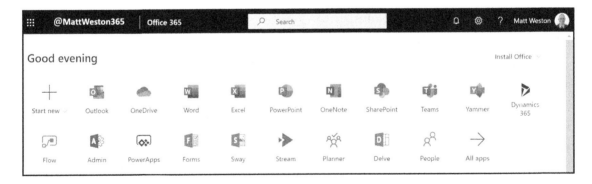

Figure 2.1 - Office 365 Portal Home Page

2. Then, select **Canvas app from blank**.
3. This will launch a modal dialogue box that will ask you for more details regarding the **App name** and the **Format** it is going to take. If you select the **Phone** canvas, then you will get a canvas that is 640 pixels wide and 1,136 pixels high, which means that it will work well on all common mobile devices:

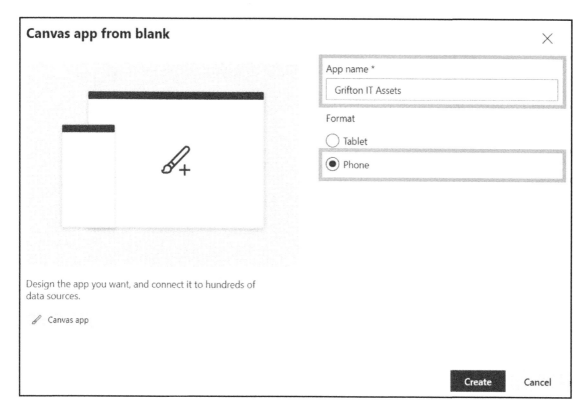

Figure 2.2 - Canvas app creation box with Phone selected

4. Now, an app with no content, other than a single screen, will be generated. This screen is known as the PowerApps Studio and is where all of the components and logic are added so that you can make your fully functional PowerApp:

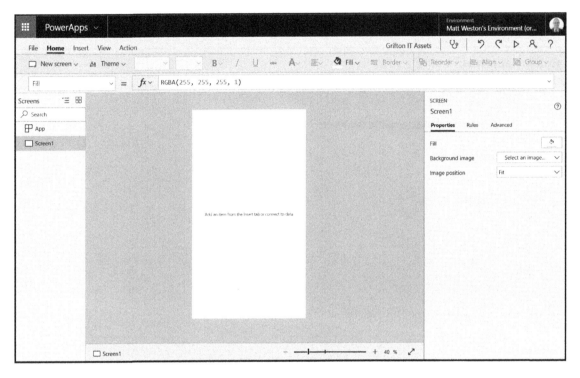

Figure 2.3 - A blank Phone canvas

5. For now, all we are going to do is save the app. This is done by clicking on **File** on the menu bar. Microsoft has done a good job of maintaining consistency between the Microsoft Office suite of applications and the online editors by maintaining the look, feel, and layout of the menus.

6. Just like in Microsoft Office, you have the ability to select **Save** or **Save as**. Regardless of which option you select, the first time you save your app, it will perform the **Save as** action. Going forward, **Save as** will allow you to save a copy of the app, whereas **Save** will append your changes to the app that you are editing.

7. While saving your app, you have the ability to save it to one of two locations. The first option (and the one that you will use the most) is the save the app to the cloud as this will immediately save your app back to tenancy. The second option is to save it to your computer. Here, we will save the app as a .msapp file:

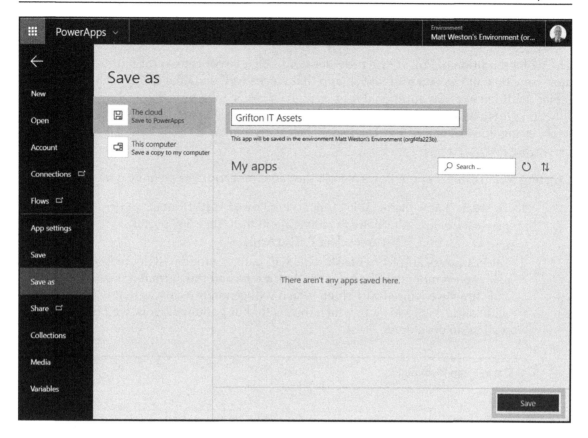

Figure 2.4 - The save screen

The purpose of saving to your local machine is to allow you to take your app and move it between tenancies or environments without the necessity of recreating the entire app from the ground up.

Once your app has been saved, you can allow others to access it or work on it by sharing it with others or by sharing it with the entire organization. Until you have a working app, do not share it with your organization because at this point, anyone who can access your tenancy will be able to start using it.

Phones are not the only type of mobile device, however, and consideration should always be given to tablet devices.

Creating a tablet app

The tablet rendition of PowerApp provides you with a larger canvas for building your app – one that allows you to create an app that works well on tablet devices. However, the tablet rendition also has additional uses as it gives you a good basis for adding functionality to SharePoint online using the PowerApps web part, or to Microsoft Teams as a tab. Using PowerApps within Teams will be covered in Chapter 4, *Publishing and Leveraging PowerApps*.

Creating a blank tablet app follows almost the same procedure as creating a mobile app:

1. To create a new blank tablet app, access PowerApps from https://web.powerapps.com. Alternatively, navigate to the Office 365 portal (portal.office.com) and select **PowerApps**.

2. Select **Canvas app from blank**. This will launch a modal dialogue box that will ask you for more details about the **App name** and the **Format** it is going to take. This time, we will select **Tablet**, which will generate a canvas that is 1,366 pixels wide and 768 pixels high, which means that our app will work well on tablets, as well as on desktop devices:

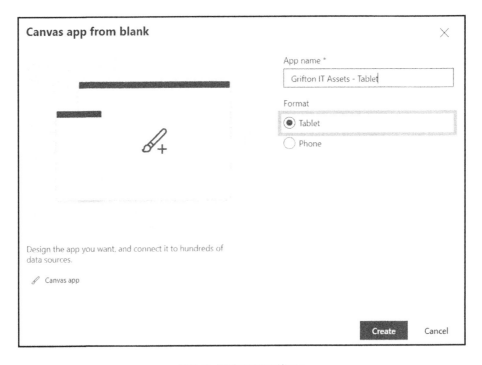

Figure 2.5 - Creating app as a tablet app

Note that I have given the app a different name to what we gave it previously, as PowerApps does not distinguish between phone apps and tablet apps. Therefore, you must give it a unique name; otherwise, you will see the following warning at the top of the canvas app:

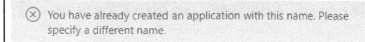

3. I usually append – `Tablet` to my tablet apps so that I can immediately see which version of the app I'm working with since you can't easily distinguish between what is a phone and what is a tablet app from the apps list:

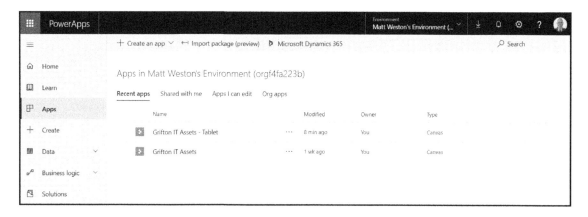

Figure 2.6 - Demonstrating different app names

4. Now, click on **Create**. The behavior that we can see is exactly the same as when we created the blank mobile app. PowerApps Studio will present us with a completely blank app; however, note that we now have much more space on the screen to place components:

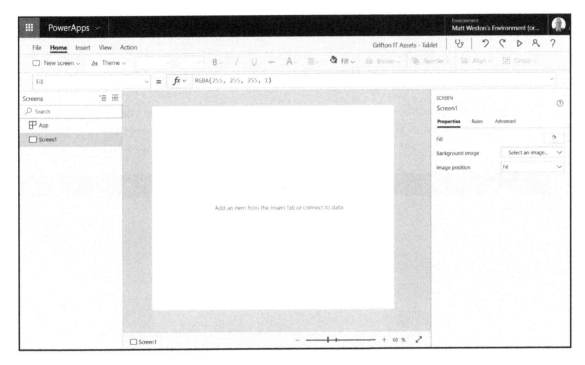

Figure 2.7 - A blank tablet canvas

From here on, we can save the app in the same way as we did previously, that is, by going to **File** | **Save** and then saving it as a draft or publishing it so that it can be shared.

Now that we've seen how we can create the two types of canvas apps, let's check out the settings that PowerApps Studio provides.

Changing the app settings

One of the easiest customizations to make to your app is to change the basic settings that apply to your app. These settings cover three key areas:

- **App name + icon**
- **Screen size + orientation**
- **Advanced settings**

App settings can be accessed from the **File** menu, which we started to explore while saving our app. However, rather than clicking **Save** from the left-hand side menu, we're going to click **App settings**:

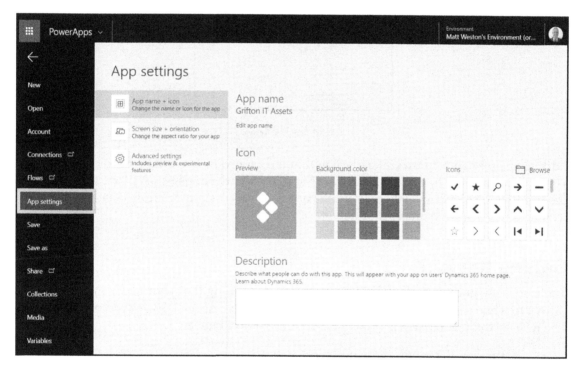

Figure 2.8 - The App settings menu

Now, let's check our first **App settings – App name + icon**.

Accessing the App name + icon setting

To access this part of **App settings**, you will need to ensure that you have selected **App name + icon** from the submenu that appears on the left-hand side of the working area. This page will open by default as soon as you have selected **App settings**.

Changing the name

When you develop an app, there will come a time where you may need to change its name, whether that's because the app's functionality or scope has changed slightly, or because you simply don't like the name that you gave it when you created it initially. At any point, you can go to the **App name + icon** screen and click **Edit app name**:

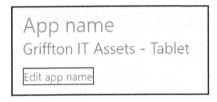

Figure 2.9 - Editing the app name

Editing an app name doesn't take place within the context of PowerApp Studio. Instead, you will be taken to the **Details** tab of your app, back in the apps list. A blade will open on the right-hand side; this is where you can change the app's name. Simply click on the pen icon next to the app's name and update it.

Setting the icon

The icon is the graphical identifier for your app – something that your user's eye will be drawn to while looking for your app in either the browser or the PowerApps mobile app. The icon customization area is broken down into three elements:

- **Preview**: This will show you what your icon looks like as you start to change its settings – whether that is the actual icon itself or the background color.
- **Background color**: This a grid of colors that allows you to select from a list of predefined colors. The selection is quite limited and there is no ability to enter a custom color, but you should be able to find a color that is close to your desired brand color if you're working to brand guidelines.

- **Icons**: This has a selectable library of icons, all of which have been provided by Microsoft. Please note that if you have your own icon set, then you can upload your own icon–you just need to ensure it's 245px × 245px in size and that it's either a `.png`, `.gif`, or `.jpg` extension.

The following screenshot shows these elements in the **App settings** menu:

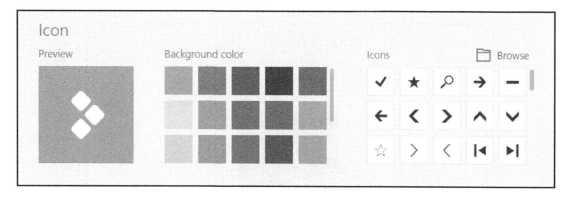

Figure 2.10 - App identity settings

 Always consider applying this basic level of branding to your app as it is the first thing your users will see.

Accessing the Screen size + orientation setting

There are occasions where you will have specific design requirements for your app; for example, you may want to explicitly develop for a specific orientation or develop a screen size for a specific device that your organization uses. To change these options, you can select **Screen size + orientation** from the App settings menu.

Using the phone app

When you access this screen for a phone canvas app, you are very limited as to what you can actually change. The phone canvas is designed to have a static height and width that can't be changed. However, you can change the orientation from portrait to landscape and back again. Installing and configuring the phone app will be covered in Chapter 4, *Publishing and Leveraging PowerApps*:

Figure 2.11 - Orientation settings

There are also two settings on this screen that are considered to be advanced:

- **Locking the aspect ratio**: This effectively means that the app will auto-scale up or down, depending on the screen size of the device the app is being used on. Keeping this on will mean that PowerApps will automatically maintain the height and width ratios to prevent any distortion.

- **Locking the orientation**: You can lock the orientation so that if your app is specifically designed to be used in a portrait orientation, then changing the angle of the mobile device won't have any effect. However, if you unlock it, the app's orientation will change, along with the mobile device's. While unlocking the orientation means that your users can use the app in whichever orientation they wish, it does mean that you need to carry out further testing and development to ensure that your app is still usable.

These settings are shown in the following screenshot:

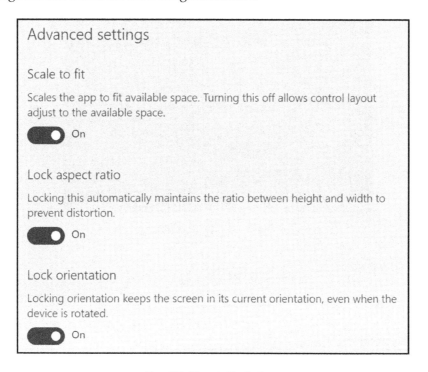

Figure 2.12 - Advanced settings for the app

Now that we have explored the available options for the mobile app, let's look at the tablet app to see how it differs.

Using the tablet app

The tablet app, like the phone app, allows you to specify the default orientation for your app. However, there are some additional options in terms of sizing the canvas:

Figure 2.13 - Tablet app orientation settings

Here, you can set up your app for specific devices, some of which are named Surface Pro, iPad, and so on, but you also have the ability to define your own height and width. This gives you the flexibility to target devices that are explicitly supported by your organization, or if you are going to work to a specific design.

You also get the same **Advanced settings** options so that you can lock the aspect ratio and orientation, just like you did within the phone canvas.

Accessing the Advanced settings

Finally, we have our **Advanced settings**, which is where we can enable or disable some of the really interesting components in PowerApps. You can access **Advanced settings** by clicking the relevant link on the **App settings** menu.

The advanced settings are broken into three key areas:

- Data row limit for non-delegable queries
- Preview features
- Experimental features

Data row limit for non-delegable queries

This option is purely there to protect your app's performance when it uses connectors that don't support delegable queries, such as the OneDrive Excel connector. A delegable query can be defined as one that pushes the processing load to the data source, rather than downloading all of the data locally to your canvas app and processing it locally.

You may want to change this number, depending on the data that you're going to pull back from your connector. For example, if you know that your data source is going to return 700, you may wish to increase this to ensure that you have all of your data available.

The lowest possible value is 1, which means that 1 item will be pulled back at a time. On the other end of the scale, Microsoft imposes a maximum limit of 2,000, which is purely used to protect the overall performance of your app. Therefore, if you wish to query a data source that is going to pull back more than 2,000 items, then you should consider moving to a connector that supports delegation.

Preview features

Before functionality is fully released, also known as being **generally available**, it transitions through a number of different release tiers, such as experimental and preview. Preview features are those that are effectively available for app developers to use for the purposes of testing, in preparation for them being rolled out.

The list of features that you see in this area changes from time to time, so it is a good idea to check them regularly and do regression testing on your apps to ensure that, when these preview features are enabled, your app still functions in the way that you expect.

When functionality is in preview, it is used within your PowerApps and will work, but may contain bugs or functionality issues that weren't picked up on during testing. Therefore, it is extremely risky to base a production app on preview features.

Experimental features

Experimental features are pieces of functionality that Microsoft is trialing on the PowerApps community. You can use features that are considered experimental; however, they should be used with caution. Effectively, you are using beta versions of the functionality, which means that the controls may break when new code is deployed to PowerApps or the actual functionality may change. There is also the possibility that Microsoft removes the functionality completely, which will mean that your app will no longer function as you initially intended.

While these components shouldn't be used for your production apps, I return to this area quite often as it's good to see what may be coming to PowerApps in the near future, as that may also shape how you design your apps in the present.

Lab 1

In this lab, we are going to start building a PowerApp that will manage IT assets for our fictional company, Griffton IT. The first thing we are going to do is create the canvas so that we can start populating it with components in Chapter 4, *Publishing and Leveraging PowerApps*.

Activity 1: Creating a blank tablet app

Follow these steps to create a blank tablet app:

1. Log in to the PowerApps portal by navigating to https://web.powerapps.com. If you are prompted to log in, please do so using your username and password.
2. In the center of the screen, beneath **Make your own app**, click on **Canvas app from blank**:

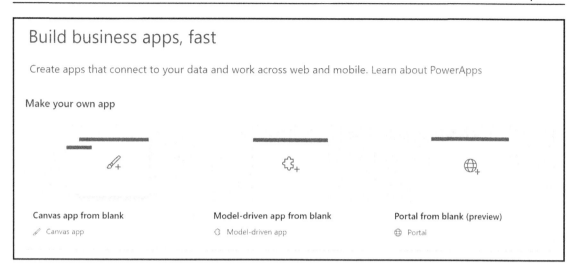

3. In the **Canvas app from blank** dialogue box, fill in the following details:
    1. **App name**: **Griffton IT Assets - Tablet**
    2. **Format**: **Tablet**:

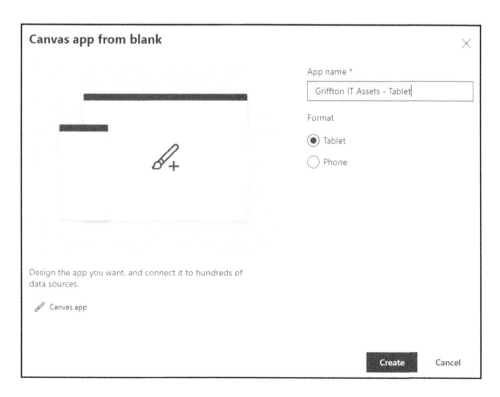

4. Once you have filled in these details, click **Create**.
5. If the **Welcome to PowerApps Studio** dialogue box appears, click **Skip**. Optionally, you can tick the **Don't show me this again** checkbox if you don't want it to appear the next time you log in.

Creating the identity of the app

Now that we've generated the app, we will create a basic identity for the app by setting the icon and color scheme:

1. From PowerApps Studio, select the **File** menu.
2. When the **File** menu loads, you will be presented with the app name and icon page. Select **Browse** from the icon selector and upload the icon, called `icon.png`, that's provided in the *Lab 1* resources:

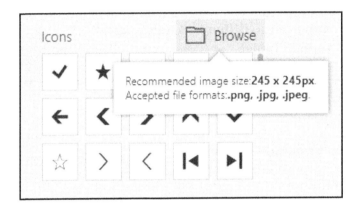

3. Set the **Background color** to crimson for your icon. Note that the preview changes to reflect the updated icon:

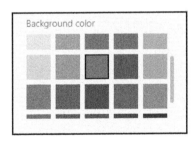

4. Our app identity should now reflect the app that we are going to create:

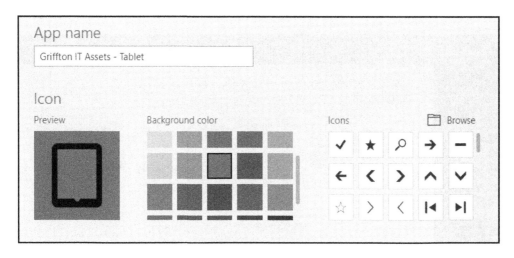

Now that we have given our app an identity, we should save it so that we can return to it in the next lab.

Saving the app

Follow these steps to save the app:

1. Let's save the app so that we can return and edit it later. Click on the **File** menu at the top of the screen:

2. Go to the left-hand side and click **Save**.
3. On the bottom right corner of the screen, click the **Save** button:

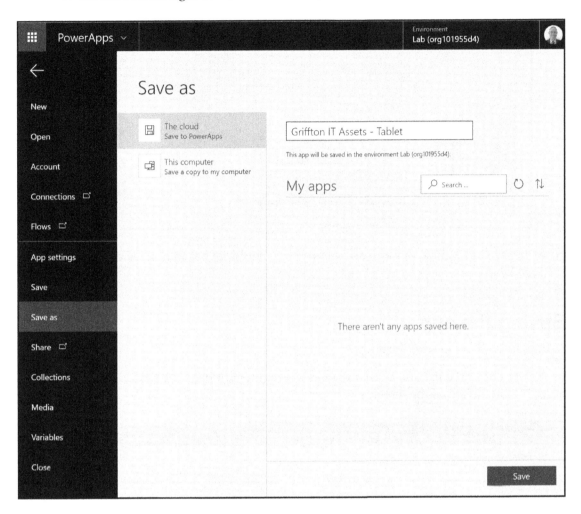

Your app has now been created and saved to the cloud. Now, your app will appear in the app list and can be viewed and edited by you, but cannot be used by anyone else at the moment.

To demonstrate the different app designs (phone and tablet), we will create a companion phone app.

Activity 2: Creating a blank phone app

Now that we've created a blank tablet app, we will create a blank phone app so that you can start to appreciate the differences between the canvas sizes:

1. Log in to the PowerApps portal by navigating to `https://web.powerapps.com`. If you are prompted to log in, please do so using your username and password.

2. In the center of the screen, beneath **Make your own app**, click on **Canvas app from blank**:

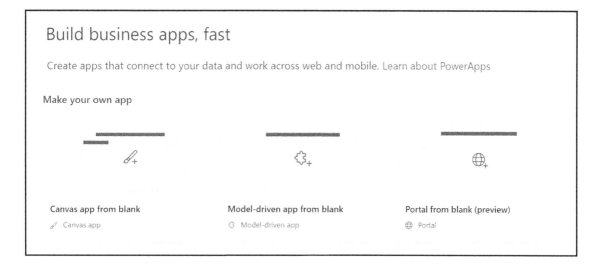

3. In the **Canvas app from blank** dialogue box, fill in the following details:
   1. **App name**: Griffton IT Assets - Phone
   2. **Format**: Phone:

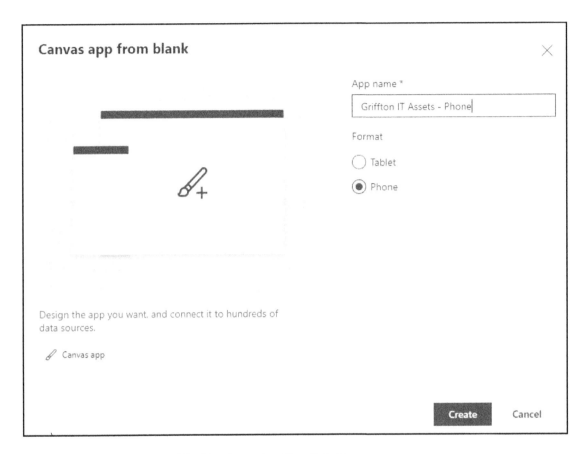

4. Once you have filled in these details, click **Create**.
5. If the **Welcome to PowerApps Studio** dialogue box appears, click **Skip**. Optionally, you can tick the **Don't show me this again** checkbox if you don't want it to appear the next time you log in.

Creating the identity of the app

Now that we've generated the app, we will create a basic identity for the app by setting the icon and color scheme:

1. From PowerApps Studio, select the **File** menu.
2. When the **File** menu loads, you will be presented with the app's name and icon page. Select **Browse** from the icon selector and upload the icon, called **icon.png**, that's provided in the *Lab 1* resources:

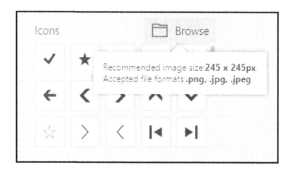

3. Set the **Background color** to salmon for your icon. Observe that the preview changes to reflect the updated icon:

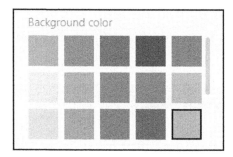

4. Our app identity should now reflect the app that we are going to create:

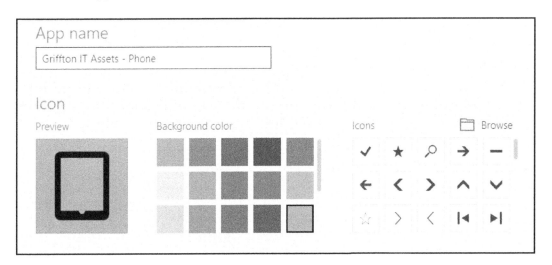

Now that we have given our app an identity, we should save it so that we can return to it in the next lab.

Saving the app

Follow these steps to save the app:

1. Now, we are going to save the app so that we can return and edit it later. Click on the **File** menu at the top of the screen:

2. Go to the left-hand side and click **Save**.
3. On the bottom right corner of the screen, click the **Save** button:

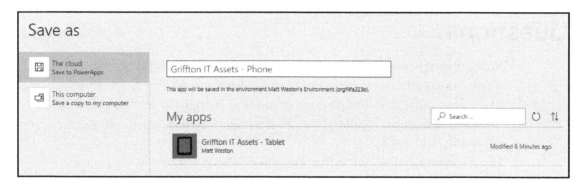

Your app has now been created and saved to the cloud. Your app will now appear in the app list and can be viewed and edited by you, but cannot be used by anyone else at the moment.

In the upcoming chapters, we will continue to build upon this lab, adding components and functionality as we go until we have a fully functioning app.

Summary

In this chapter, we created our first PowerApp and did so with two different canvas apps. First, we created a mobile canvas app that has a fixed size, regardless of the size of the device that we are going to use the app on. Then, we created a tablet canvas app that allows us to change the dimensions of the canvas to suit specific devices if we don't use one of the predefined ones. Both types of apps can be set to always portrait, always landscape, or so that they allow rotation.

We started to apply basic customization to the app by assigning a customized icon and background so that we have our basic branding.

There are also two areas to be aware of to ensure that your PowerApp is going to continue to work as new changes roll out. The first is the preview features area, which you should periodically turn on and test your app in to ensure that it will continue to work if Microsoft deploys new updates. The second is the experimental features area, which allows you to take a look at what may be coming in the future. However, it isn't recommended that you use these features in a production app as the components may change or disappear entirely.

In the next chapter, we will learn how to create another type of PowerApp: model-driven apps.

Questions

1. What are the two types of canvas that can be created within PowerApps?
2. Which canvas allows you to define custom dimensions?
3. Which app setting would you go to in order to change the icon of your app?
4. Which set of features should you test on a regular basis to ensure that your app will continue to work?
5. Which option should I set so that my app rotates when the device rotates?
6. What is the largest number of items I can return from a non-delegable query?

Creating Apps from SharePoint

3

In the previous chapters, we have looked at how we can create a new canvas app from a blank canvas. In this chapter, we will investigate the relationship between PowerApps and SharePoint, and how you can quickly and effectively create apps based on your data.

In the past, customized interfaces for SharePoint have been created using InfoPath or by using customizations such as web parts to allow a richer creation and edit experience. While InfoPath still exists and will still work with Office 365, the user experience of the created forms, which has its own styles and is not mobile responsive, means that it did not really fit into the bigger Office 365 picture. PowerApps is now starting to fill the void for that lack of tooling for creating customized forms.

To create an app from your data stored within SharePoint, you will first of all need to have a list that contains the fields that you wish to pull through into your app. The ability to create an app directly from SharePoint is only available if you are using the modern SharePoint user experience, so classic lists such as tasks will not support this approach.

I should point out that you can still use classic lists as a data source, it is only the app generation that requires the modern user experience.

In this chapter, we will be covering the following topics:

- Preparing your list within SharePoint
- Automatically generating an app from SharePoint
- Customizing SharePoint forms

By the end of this chapter, you will be able to quickly and easily generate PowerApps that will serve as an interface to your SharePoint lists. This will take the form of a standalone app for your phone or will allow you to recreate the input forms for your list items.

Technical requirements

To follow through this chapter, you will need an Office 365 license, which will give you access to SharePoint Online. The demos in this chapter rely on the creation of a SharePoint Online site or team or communications site but specifically require to be running in the modern experience.

Due to the close working nature of PowerApps and SharePoint, this chapter will assume some basic working knowledge of SharePoint Online.

Preparing your list within SharePoint

This is the first time that we will look at creating an app based on data that we have already created, and for that, we will need to create a list within SharePoint. As previously mentioned, if the list can be viewed in the modern user interface, then you can access the PowerApps menu and customize the form. There are two ways to tell whether you are using the classic or modern experience. The first is that the classic experience, illustrated in *Figure 3.1: A SharePoint site using the classic experience*, will still contain the ribbon at the top of the screen, which was introduced with SharePoint 2010:

Figure 3.1: A SharePoint site using the classic experience

The second is that the search bar, which in the classic experience appears in the top-right, can be found at the top of the left-hand menu when using the modern experience. The modern experience is illustrated in the following screenshot:

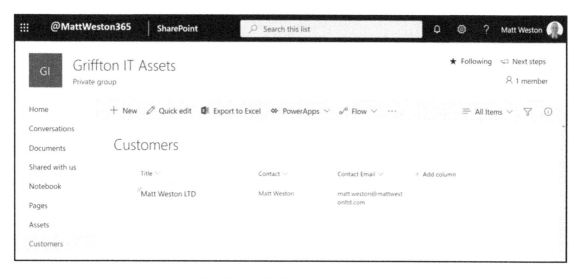

Figure 3.2: A SharePoint site using the modern experience

Once we are using SharePoint, we need to start building our lists to hold our data, which could either be a single list or a list that uses lookup columns to reference from other lists on my SharePoint site. We can create columns using all of the SharePoint data types; however, there are some limitations that you should be aware of. The more complex fields such as calculated columns and the managed metadata columns, and the newer fields types such as location, can be used by PowerApps, but will only be created as read-only fields.

We can go ahead and create a basic list which we can then use to generate our app. For the purpose of this example, I'm going to use a single list that contains several different fields so that we can see how they are built within our app.

My list is going to be called `Customers` and contains the following fields:

- `Title` (default field associated with all SharePoint list items): Required
- `Contact Name`: Single line of text—Required
- `Contact Email`: Single line of text
- `Address`: Location
- `Date of Agreement`: Date

- Expected Revenue: Currency
- Active: Yes/No

Once our list has been created, we can then use the built-in mechanism for creating a PowerApp.

Creating your app

Creating the app from SharePoint could not be more simple, which is a credit to Microsoft and shows the importance of the relationship between SharePoint and PowerApps. Simply follow these basic steps:

1. Simply navigate to your list with SharePoint using a browser.
2. On the list actions running across the top of the list, click on the drop-down menu titled **PowerApps** and select **Create an app**.
3. If you can't see this menu, then it is likely that you have a list item selected, indicated by a tick against a row.
4. Simply deselect that list item, and the list menu will return:

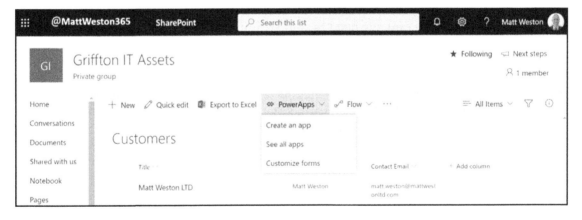

Figure 3.3: Create an app from a list

5. Upon clicking **Create an app**, a blade will appear on the right-hand side of the screen emblazoned with the PowerApps branding. This blade only requires you to give the app a unique name, that is, a name that hasn't been given to any other PowerApp, not just any apps that have been created from the current site.

6. Once you have given it a name, we can hit **Create**:

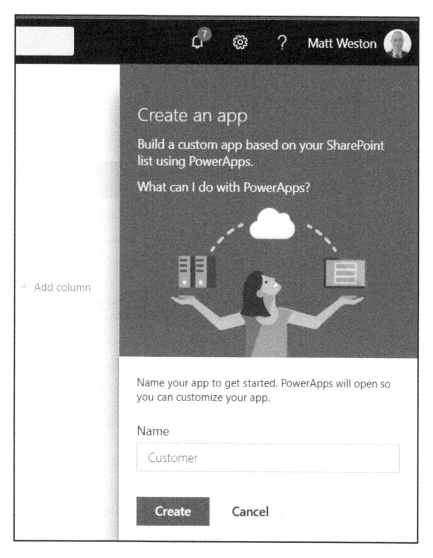

Figure 3.4: The Create an app blade

PowerApps will then open in a new browser tab and will begin to build an app based on the data structure that we created within SharePoint. There are no other interactions or configuration settings required; the built-in engine will simply create several screens based on your SharePoint configuration:

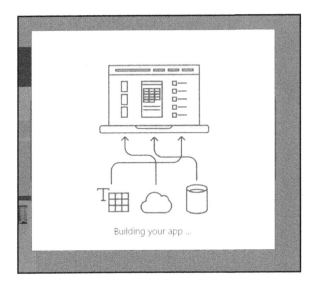

Figure 3.5: The app automatically building

Following a short pause, the PowerApps Studio will open and will display a fully formed and fully functioning app for you to start to use. So, let's have a look at what has been created for us in this automatically-generated PowerApp.

Exploring the auto-generated PowerApp

When the build functionality has completed successfully, you will have a PowerApp created for you that has several screens along with several components on those screens. However, the key thing to notice is that the generated app will always be created on a mobile canvas; you don't get the option to create a tablet version.

The generated app contains all of the functionality which you would expect to be able to carry out in SharePoint itself, being able to add, edit, and delete data from the list which the app was generated from. You can press play in the top-right corner of the studio, or run the app and you will be able to interact with the data in SharePoint.

Browse screen

Assuming that you have placed some data into your list, you will see several controls on the screen, which will allow you to browse your data. There are several key learning areas on this screen, which we will investigate later in this book and they are the ability to search and sort data, as well as being able to navigate between various screens. The purpose of this screen is to show high-level data that you can then interact with to drill down to more information:

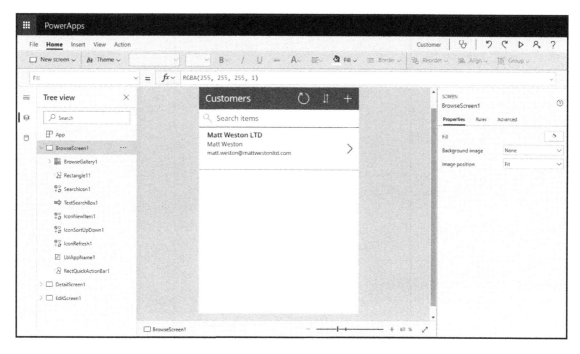

Figure 3.6: The generated app. which has all of the key elements added to it

The logic has already been built into the app to allow us to navigate between the screens. So, clicking on an item on the browse screen will take you to the detail screen.

Detail screen

The detail screen gives you a read-only view of an individual list item, displaying all of the fields that have been created within SharePoint. This screen now also starts to bring in more contextual types of control such as the ability to edit or delete the item that is being displayed:

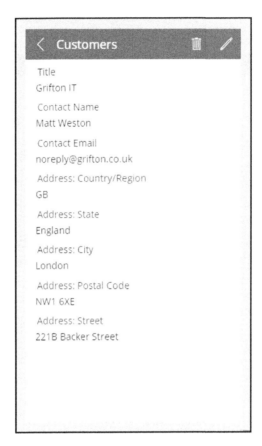

Figure 3.7: The auto-generated details screen

As well as having the ability to view data within the app, the auto-generated app will give us the ability to edit the data as well. By clicking on the edit icon in the top-right of the app, we will be directed to the edit screen.

Edit screen

This is the first time that we will see how some data types differ when they're generated in PowerApps; for example, the location field is represented in a read-only format whereas the text and more conventional data types are all editable. You will notice that there is not a *new* screen, and that is because the edit form can serve both *new* and *edit*. When editing, the fields will populate with data; otherwise, when in *new* mode, the fields will be blank:

Figure 3.8: The auto-generated edit screen

From here, you now have the grounding of a fully functional app that you can either deploy or start to build upon. All controls, logic, and appearance within the app can be modified and tailored to meet your exact needs.

As well as being able to generate a standalone app, the integration between PowerApps and SharePoint means that I can also use PowerApps to create customized forms for my SharePoint list to replace the out-of-the-box forms.

Customizing forms

As well as creating fully functioning apps based on SharePoint data, PowerApps can also be used to customize specific list form experiences such as being able to create a customized *new* form or a customized *edit* form. This is so that you can build much more functionality into the form itself, for example, showing and hiding specific fields based on an input elsewhere.

 Consider using this if you want to add more styling to your SharePoint list form as you will be able to use icons and geometric shapes to add more character to your form.

To create our customized list form, we will start in the same way as we did previously:

1. Simply navigate to your list with SharePoint using a browser.
2. On the list actions running across the top of the list, click on the drop-down menu titled **PowerApps**; however, this time, select **Customize forms**, as seen in *Figure 3.9: The PowerApps menu showing the Customize forms option.*
3. If you can't see this menu, then it is likely that you have a list item selected, indicated by a tick against a row.
4. Simply deselect that list item, and the list menu will return:

Figure 3.9: The PowerApps menu showing the Customize forms option

5. Again, PowerApps Studio will launch in a new tab so that you can customize the app; however, there are some key differences. Firstly, you will notice that there is a navigation link above the normal menu allowing you to navigate **Back to SharePoint**. This will close the app for you and return you to your list.

6. Secondly, below the usual app object under screens, there is now an additional item called **SharePointIntegration**, as illustrated in *Figure 3.10: The SharePointIntegration properties*. Notice that there are also multiple events that you can build functionality around, such as **OnView**, **OnSave**, **OnCancel**, and more:

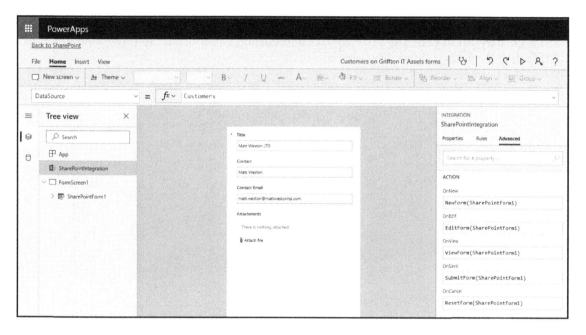

Figure 3.10: The SharePointIntegration properties

 SharePointIntegration is designed to set the global SharePoint settings for this particular app, in a similar way that *app* allows global settings for the app as a whole. This option will only appear when customizing a form from SharePoint; it won't appear if you are simply using SharePoint as a data source like we did earlier in this chapter when we created the auto-generated app.

Now that we have looked at how we can create the customized form, we need to modify the form to make it bespoke to our needs.

Modifying forms

Now that we have the basic form open in PowerApps studio, we can start to modify it. The idea is that we can add or remove fields from the form to create a bespoke data entry experience, which will generate controls within a form. For the controls to appear within SharePoint, they must be contained within a form control, but what you do within that form is entirely up to you. The form control and editing capabilities are illustrated in *Figure 3.11: Editing the fields within a form control*:

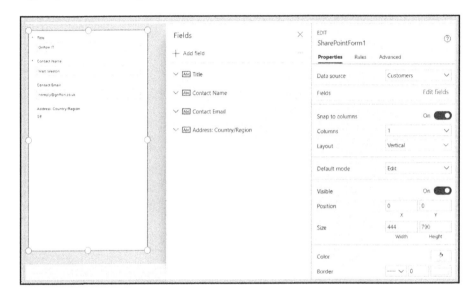

Figure 3.11: Editing the fields within the form control

 We will learn more about the form control in `Chapter 5`, *Exploring Controls*.

Modifying the form allows you to change the controls that you use to enter data or to enhance the styling of the form by adding additional formatting or information, or by hiding and showing other controls based on logical conditions. All of these were previously made possible by using InfoPath or by customizing; however, this is now possible through PowerApps and will help you to greatly enhance the SharePoint user experience.

As mentioned in *step 6* of the form creation, there are several events that we can add functionality to, and these are accessible by going to the advanced options available to the form.

Advanced options

While **SharePointIntegration** does not show any options under properties, it will allow you to edit some key features when you select **Advanced** within the properties pane on the right side of the screen, as shown in *Figure 3.12: Advanced options for SharePointIntegration*. These are the forms that are used for the various inputs when interacting with SharePoint, all of which will default to **SharePointForm1**. Effectively, you can build out several different forms within the PowerApp and then tell SharePoint which one to use; that is, you may wish to display different fields on the new form compared to the edit form:

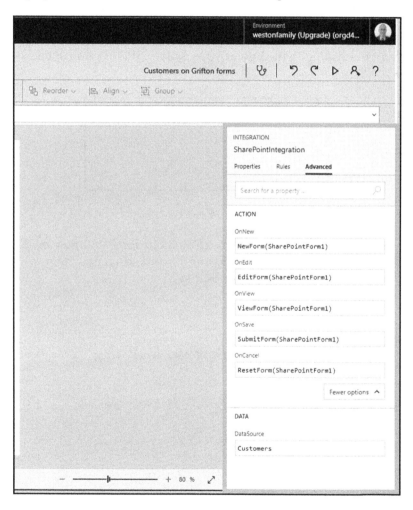

Figure 3.12: Advanced options for SharePointIntegration

Once again, you can customize the app and the forms as you see fit, to introduce additional logic, controls, or styling to provide your users with the functionality they require.

Once we have made any changes to the SharePoint form, we need our users to start using it. But before that happens, the form needs to be published.

Publishing the app

Once the app has been developed, it will need to be published before it is available to users through SharePoint. This is done in exactly the same way as a standard PowerApp, by going to the **File** menu and then clicking **Publish to SharePoint**. The main difference here is that, rather than publishing to the PowerApps gallery, it will publish back to SharePoint, as follows:

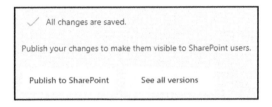

Figure 3.13: Publish app dialog box

Once we close PowerApps and return to SharePoint, our form will now be the default form when interacting with the list. So, if we go to our list and add a new item, we will see the customization that we made in PowerApps Studio:

Figure 3.14: Demonstrating the PowerApps form in SharePoint

I have now started to build on the close relationship between PowerApps and SharePoint to start to build a better user interface for my users to interact with my lists. We will learn more about the types of controls that we can use in our SharePoint forms in `Chapter 5, Exploring Controls`.

Lab 2

In this lab, we are going to create a list within Microsoft SharePoint, and then generate an app from it. This will result in your first working PowerApp; however, after this chapter, we will continue to build our app from scratch. This lab assumes no prior experience with SharePoint Online, therefore, it will walk you through step by step how to create the list ready for the app:

1. Navigate to `https://portal.office.com` and log in using your credentials:

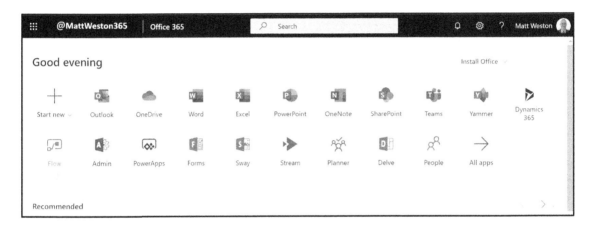

2. From the apps list, select **SharePoint**, which will load the SharePoint home screen:

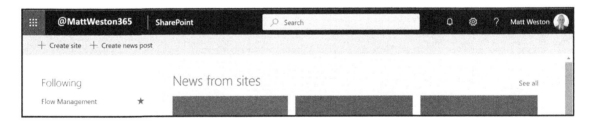

3. Click on **+ Create site** and, in the site creation blade that appears on the right of the screen, select **Team site**:

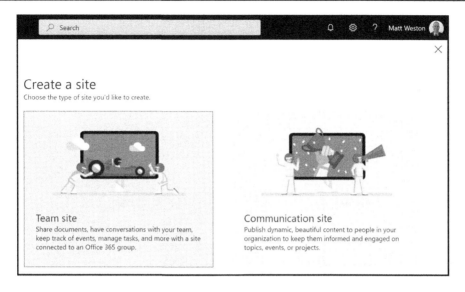

4. Create a new **Team site** named it `Griffton IT Assets`:

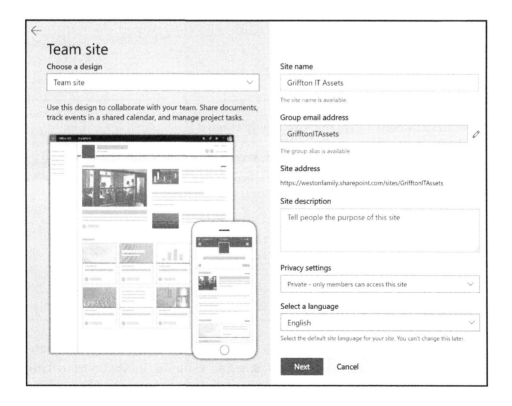

5. You will then be presented with a new SharePoint site:

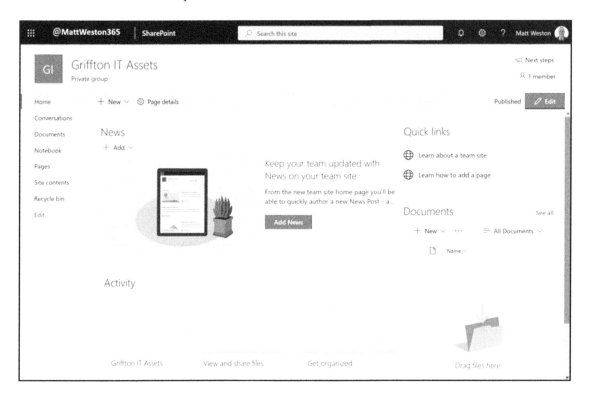

6. From the **+ New** menu on your newly created homepage, select **List**:

7. On the new list blade, enter the list name as Assets and then click **Create**.
8. Once your list has been created, click **+ Add Column** (located next to **Title** in the main display):

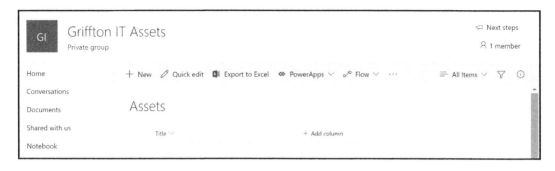

9. Select the column **Type** of **Choice** (drop-down) and use the following configuration:

- **Name**: Asset Type.
- **Description**: The category of the asset.
- **Choices** (create one on each line): Laptop, Desktop, Monitor, Camera.

10. Click **Save**:

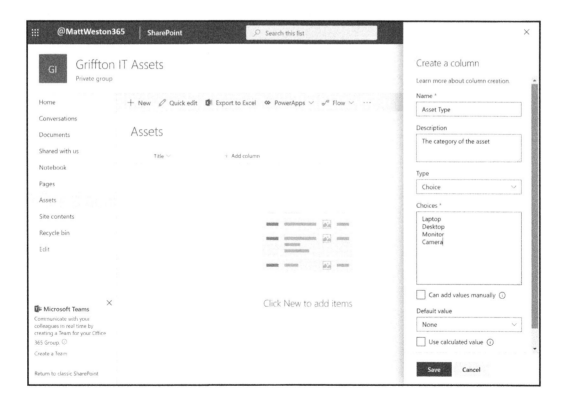

11. Repeat *step 8* to *step 10* for the following additional columns:
    - Item Description: Use the following:
        - **Type**: **Multiple lines of text**.
        - **Description**: Description of the item in as much detail as possible.
    - Received Date: Use the following:
        - **Type**: **Date**.
        - **Description**: The date which the asset was received into Griffton.
    - Issue Date: Use the following:
        - **Type**: **Date**.
        - **Description**: The date when the asset was issued.
    - Issued To: Use the following:
        - **Type**: **Person**.
        - **Description**: The person who the asset has been issued to.

12. You will now see your fields displayed within your SharePoint list:

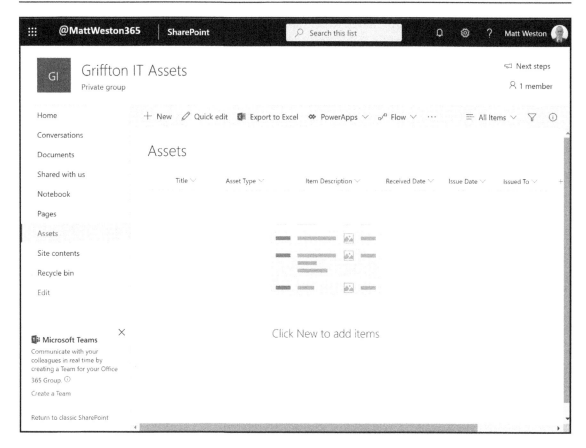

13. Now that you have the basic structure of your list created, click on the
    PowerApps button on the list command bar and select **Create an app**:

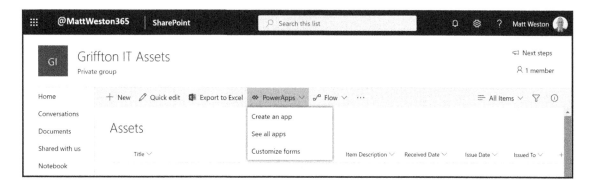

14. In the **Create an app** blade, which appears on the right-hand side of the screen, name the app `Griffton IT Assets - Phone`:

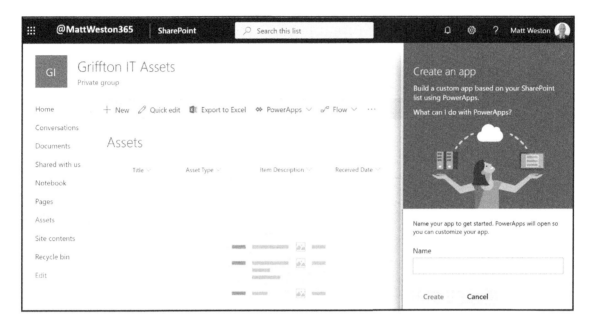

15. From the drop-down menu, select **Create an app**. Observe that the app will now automatically be generated and will create the relevant field types for you:

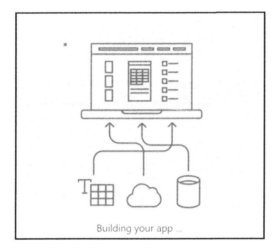

Building your app ...

16. Once your app has generated, you will have a fully working PowerApp that is connected to your SharePoint list. It will have all of the functionality built into it to allow you to add, edit, and remove items from the list. Test this functionality by pressing the play button in the top right of the screen:

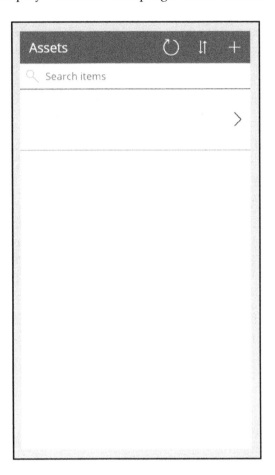

We have now generated an app by using SharePoint as a way of modeling our data structure using simple lists. This can quite often be the quickest way of getting a PowerApp up and running so that you already have a foundation from which to build.

Summary

Within this chapter, we have explored the close relationship between SharePoint and PowerApps, and the way that PowerApps can greatly enhance the way that you work with data. First of all, we explored how we can create an app directly from SharePoint, which is different from how we created apps in previous chapters, either from blank or from a template. This is especially useful if you are concentrating on getting your underlying data correct first before starting to develop the app itself. Just remember that not all of the data types within SharePoint will map automatically into your PowerApp form, so complex data types such as managed metadata or new data types such as location will be created but will be read-only.

Also, when generating apps from SharePoint, keep in mind that it will generate an app based on the mobile canvas, so if you need a tablet canvas, then you'll need to create that from blank and select **SharePoint** as the data source.

We also looked at how we can use SharePoint to customize forms that are used directly within SharePoint, for example, the *new* form or *edit* form. These forms are created in SharePoint within form controls, which are then referenced internally by SharePoint. They can contain logic, styling, and controls in addition to that which you get from the auto-generated app. By publishing back to SharePoint, your users will now be able to take advantage of a much richer add and edit experience.

In the next chapter, we will see how the publishing of the app takes place on different platforms.

Questions

1. Which user experience does SharePoint need to use to allow auto-generation of an app?
2. Which canvas is the app generated on?
3. What do I need to do to allow users to use my new form?
4. What is the key addition to the screens picker on the left-hand side of the screen?
5. True or false: managed metadata fields are fully supported by PowerApps?
6. If I wanted to change which form was used by SharePoint for editing, where would I go?

4
Publishing and Leveraging PowerApps

In this chapter, we will look at how we can use our apps once they have been created and published. Until an app is published, it cannot be used by anyone else, so we will also discuss what it means when an app is published and how you can review the history of the app, as well as identify which app is currently live. In case of any issues, we will also look at how apps can be rolled back to previous versions in the simplest of ways.

We will also look at how our users will interact with the app once it has been published and how users can get the most from the PowerApps functionality available to them. The three key ways of interacting will be the following:

- SharePoint
- Microsoft Teams
- Mobile device

The following topics will be covered in this chapter:

- Publishing a PowerApp
- Accessing your app through SharePoint Online
- Microsoft Teams
- Using the mobile app
- Lab 3

By the end of this chapter, you will know how to publish your app and access it through several key interfaces. This will allow you to make your apps available to a wide range of users, thus allowing them to use your functionality in the way that they feel comfortable working with.

Technical requirements

To follow along with the examples in this chapter, it is assumed that you have an Office 365 subscription that grants you access to SharePoint Online and Microsoft Teams and that you have a mobile device that you can test our app on. This device can be either a phone device or tablet and can be iOS or Android-based.

Due to the close working nature of PowerApps, SharePoint, and Teams, this chapter will assume you have some basic working knowledge of SharePoint Online and Microsoft Teams.

Publishing a PowerApp

Before we can utilize our PowerApp in any application, we need to ensure that it is published. Publishing works in very much the same way as how SharePoint publishing works, whereby you can work on the app and have multiple versions associated with it. This means that you don't need to maintain multiple copies of an app; you can happily work on an app in its *draft* state while your users are still using the last published version. Each time you save your app, it will create a new version that allows you to revert to previous versions if you need to:

Figure 4.1: Version history of an app

Now that we have seen what the version history screen looks like, let's take a look at how we can get there and start using it.

Version history

To view all of the versions of an app, navigate to the **Apps** list on your PowerApps portal. This can be found by clicking the **Apps** link on the left hand, which will allow you to find your apps quite easily. Once you have your list of apps on the screen, you can click the ellipsis (...) to the right of your app to bring up the menu:

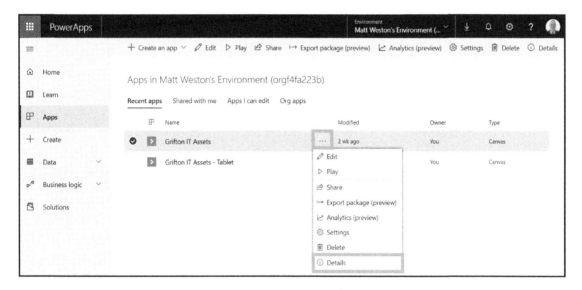

Figure 4.2: The context menu for the app showing the Details option

Once the app details are on the screen, we can review the version history of our app by selecting **Versions** from the horizontal menu bar:

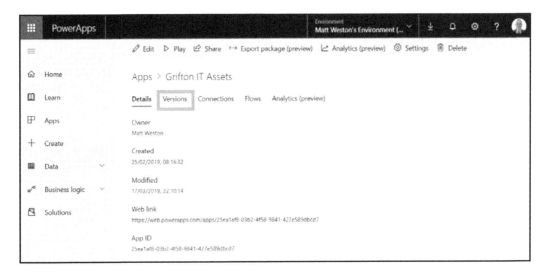

Figure 4.3: Location of the Versions menu

The **Versions** page is particularly useful because we can see what version of the app we are currently editing and see what is live. A PowerApp isn't considered live until it has been published. We can save apps in the draft, safe in the knowledge that only the creator and other editors can see the draft versions when editing. If we were to use the app ourselves, we would still be using the last published version, which is indicated as **Live** in the published column:

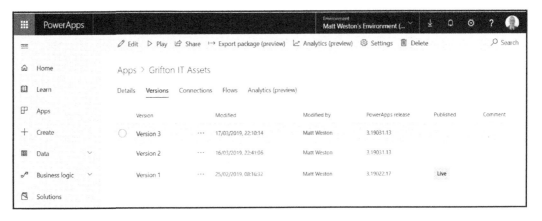

Figure 4.4: Version history in the PowerApps portal

Also, much like version control has been made available within SharePoint, we have the ability to restore a previous version, so should we ever need to roll back, we can do so. When we restore a previous version, a new version of the app will be created and will become the latest draft. It will not go **Live** until we have gone back into the app and published it.

Now that we have made our app live, we need to make it as easy as possible for our users to be able to access it. One way to do that is through SharePoint Online.

Accessing your app through SharePoint Online

SharePoint allows us to embed our PowerApps directly onto a page so that we can enhance the functionality of a page, all without having to take the user away from PowerApps itself. This is a really good way of surfacing data through your PowerApp or introducing ways for your users to interact with a page.

 Commonly, we see PowerApps becoming a key part of SharePoint Online-based intranets, which allows forms functionality to be embedded into a page.

Before we begin, however, we need to be able to identify our app so that we can bring it into SharePoint.

Getting the PowerApp ID

Before we start making any changes to SharePoint, there are some basic details that we need to find out about our app. For SharePoint to use our PowerApp, we need to provide either the **Web Link** or the **App ID** for our app. This is a shortcoming of the user experience for adding our app to SharePoint at this time, and I fully expect this to be improved in the future.

To get the details we need, return to the main apps list by selecting **PowerApps** from the app launcher in the top-left corner of the screen. If your app appears on the home page, then you can perform the following actions from there; otherwise, click **Apps** on the left-hand menu and locate your app.

Once you have located your app, select the ellipsis (**...**) to the right of the app name, which will expand out the app menu, exactly the same as when we were accessing the version history. From there, click on **Details**, which can be found at the bottom.

The **Details** screen displays some key pieces of information; the most important for this task is to capture the **Web link** or the **App ID**. Either of these details can be used, so either copy one of the identifiers to the clipboard or paste it into Notepad if you want to be sure that you're not going to accidentally clear it:

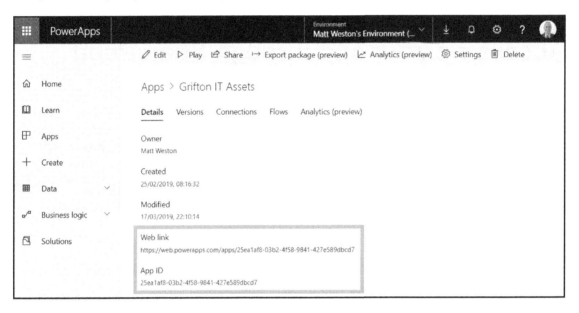

Figure 4.5: Location of the Web Link or App ID within the app details screen

Now that we have this information, we can go to SharePoint and surface our app on a page.

Adding the PowerApp to SharePoint

To put our app on a page within SharePoint, we need to use a modern page. Modern pages are those that are completely mobile responsive and are designed to function within the SharePoint mobile app, as shown in the following screenshot. They differ greatly to the *classic* pages, which make use of web part zones to place components on the page.

When you create a SharePoint site from the SharePoint home page, you can create either a communication site or a team site. Both of these site templates are *modern*, therefore allowing you to use your PowerApps.

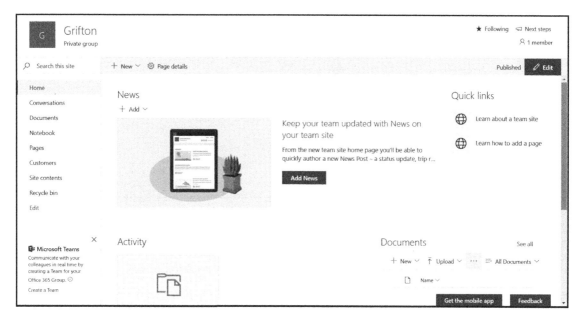

Figure 4.6: A modern SharePoint team site

When we edit the page, we can add components to the page in the form of web parts. These modern web parts include a PowerApps web part, which at the time of writing is in preview. To add a web part to a page, you must begin editing the page using the **Edit** option in the top-right area of your SharePoint page:

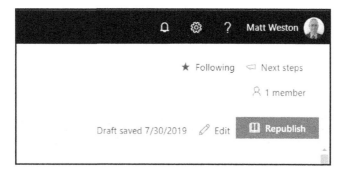

Figure 4.7: The edit option in SharePoint Online

Once the page is in edit mode, you can add new web parts to your page. This is done by hovering over the desired area so that you see the **+** icon, which you can then click on to open up the web part toolbox:

Figure 4.8: Add a web part button

Once the toolbox is open, you can either scroll down until you find the Microsoft PowerApps web part or use the search box at the top of the toolbox to filter:

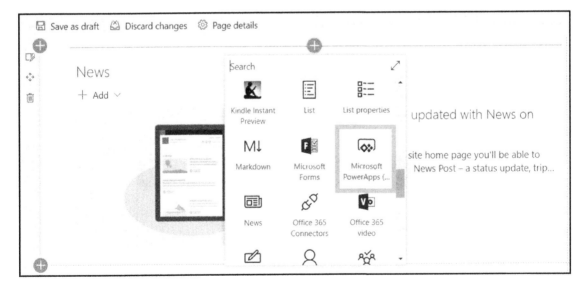

Figure 4.9: The PowerApps web part in the toolbox

Once you have located it, click on the web part so that it will be placed onto the page. The web part properties blade will automatically open on the right-hand side of the screen. The web part properties section is where you can add either the **App web link or ID** that we identified earlier, and where you can specify whether there is a border around the app or not:

Figure 4.10: Configuring the PowerApps web part

As soon as you paste in the **App web link or ID**, it will immediately start to render on the page and display the last published version of the app. This is then available to you and your users to interact with on your SharePoint site, as shown in the following screenshot:

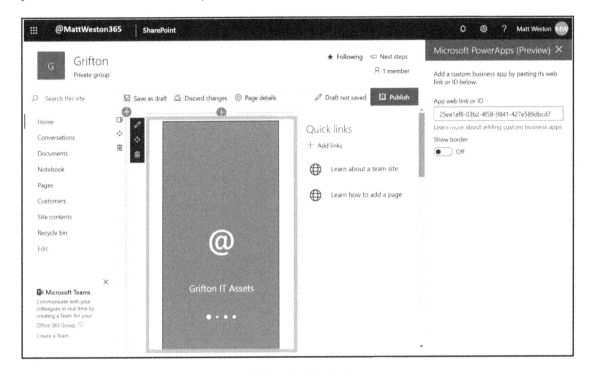

Figure 4.11: The app being displayed on the page

 It is worth keeping in mind that it can take a second or two for your app to actually load, so consider the burden on the browser if you have multiple PowerApps embedded on a single page.

The final step is to publish your SharePoint page, which is achieved by pressing **Publish**, which can be found in the top-right corner. Once that has been done, any standard users of your SharePoint site will be able to use your app without having to leave SharePoint.

SharePoint provides just one of the key collaboration areas within Office 365; the other key area is Microsoft Teams.

Microsoft Teams

Microsoft Teams is the central collaboration hub for users. It is cited as being the fastest growing product, in terms of user adoption, of all of the Microsoft products throughout its history. For Office 365, Microsoft Teams provides a window to all of the productivity tools that your users need; therefore, it makes sense for you to allow your users to interact with your PowerApp without ever leaving Teams. This can be achieved by adding it as a tab.

As a brief introduction to Microsoft Teams, collaborative areas are broken down into high-level areas called teams. Behind the scenes, Teams creates a SharePoint site and an exchange mailbox to provide the key collaboration and communication tools that have made Microsoft Teams so successful. These teams are then broken down into sub-areas called channels, which allow you to separate out your conversations and files. An example is shown in the following screenshot, where we have individual channels for infrastructure and policies:

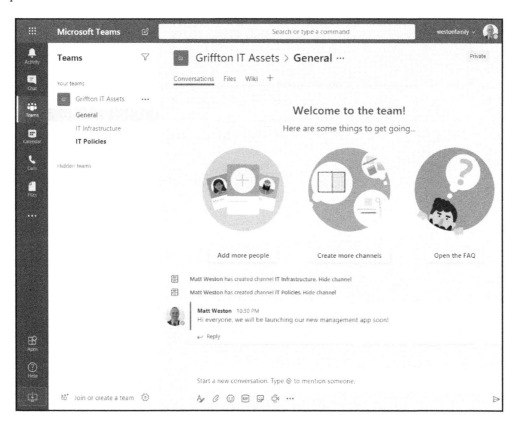

Figure 4.12: The Microsoft Teams interface

Each channel allows you to bring in additional resources to complement the way that your users work within Teams, and this is achieved by adding new tabs to a channel.

Adding a PowerApps tab

Adding the PowerApps tab to your Teams channel means that your app will be displayed within the Microsoft Teams interface. This is designed to be an additional way of accessing your app, rather than through the browser, SharePoint, or mobile app.

 If your Microsoft Teams and your PowerApp are key to your users' day-to-day activities, consider implementing a PowerApps tab to make it as easy as possible for your users to do everything in one place.

Compared to SharePoint, the user experience for adding a PowerApp is much richer and easier. If you haven't already got a team, then you can create one from within Microsoft Teams itself, or if you have a modern SharePoint team site, then you can create a team from there.

Once you're within Microsoft Teams, your PowerApp can be added as a tab to one of your channels. You can add your app to any channel, and you can add it in several places if that is what you want to do. To add your tab, click the plus (+) to add a new tab to your channel, and then either scroll or search for the PowerApps tab. Notice that, unlike SharePoint, this is not in the preview:

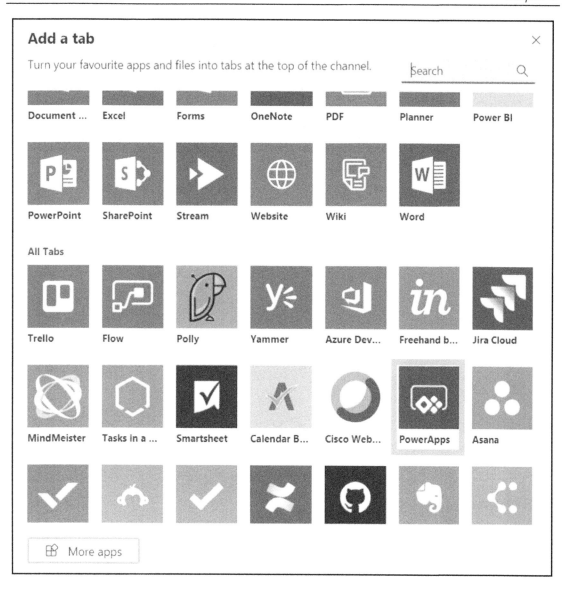

Figure 4.13: The PowerApps tab available from the Add a tab dialog box

If this is the first time that you've added PowerApps to your team, you will be asked to install it. This effectively goes through the normal checks that all the tabs do, which is to ensure that you're happy with any data being shared or displayed. If you're happy to proceed, click **Install** at the bottom-right corner of the dialog box:

Figure 4.14: PowerApps installation from Microsoft Teams

Once the app has been installed, you will be able to surface your PowerApp into Microsoft Teams. You will be faced with a selection box that allows you to pick the exact app you want to use. Your apps will be available from all the environments that you have access to and are consolidated in this one window. You can also search if you have a large number of apps, or use the filter to identify **My apps**, **All apps**, or even directly install one of the sample apps. Simply select the app you want to install and press **Save** in the bottom-right corner. If you have left the **Post to the channel about this tab** checkbox ticked, then this also posts a message in the conversation tab about the app being added:

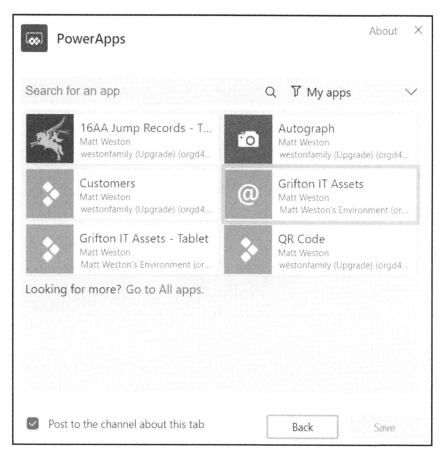

Figure 4.15: PowerApp selector screen

Once you have added your app to your team, it will appear as an additional tab along the top of the team window and will be visible to everyone who has access to that team, as shown in the following screenshot. When you select it, your app will load and will give you the ability to use and interact with it exactly as you would on any other platform:

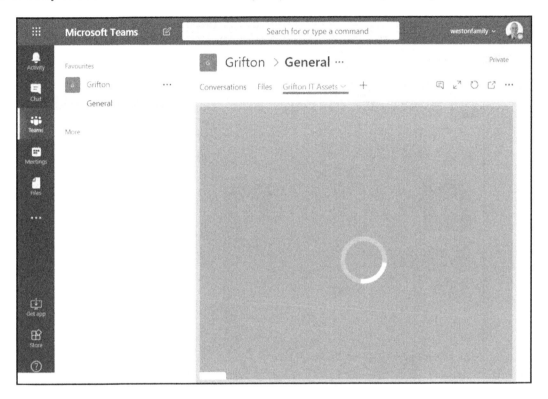

Figure 4.16: The PowerApp being displayed in Microsoft Teams

Now that we have looked at SharePoint Online and Microsoft Teams, let's look at how we can leverage our PowerApp on the move using the mobile app.

Using the mobile app

One of the biggest drivers for the adoption of PowerApps within organizations is the ability to create mobile apps without the need to pay large development fees. PowerApps, much like other areas of Office 365, has its own dedicated app, which can be downloaded from the relevant app store. Both iOS and Android devices are fully supported, meaning that the reach your app can have can be vast.

The screenshots in this section have been taken using an iOS device:

Figure 4.17: A PowerApps app that has been installed on a mobile device

Once the app has been installed on your device, you can immediately start to use it by launching it from your home screen.

Using the app

When you first launch the PowerApps app, you will be asked to authenticate using the Office 365 credentials that you normally use within the browser. There are a lot of similarities in the user experience between what we saw in Microsoft Teams and what we can see in the mobile app. The first thing we can do is view the list of apps that we can access. Once again, we can filter on **MY APPS**, **All Apps**, and **Sample apps**, as well as search. Once you have identified the app you wish to use, we simply need to tap it, and it will launch:

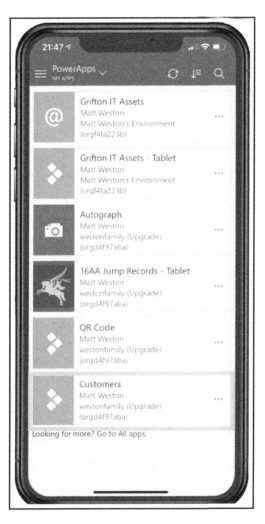

Figure 4.18: PowerApps available in the mobile app

The app will momentarily display the splash screen before actually being ready to use. Once the app has loaded, you can use it in exactly the same way as you would through the browser, SharePoint, or Microsoft Teams. One of the most endearing qualities of PowerApps is that the user experience is consistent, regardless of the medium in which we use the PowerApp:

Figure 4.19: The phone app that was generated in Chapter 3, *Creating Apps from SharePoint*, being displayed through the PowerApps mobile app

To exit the app and return to the app selection screen, we simply need to swipe from the right edge of the device and launch another app.

For you to make it even easier to access your PowerApp, your users can make it look like a native app by pinning it to home.

Pinning to home

One of the nicest things about the PowerApps native app is that we can pin any apps that we can access to the home screen. For most users, this gives the impression that the PowerApp is installed on the device. What it's actually done is create a shortcut to the app. The shortcut will still launch the PowerApps app; however, it will quickly redirect the user to where they need to be. This effectively makes the journey for the user much more friendly as they are reducing the number of taps.

To pin the app to the home screen, open the PowerApps app and tap the ellipsis (**...**) to open the menu. Here, you will see **Pin to Home**. The process for pinning to the home screen will differ depending on the device's OS, but, the basic process is to add it to the home screen, give it a name if you want to rename it, and then it will appear as an icon. Now, the app is only ever one tap away from being used. The relevant screens can be seen in the following image::

Figure 4.20: Adding an app to the home screen on an iOS device

Now, we have added access to the app through a mobile device, Microsoft Teams, and SharePoint Online.

Lab 3

Within this lab, we are going to install and configure the PowerApps mobile app so that we can experience using our PowerApp as we build it throughout this book. This lab assumes that you have completed *Lab 1*, and therefore have created the Griffton IT Assets app. However, you can follow these steps for any other app that you create. We will install the PowerApps app and then pin our tablet app to the home screen.

First of all, let's install the mobile app.

Activity 1: Installing the mobile app

This first activity will allow us to install and configure the PowerApps mobile app onto our chosen device. The screenshots in this lab have been taken from an iOS device:

1. On your mobile device, open the app store that's relevant to your device.
2. Search for `PowerApps`:

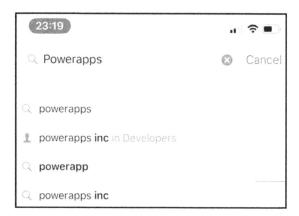

3. Select **PowerApps** from the search options and select to install it:

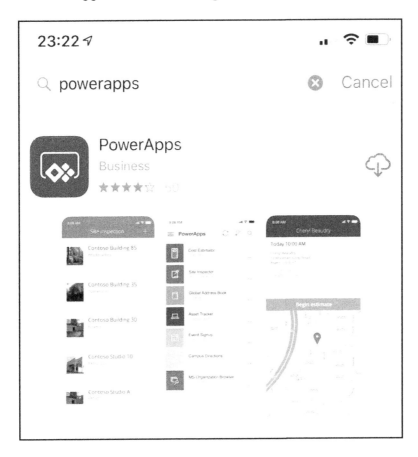

4. Once the app has been installed, open the app from the app store or the home
   screen:

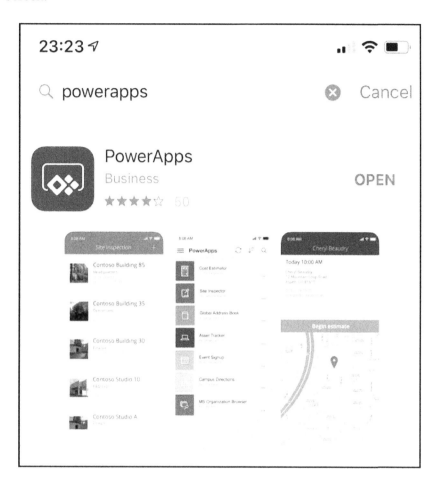

5. When the app opens, sign in using your Office 365 credentials:

6. Once loaded, ensure that you can see the apps named **Griffton IT Assets**:

Now that we have our app installed and we have signed in, we will pin the tablet app to the home screen.

Activity 2: Pinning the app

In this activity, we will practice pinning an app to the home screen so that we can easily access our app again in the future:

1. If the PowerApps app is not open, open it now by selecting it from your home screen:

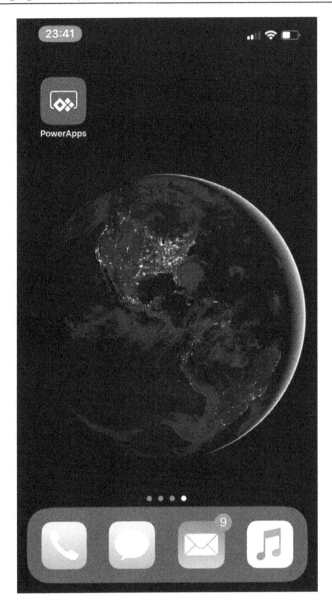

2. From the app selection screen, click on the ellipsis (**...**) on the **Griffton IT Assets - Tablet** to display the menu:

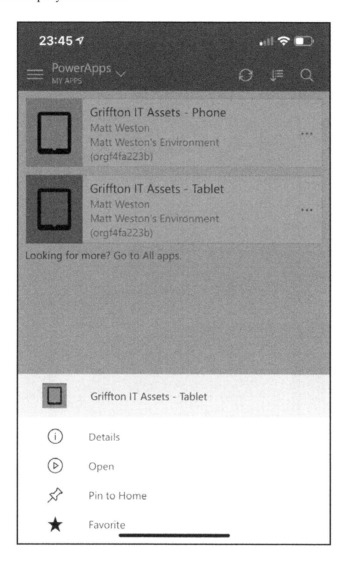

3. Select **Pin to Home**.
4. From this point on, follow the procedure that's relevant to your device, which will pin the app to the home screen:

5. Confirm that the app now appears on your home screen:

Here, we have gone through the process of adding an app to our mobile device. We can use this same process for testing and using the app, which we are going to build as we progress through the rest of the labs.

Summary

In this chapter, we looked at the version history and what that means for our PowerApp. We identified that we can happily work on our app in the draft stages without users being able to see our changes. Once the app has been published, it will be marked as **Live** and will be available for our users to start using. Should the worst-case scenario be realized and we have an error in our app, we can easily revert to a previous version by selecting **Restore**. The restored app will then become a new version, but won't be visible to our users until we click **Publish**.

We also looked at the key ways in which our users can exploit the functionality that's created using PowerApps. First, we focused on SharePoint, which uses a web part within the modern experience to embed the PowerApp onto the page. This is done by providing the web part with the **App web link or ID**, which is obtained from the app **Details** screen. This experience may be due to the web part still being in preview and may change as it is developed further.

The second method was using Microsoft Teams, where we can add a tab to a channel and select **PowerApps**. This will install the PowerApps app to the team and will allow us to select one of our apps or one of the sample apps that are available to us. Anyone who has access to the team will be able to access the tab.

The final method was using a mobile device, where we can use the PowerApps native app, which is one of the many native apps provided by Microsoft for Office 365. When the app is loaded, it will, just like Microsoft Teams, give you the ability to select from any of the apps that you have access to and to the sample apps. Your users can pin the app to the home screen, giving the impression that it is installed locally; however, what it has actually done is create a shortcut. The shortcut will still launch the PowerApps app, but it will immediately direct the user to the relevant app.

In the next chapter, we'll learn about the controls that can be used in PowerApps.

Questions

1. What information do I need to provide to the SharePoint web part to render the PowerApp?
2. How is an app identified as being the current version that users are actively using?
3. Can I add a sample app to a Microsoft Teams channel?
4. Is the PowerApps app available for Android?
5. What would I do to create the illusion of having the app installed locally on the device?
6. True or false: A PowerApp can be installed on a Classic SharePoint page.
7. If I have three versions of an app that is, 1.0, 2.0, and 3.0 (live), what happens if I restore version 2.0?

Section 2: Developing Your PowerApp

2

Within this section, we are going to build upon the basics covered in Section 1, *Getting Started with PowerApps*, and start to focus more on the key building blocks of PowerApps.

In the first chapter of this section, we will undertake an in-depth exploration of the various controls that you can use to build the desired functionality within your PowerApp. As we explore the various controls, we will also highlight where these controls could be used.

In Chapter 6, *Exploring Formulas*, we will be focusing on how we can build logic within PowerApps by using formulas. We will begin with basic formulas such as interacting with text. From there, we will build on those skills and introduce branching logic such as using conditions to allow us to build more complex formulas.

Chapter 7, *Working with Data*, will see us starting to work with data, first of all by being able to create structured data within our apps, but then also looking at ways in which this data can be output into the app.

Finally, in Chapter 8, *Introducing Connectors*, we will look at how we can start to use other data sources and services to provide functionality to our apps by exploring connectors. This chapter will look at the connectors that are provided natively through PowerApps and will then look at how you can create your own connectors to connect to your own services.

This section includes the following chapters:

- Chapter 5, *Exploring Controls*
- Chapter 6, *Exploring Formulas*
- Chapter 7, *Working with Data*
- Chapter 8, *Introducing Connectors*

5
Exploring Controls

In the previous chapters, we looked at PowerApps Studio and created canvas apps using SharePoint and a blank canvas. In this chapter, we will look at PowerApps controls, what they are, how they are used, and some of the ways in which you can interact with them.

Controls play a critical role in the development and functionality of your app as they allow users to interact with data or trigger actions. Choosing the right control for the right job is extremely important for the functionality and the look and feel of your app, as it ensures that you're making the user experience as rich and easy as possible.

In this chapter, we will focus on the main control groups. We will cover the following topics:

- Control properties
- Text controls
- Controls
- Gallery controls
- Icons controls
- Lab 4

In each section, we will learn how these controls work and how we can use them to start adding rich functionality to our app. We will also explore the basic properties that are associated with every control and then start to look briefly at how some of the controls differ from their own key properties.

Technical requirements

To follow along with this chapter, you will need an active PowerApps subscription and have completed *Lab 1*, which can be found in `Chapter 2`, *Creating Your First Canvas PowerApp*, where we created a blank canvas app.

Let's start off by looking at the common configuration settings of the controls, which are called properties.

Control properties

Every control has a multitude of properties associated with it that allow us to define its look, feel, and behavior. Some of the properties are style-related and govern the appearance of the control while it's being viewed by a user, while others are action-related and require the user to interact with the control for it to take effect.

Every control shares some very basic styling properties:

- **X**: This is the horizontal position of the control on your canvas and is expressed as a number of pixels (in terms of distance) from the left side of the app.
- **Y**: This is the vertical position of the control on your canvas and is expressed as a number of pixels (in terms of distance) from the top of the app.
- **Width**: The width of your control.
- **Height**: The height of your control.
- **OnSelect**: This action is taken when a user clicks or taps the control. This is set to *false* by default, which means that no action will be taken.

All of these properties allow you to define either static entries or a formula that calculates the value. In `Chapter 6`, *Exploring Formulas*, we will explore how we can use a formula to make our controls more dynamic. However, for the basic concepts, we will use static values. Now that we have looked at properties, let's take a look at the controls themselves. We will look at what they are and how they're used, and then look at the key properties that apply to them.

Text controls

Text controls are the most common types of control that you will use within your canvas app. They are designed to display textual information, as well as receive inputs from a user, and provide the mainstay of any app. They are commonly used throughout the web to present and allow interaction with data, so, from a user experience point of view, their behavior is well understood by even the most basic of users.

The first control we will look at is one of the most common controls you will use in an app: a label.

LABEL

A **LABEL** is a control that is read-only and allows you to output text to the user but not collect input. The label text is a string; therefore, it can contain alphanumeric and special characters and can either be directly assigned a value or can use a formula to generate an output.

Labels are one of the most versatile controls because there are a lot of properties that can be configured to achieve the desired effect. This could be something as simple as putting a line of text on a page, as shown in the following screenshot, or could be used to display a larger block of text that we can scroll through:

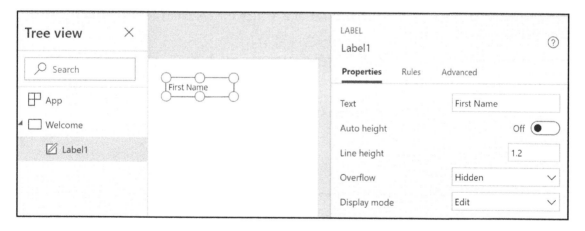

Figure 5.1: LABEL control

Allow your labels to grow with their content by setting the **Auto height** property to *true.*

Typically, labels will be used to introduce another control on a page. For example, when a form is generated, it will use a label for the name of the field. They are also often used to put textual blocks onto your screen. For example, if you wanted to have a piece of introductory text, you would place that text within a label.

The prefix that most developers commonly add when naming a label is `lbl`, for example, `lblFirstName`.

As well as being able to output text, we can also capture inputs using the **TEXT INPUT** control.

TEXT INPUT

TEXT INPUT controls are your standard way of interacting with your app and allow your users to provide textual input that can then be used with a data source or within a formula. **TEXT INPUT** controls are single-line by default, as shown in the following screenshot, but can be expanded so that they become multi-line, which makes them very versatile when we're building out our app:

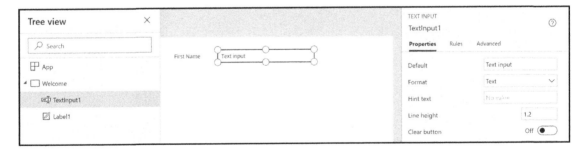

Figure 5.2: TEXT INPUT control

Much like a label, text boxes are extremely versatile controls that have a wide range of uses, from storing temporary data to displaying data from a data source. They have the ability to define the type of data that you are expecting from the user – regardless of whether it's text or a number. This allows you to govern what inputs you receive from the user.

Restrict the number of characters that your users can put into a text box by setting the **Maximum length** property.

Text controls in PowerApps share similar functionality to text controls on a web page, where you can configure the text box to receive a secured string, such as a password. This means that any textual input will be obscured so that it can't be read by someone else just by them looking at the screen. Let's take a look at what a text input control will look like in PowerApps Studio.

To provide a richer user experience with this control, you can also switch on the **Clear button** property and add a tooltip. The clear button renders an **X** when the text box is populated so that you can easily clear any content within it, while the tooltip will add some bespoke help text that is automatically cleared when the user begins typing. These two very simple properties allow you to provide a rich user experience for your users and are practices that are now routinely included on websites and apps across the internet.

 The prefix that most developers commonly add when naming a label is `txt`, for example, `txtFirstName`.

As well as plain text, we also have controls that are able to handle text strings, which contain markup such as HTML.

HTML text

The **HTML text** control is very similar to a standard label; however, it allows you to define HTML within the text property. This allows you to add additional styling and markup beyond the basic formatting tools that are available through PowerApps Studio.

As shown in the following screenshot, you can use standard HTML encoding to add additional styling to specific parts of your text. With the label control, you can apply styling to the entire control, whereas with the HTML text control, this will give you the flexibility to change the color or boldness of the text in the middle of the string.

The key property for this control is the **HTML text** control:

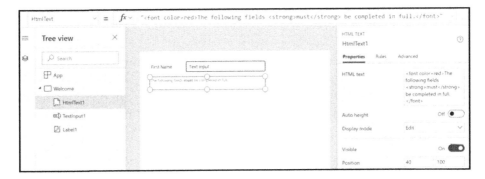

Figure 5.3: HTML text control

The **HTML text** control can also be used for drawing **Scalable Vector Graphic (SVG)** images, which are responsive graphics that are constructed using XML.

As well as being able to output text using HTML formatting options, we are also able to have our users enter markup text using the **RICH TEXT EDITOR**.

RICH TEXT EDITOR

The **RICH TEXT EDITOR** provides a **What You See Is What You Get (WYSIWIG)** editor for your PowerApp, which allows your users to provide their own formatting when entering text. The text and effects that are added to this control are output and rendered in the same way that HTML would be rendered in a browser. As shown in the following screenshot, this control gives you the ability to select what type of formatting you want to use from the toolbar across the top of the control, such as the ability to apply styling, make the text bold, or include bullet lists:

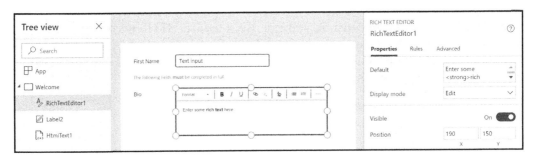

Figure 5.4: RICH TEXT EDITOR control

Pasting content from another source (such as another web page) will retain the source's formatting. This also applies to content that's created within Word; any styling will be copied to the **RICH TEXT EDITOR** control.

Rich text editors provide perfect control if you're looking to give your users the ability to provide structure around their input. As an example, if you are using this in a service desk app, then your users could list recreation steps using numbered lists.

Finally, we have the ability to give our users a more free-form type of textual input with the **PEN INPUT** control.

PEN INPUT

PEN INPUT is a control that allows you to accept non-textual input for a selected area. This type of control provides a free-form tool that can be used for whiteboarding, signatures, or general drawing. Often, I have seen this being used to capture wet signatures on a mobile device, which is where someone actually signs their signature directly onto the screen.

The key properties that are used with this type of input are as follows:

- **Mode**: This defines what the default tool is, whether that is the draw tool or the erase tool.
- **Show controls**: This defines whether the toolbox is presented at the bottom of the control. When applying signatures, I have turned the toolbox off:

Figure 5.5: The PEN INPUT control showing a signature

The output from this control will produce an image that is stored locally as a **Binary Large Object (BLOb)**.

Now that we have looked at the most common types of controls, that is, text-based controls, let's explore the other controls that we can use to add more functionality to our app.

Controls

Controls are key components that are used to build the basic functionality and interactivity of your app. While text controls are the most common components we'll use, the following controls will allow you to customize the input experience so that you can take other data types and other input methods into account.

BUTTON

Buttons are one of the most simple controls that you can work with; they are designed to be a focal point for a click or a tap and are generally used to instantiate an action. The default styling on a button makes it stand out as a clickable control, as shown in the following screenshot. However, this styling can be changed to suit the look and feel of your page:

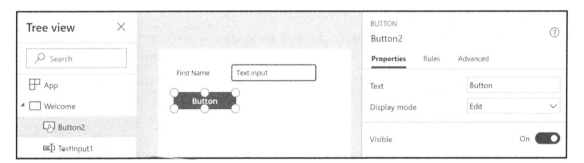

Figure 5.6: BUTTON control

While the ability to edit the styling of the button is available, the most important aspect of this control is the **OnSelect** property. **OnSelect** allows you to define the behavior of the button using a formula; for example, when a button is clicked, it will save an item. As a result, buttons are used a lot throughout apps, even to the point of interacting with other controls on the screen.

There are numerous other types of interaction we may want within our app. One of them is related to inputting dates.

DATE PICKER

The **DATE PICKER** is a good alternative to a text box if you are asking the user to provide a date. This allows you to ensure that the date is entered in the correct format. The date picker is a calendar that the user can navigate through and click on, rather than having to type anything.

While using the date picker, the user can navigate forward and backward one month at a time. Alternatively, they can click on the month or the year to directly change those values:

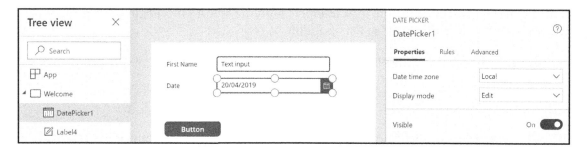

Figure 5.7: DATE PICKER control

The key properties for this control are as follows:

- **DefaultDate**: The date that's displayed when the control is rendered.
- **Format**: How you wish the date to be displayed once it's been entered.
- **Language**: If you are using the long date format, where the month is displayed textually, the language property will change the date depending on the language that's selected. If this is left blank, the default behavior is to use the native language of the device.
- **Start Year**: This is the starting year that the user selects using the date picker and will default to 1970. Be aware that if you need to select dates before 1970, then you will need to change this property.

There are times where you will want to govern what inputs are provided by your users by making them select predefined answers. These are classed as multiple choices.

Presenting multiple choices

Often, to maintain the integrity of the data being captured, you will want to present options to your users. This will ensure that the data you're taking in is correct, in the right format, or to avoid ambiguity.

Multiple choice controls are best used when you have a defined list of options, or where a text box would allow ambiguous and varied options to be entered. For example, "United Kingdom" could be expressed as "United Kingdom", "UK", "Great Britain", and so on.

DROP DOWN

A **DROP DOWN** is designed to allow a user to select something from a number of predefined options. The intention is very much to avoid long lists of options being displayed on a screen, thereby collapsing all of the available options into a small amount of screen real estate. Only when the user interacts with the control by clicking on the chevron will the user see the full scrollable list of options.

 DROP DOWN controls will support a maximum of 500 items.

When providing options to PowerApps directly, you must provide them as an array of strings, with each option being separated by a comma. Therefore, if I wanted to supply a list of days of the week, the **Items** property of the **DROP DOWN** would look like this:

```
["Monday","Tuesday","Wednesday","Thursday","Friday","Saturday","Sunday"]
```

An example of the **DROP DOWN** control in action is shown in the following screenshot:

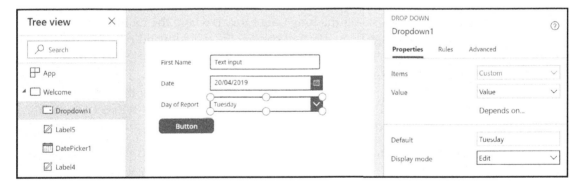

Figure 5.8: DROP DOWN list control

The key elements of this control are as follows:

- **Items**: These are the options that are available to the user. Entries for items can either be manually entered or bound to a data source. If you're using a data source that contains several columns, then you will simply need to select the data field that contains the date you wish to show.
- **Default**: This is the default value that is displayed when the control is first rendered and will be the value that's submitted by the control if the user doesn't change it. If you leave the default value empty, there will be no default displayed in the control when it is first displayed.
- **Selected**: If you are retrieving data to display in this control, setting the **Selected** property will ensure that the current item is displayed in the control rather than a default value, if one has been provided.

Dropdown boxes don't really offer the best user experience if you have a lot of options to choose from due to having to scroll up and down to find your selection. In a scenario where we have a lot of options, we should consider a combo box instead.

COMBO BOX

A **COMBO BOX** behaves similarly to that of a **DROP DOWN** control, whereby you can define a list of potential options for a user to select from. The advantage that a **COMBO BOX** has is that you can click it and search for an entry. Unlike a **DROP DOWN**, a **COMBO BOX** needs to be bound to a data source that it will search for, based on the user's input.

There are a number of different display templates that can be selected when you're using a **COMBO BOX** and they can really tailor your user experience. Some of these are as follows:

- **Single data value**: Provides just a single line of text
- **Two values**: Allows two lines of text in the selection, with one being the option and the other being a subtitle
- **Two values (person)**: Allows the same layout as **two values** but also allows the use of an image

There are several key properties that need to be configured when you're using a **COMBO BOX**:

- **Items**: The source of data that is going to provide your options.
- **DefaultSelectedItems**: The option/s that are selected when the control is rendered for the first time.

- **SelectMultiple**: Defines the selection behavior in terms of whether the user can select one or multiple options from the control.
- **IsSearchable**: Defines whether the user can use the search functionality that's available for the control.
- **SearchFields**: If the user can search, then you need to define how the search will work. The data source is defined within the Items property, so you need to provide this property with a string array of columns; for example, `["Country","Region"]`:

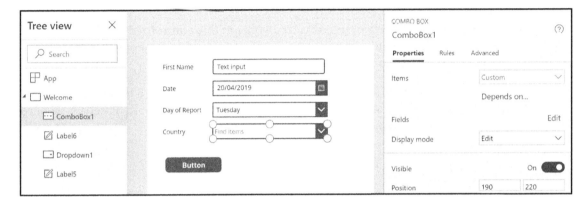

Figure 5.9: COMBO BOX control

Consider using this control when there are a large number of options that the user can select from to avoid having the user spending large amounts of time scrolling up and down a list.

The **DROP DOWN** and **COMBO BOX** controls hide all of the available options until the user clicks on the chevron to expand them. Your app may require you to display the options in a more visible way but still allow a controlled set of options to be selected. This can be achieved by using the **LIST BOX** control.

LIST BOX

A **LIST BOX** is another way of being able to present and select options from a predefined list. The major difference, however, is that because more of the options are shown in a single control, you will take up more real estate on the screen. An example of the **LIST BOX** control is shown in the following screenshot:

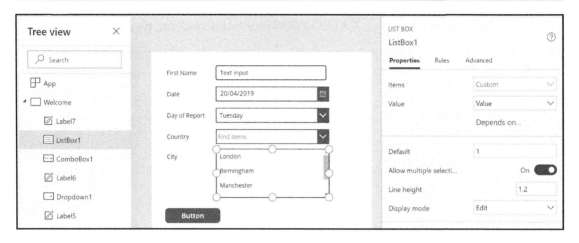

Figure 5.10: LIST BOX control

The key properties associated with this control are as follows:

- **Items**: The source of the options that are presented in the control, much like the **DROP DOWN** control
- **Default**: The option that's selected when the control is rendered

If we have multiple options available to us but we only want to allow the selection of one, then we could consider using a **RADIO** button control.

RADIO

RADIO buttons are very common on HTML forms and will provide a list of options where only a single item can be selected. Each of the options will be displayed within your app, meaning that it can take up a large amount of real estate.

The key properties for this control are as follows:

- **Items**: The source of the options that are presented in the control, much like the **DROP DOWN** control
- **Default**: The default value that's selected when the control is rendered
- **Layout**: Allows you to define whether the options are listed horizontally or vertically

The following screenshot shows a **RADIO** button control displaying two options:

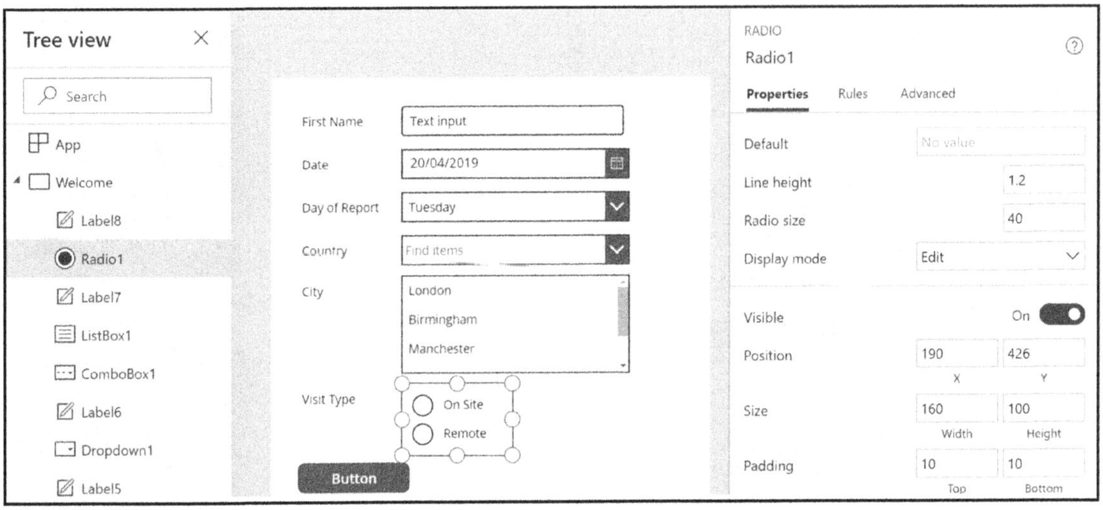

Figure 5.11: RADIO control

> Consider using this control when the number of options is relatively small and where only one option can be selected.

All of the controls that we have looked at so far have allowed us to use a range of different methods to capture alphanumeric input from the user. Often, in development, you will need to capture Boolean (yes or no) values. PowerApps has some controls that allow us to do this.

Boolean controls

There are times when you need to take in a binary response from your users, whether the result is either true or false. Rather than creating our own control to handle this type of input, we can use the **CHECK BOX** or **TOGGLE** control.

CHECK BOX

A **CHECK BOX** is a very simple control that can either be set to true or false by the user ticking or unticking it.

The key properties of this control are as follows:

- **Text**: The descriptive text that is placed next to the checkbox.
- **Value**: Just because the control is Boolean in nature doesn't mean that an alternative value can't be assigned.
- **Default**: This is either true or false and specifies whether the checkbox is ticked or not when it is first rendered.

When this is rendered onto the screen, it will provide a square box that the user can either tick or untick based on their selection. This is shown in the following screenshot:

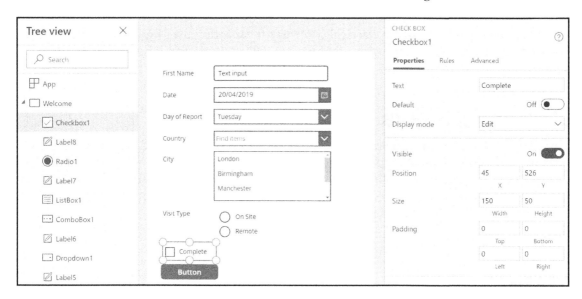

Figure 5.12: CHECK BOX control placed on the canvas

Consider using this control when the input that's required from the user is a simple yes or no; for example, do you agree to the terms and conditions?

As an alternative control to a checkbox, a common control that's used for yes and no values, especially on mobile apps, is the **TOGGLE** control.

TOGGLE

TOGGLE is a graphical improvement of the checkbox whereby the user can switch control between true and false by moving the handle. This has the same behavior as the checkbox, but it doesn't have a text property. If you need to add some supporting text, you will need to use another control, such as a label.

 Consider using this control when you're collecting Boolean input and need to conserve screen space.

As well as being able to use the classical controls for capturing user inputs, we can also use some of the more modern controls so that we can collect numerical inputs from a user.

Numerical inputs

Unlike text boxes, which allow us to input alphanumeric strings of data, numerical inputs are bound to numerical data types. Correctly using this type of control will ensure that you are supplying the correct data formats to your data source and ensure that any calculations based on your inputs can be executed correctly. Let's take a look at a couple of input methods that act as alternatives to standard text boxes.

SLIDER

A **SLIDER** is designed to be an interactive user control whose value will change if we drag its handle. The control can be defined with a minimum and maximum value, which equates to the left and right extremes of the slider, with the user selecting the value by positioning the handle between the two extremes.

The key properties associated with this control are as follows:

- **Minimum**: The number that's associated with the left-hand side of the slider scale
- **Maximum**: The number that's associated with the right-hand side of the slider scale
- **Default**: The value where the slider control starts, which must be between the minimum and maximum values:

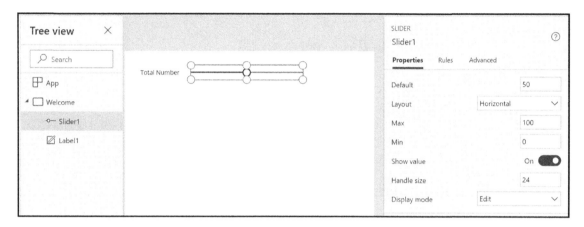

Figure 5.13: SLIDER control placed on the canvas

 Consider using this control when you require your users to select a numerical value within a distinct range.

Another common way of providing numerical input, especially within modern shopping apps, is by using a rating system, which can be used to capture scores or ratings that can be fed into the system.

RATING

A **RATING** is a control that allows a user to select a value between 1 and your maximum value in a graphical way.

The key properties of this control are as follows:

- **Maximum**: The upper limit that your users can select. The highest number that can be defined is 200.
- **Default**: The default value that's selected when the control is rendered:

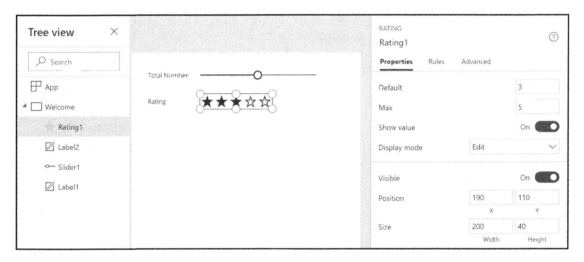

5.14: RATING control using stars to collect user input

 Consider using this control when you are adding visual richness to your app and need to get a numerical value back from the user when the maximum number that can be chosen is relatively small.

There are times where you will need to be able to use timings to add functionality to your app. This is provided by the **TIMER** control.

TIMER

TIMER controls allow you to use periods of time to perform actions within your PowerApp. For example, they can be used to determine when something appears or disappears or can be used to interact with other controls when a given amount of time has passed.

The key properties associated with this control are as follows:

- **OnStart**: Definition of what happens when the timer begins
- **OnTimerEnd**: Definition of what happens when the timer has completed
- **Duration**: How long the timer will run for in milliseconds
- **Repeat**: Whether a timer will automatically restart upon completion
- **AutoStart**: Whether the timer will start automatically or whether it requires an action to start it

Consider using this control for timer style functionality or for creating basic animations within PowerApps.

As well as using controls to interact with data within our app, there will be occasions where we need to facilitate importing and exporting data too.

IMPORT and EXPORT

The **IMPORT** and **EXPORT** controls allow you to interact with data and effectively share it locally between two apps. To prepare data to be exported, you must save your data within a collection, which we will explore further in `Chapter 7`, *Working with Data*.

The **EXPORT** control will create a local compressed file. If you have access to the file system, this file can be picked up and transferred elsewhere, but it can only be opened by PowerApps. The **IMPORT** control can then be used to bring that file back into your app:

Figure 5.15: IMPORT and EXPORT controls

While these controls can be quite useful, there are security practices that should be enforced upon the users who use it to ensure that only trusted files are imported into apps.

One of the most important controls that you will use within PowerApps will be galleries.

Gallery controls

Gallery controls are designed to allow the consistent repetition of data to be displayed on the screen, for example, when displaying data from a data source. Galleries can be used to display multiple types of data using multiple types of controls to build up a feature-rich display within your app. Changes to the layout are made within the gallery template, which is the first item within the gallery. Any changes that you make within the template are automatically reflected through each repeating section, which means that you don't have to manually update every single row.

Gallery controls allow you to use three different types of layout within your app:

- **Vertical**: Each row of data is displayed vertically down the canvas.
- **Horizontal**: Each row of data is displayed horizontally across the canvas.
- **Flexible height**: Each row of data is displayed vertically down the page. Here, the row's height will grow with the content:

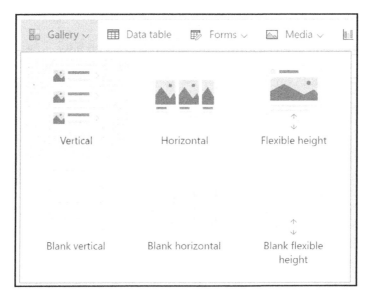

Figure 5.16: The display options that are available when inserting a gallery

Each type of gallery style has the option to auto-generate its content based on the data field that's selected. For example, if my data source is textual, then it will automatically place a text control in the gallery.

Galleries can be connected to a number of different data sources, that is, externally to your PowerApp, but also internally, such as when connecting to a collection. When we are working with external data sources, we use connectors to read data into the gallery and display it. We will talk about connectors in more detail in `Chapter 8`, *Introducing Connectors*.

As well as being able to select the display orientation of a gallery, you can also select a number of predefined layouts, ranging from blank layouts to layouts containing images. These layout templates are usually a good place to start from when you're creating your apps and they can then be customized so that you can create your desired layout:

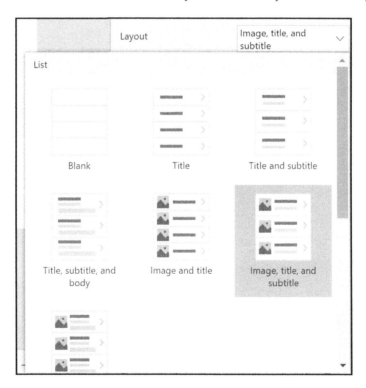

Figure 5.17: The layout types that can be applied to a gallery

We will look at the **Gallery** control in more detail in `Chapter 7`, *Working with Data*, when we start looking at how we can work with data.

Icon controls

Icons are one of the key ways in which you can add graphical and visual depth to your apps. The icons menu contains a number of icons, as well as geometric shapes that can be laid on top of each other to create effects. There are a large number of icons, many of which will satisfy the graphical requirements of your app without you having to develop your own images.

Within PowerApps, icons are used to provide various elements of functionality, for example, to sort, search, apply filters, or to open a menu.

The shape icons are generally used for creating styling and visual effects within PowerApps so that we can add header areas, backgrounds, or zones within our apps:

Figure 5.18: The icons and geometric shapes that are available within PowerApps

Each of the icons is effectively SVG in nature, which means you can make them as large or as small as you like without any distortion taking place. This also means that you can apply your own background and foreground colors to give the icon the color effect that you desire.

 Icons have additional properties, such as rotation, which give you more control over how your icon appears within your app.

The key properties of this control are as follows:

- **OnSelect**: This will allow you to define a formula that allows your icons to interact with other parts of the app.
- **Fill**: This will change the background color of the icon.

There are other controls also available to us, such as **FORMS** and **DATA TABLES**, which we will look at in Chapter 7, *Working with Data*, but these are the key components that allow us to start building our user interfaces within a canvas app.

Lab 4

In this lab, we are going to build on the blank app we created in *Lab 1* by creating a welcome screen for our app. Begin by opening the app we created in *Lab 1* in PowerApps Studio.

Activity 1: Building basic branding

The first thing we are going to do is build a basic look and feel for our app by placing some shapes onto the canvas. To begin with, we will create a header.

For this, we will insert a **Rectangle** we will use as a header. Follow these steps to do so:

1. Open the **Insert** menu.
2. From the **Icons** menu, select **Rectangle**:

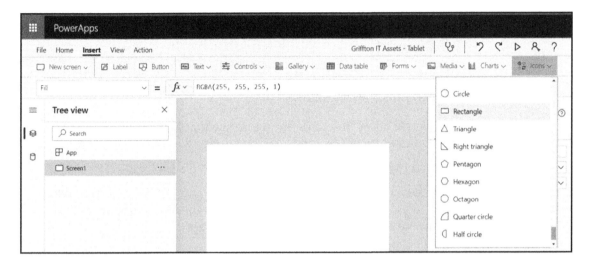

3. When the rectangle appears on the canvas, drag it to the top left corner or change the **X** and **Y** properties to 0:

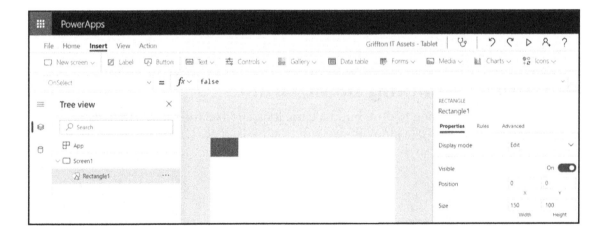

4. Use the right handle to drag the width of the rectangle until it is the full width of the canvas:

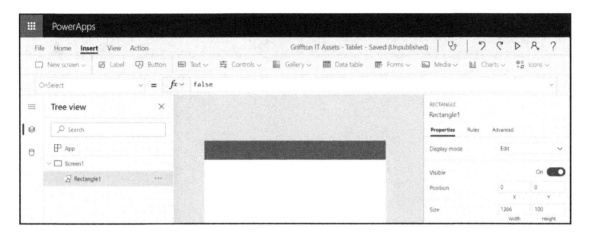

Now, we need to place a **Hamburger menu** on the screen that will serve as our navigation menu. Let's get started:

1. Open the **Insert** menu.
2. From the **Icons** menu, select **Hamburger menu**:

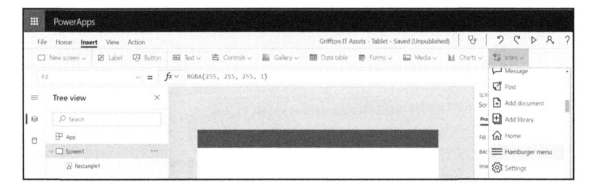

3. When the icon appears on the screen, change the **X** property to 20 and the **Y** property to 15 so that it will be positioned at a good distance from both the left and top edges of the app:

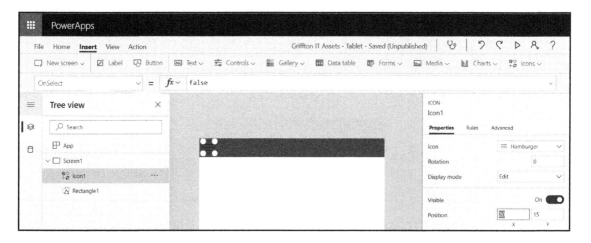

4. In the **Properties** pane, change the font color to white:

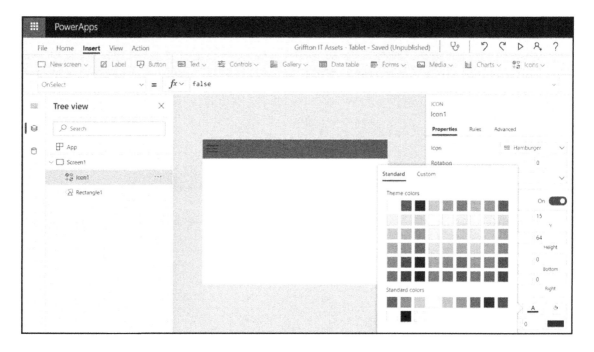

This will give us a basic header. We will be developing this further in later labs:

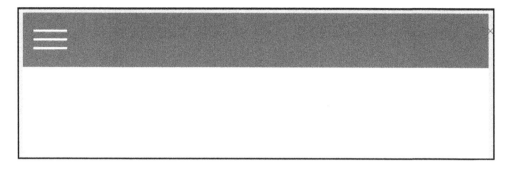

Now that we have created the header, we can add more controls to the canvas and start adding content to the app.

Activity 2: Adding the name of the app

We will use this welcome page as an entry point for our users, so we will add some basic controls to welcome them. We will start by adding the name of the app to the header to help with identification.

First, we need to insert a **Label** for the app title. Let's get started:

1. Open the **Insert** menu.
2. From the **Text** menu, select **Label**:

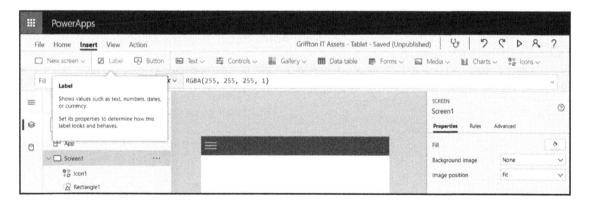

3. When the label appears, set the **Text** property to Griffton IT Assets:

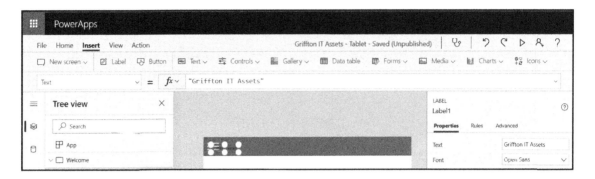

4. Set the **X** property to 500 and the **Y** property to 25:

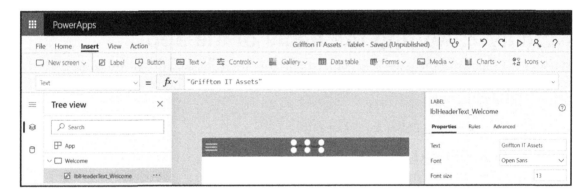

5. With your label still selected, click the **Home** menu.
6. Increase the **Font size** to 32, make it **Bold**, and change the color to white:

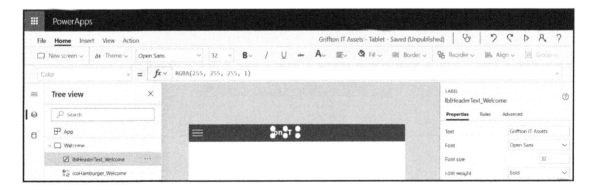

7. Using the right handle, increase the size of the label so that the text fits onto a single line:

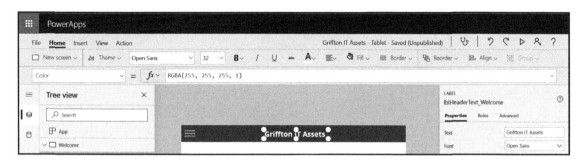

Now, we have created our header bar, including the controls that will eventually launch our menu. We've also added the title of the app. We will now add a control to allow our users to begin interacting with the app.

Activity 3: Inserting an enter button

As part of the home screen, we will allow our users to enter the app by pressing a button. We will add the navigation logic in `Chapter 6`, *Exploring Formulas*, but for now, we will place the control on the screen. Let's get started:

1. Open the **Insert** menu.
2. From the control menu, select **Button**:

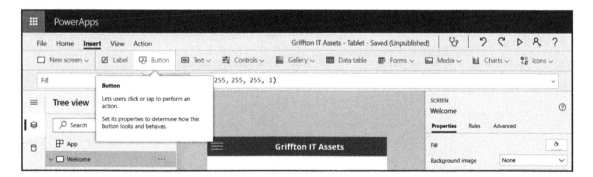

3. When the button appears, change the **Text** property to Enter:

4. Change the height to 200.
5. Change the width to 550:

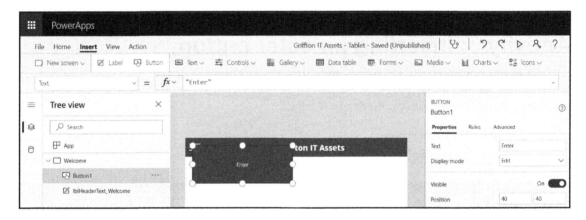

6. Change the **X** property to 407 and the **Y** property to 284:

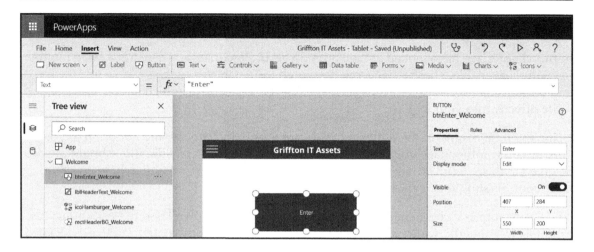

7. Increase the **Size** property of the button to `38`:

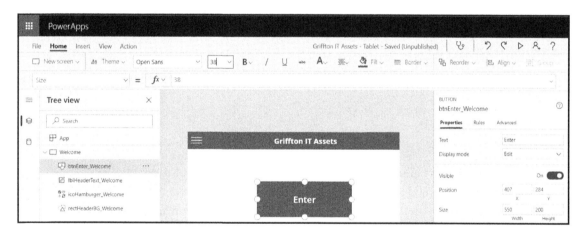

Now, we can preview the app by pressing the play button in the top right corner, as well as **Save** and **Publish** the app so that it can be tested on a mobile device.

Now, we have the first screen of an app that we will add further functionality to as we progress through this book. In the next lab, we will start to add some functionality to our app using formulas.

Summary

In this chapter, we have looked at the key controls in PowerApps. There are a large number of controls available. These range from basic web form controls such as labels, text boxes, and buttons to more complex types such as **PEN INPUT** control, which allows users to write directly into your app.

Using the right control at the right time is paramount to the success and adoption of your app, as you want to make your app as easy as possible to use. Consideration should always be given to the amount of real estate that's being used on the screen and, where possible, large controls should be avoided.

All of our controls share some basic properties that are normally related to positioning, for example, X, Y, height, width, and so on. However, most controls have properties associated with them that are specific to that control.

Controls provide a large number of icons that can be used to create visual effects and to stylize your app in the way that you want. These icons include a number of geometric shapes that can be layered on top of one another in order to make your app visually appealing to the end user.

In the next chapter, we'll learn how formulas can help us create PowerApps.

Questions

1. Which control allows you to capture either a number or a string of text?
2. What is the maximum value for the rating control?
3. Why would you use a drop-down control over a list control?
4. What is the main difference between a combo box and a dropdown?
5. What can I use to build up visual effects within my PowerApp?
6. What two values can a checkbox take?
7. Which control should I use to capture a signature from a user?

6
Exploring Formulas

In previous chapters, we looked at how to build the skeletons of the apps by using screens with controls to build up the user interface. In this chapter, we will now begin to look at how we can use functions with PowerApps to begin building up functionality within our app.

While there is a multitude of functions that exist within PowerApps, this chapter will focus on the more commonly used functions and look at how they can be used to create formulas. Many of the formulas will be illustrated using examples.

The following topics will be covered in this chapter:

- Using text functions to cast data and then perform a basic transformation on that text
- Undertaking mathematical calculations using arithmetical functions
- Working with dates, including getting the current date and time and formatting them
- Understanding conditional logic and how you can define branches using `If` and `Switch` statements

By the end of this chapter, you will have an understanding of how to write formulas to add functionality to your app. You will also have had an introduction to the syntax, and some of the key formulas that will aid you whilst creating your own PowerApps.

Technical requirements

To follow along with this chapter, you will need an active PowerApps subscription and you must have completed *Lab 1* from the previous chapter where we created a blank canvas app.

The function browser

Before we get delve into the world of functions, note that you—as a developer of PowerApps—are not expected to remember all of the functions that can be combined to create a formula.

The PowerApps Studio has a selection drop-down menu next to the formula bar, as shown in *Figure 6.1: The formula selector,* which allows you to browse and select which function you would like to use. Each function is categorized by type, which means that you can select the correct function based on what you're trying to do. For example, if we wanted to concatenate two string values, we could select **Text** from the drop-down menu and then select **Concatenate** from the browser:

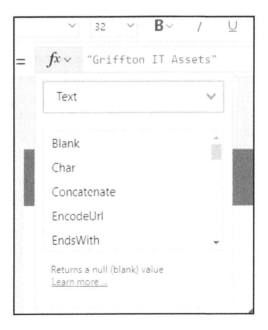

Figure 6.1: The formula selector

There are two actions that I can trigger when interacting with the function browser. If I single-click on a function, it will provide a basic description at the bottom of the menu and supply a hyperlink to tell you more about that particular function. If I double-click the function instead, it will be placed into my formula bar so that I can then use it or modify it as I see fit.

Using the formula bar

The formula bar is where you will build your formulas by combining one or several functions together to create functionality. When typing into this area, you will see an amount of predictive text appearing (or IntelliSense, if you're used to development environments), as in *Figure 6.2: Example of a formula triggering IntelliSense*. Formulas can be used in any property to help to set values, whether that is by calling a function, calling data from a data source, or interacting with another control on the screen:

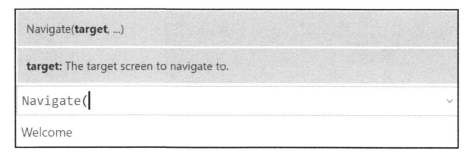

Figure 6.2: Example of a formula triggering IntelliSense

Formulas with PowerApps feel very much like writing formulas within Excel since it shares many of the same pitfalls. When writing formulas, keep in mind the following things:

- All functions and objects are case-sensitive.
- Consider some of the language nuances that apply; for example, French separates characters with commas. In these situations, consider changing commas in your formulas into semi-colons.

A basic formula will always consist of a function name and potentially several arguments that need to be provided. A basic example is navigation, where the `Navigate` function can be used. When you type `Navigate`, it will then prompt you to provide a target and a visual transition:

```
Navigate(Welcome,ScreenTransition.Cover)
```

If there are errors in your formula, the formula will be underlined with a red line similar to spelling mistakes in Microsoft Word. There will also be a tooltip, as can be seen in *Figure 6.3: Formula bar showing a tooltip on an error*, which will give you some guidance as to what the issue might be:

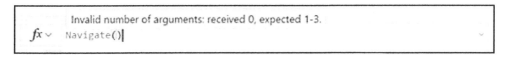

Figure 6.3: Formula bar showing a tooltip on an error

You can format your formulas so that they are not always on the same line by using the **Format text** button. This is designed purely to improve the readability of your formula by applying carriage returns and indents:

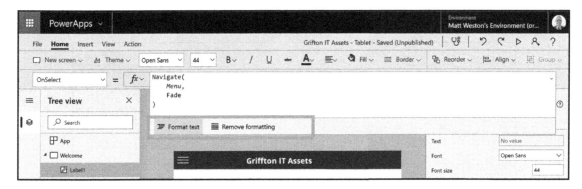

Figure 6.4: Formatting options

 You can add your own carriage returns by holding *Shift* and pressing the *Enter* key.

Now, my feeling is that it's a good practice to add comments to your formulas. This can help others to develop your app and understand the functionality without reading each formula. The notation used is identical to that of C#, which uses two forward slashes (//) to denote a comment. Comments are easily identifiable as the text turns green.

If you wish to continue to add formulas after a comment, ensure that you start a new line.

Formulas can be used to add functionality to any property of the controls you place on the screen, which means that you can start to build up a rich dynamic interface for your users. As well as setting properties, you can also refer to them by using the name and the property name of a control; for example, if I want to get the X position of a label, I can use the following code:

```
Label1.X
```

When using formulas with controls, you can easily select the parent control by using the `Parent` keyword. All controls have a parent, which, most of the time, will be the screen where the component is placed. This becomes more apparent when you start using form controls and other nested components. If I had a label on the screen and wanted to dynamically set it to the same width as the screen, I could use the following in the label `Width` property:

```
Parent.Width
```

The result of using `Parent.Width` is that the control will automatically adopt the width of the parent. Therefore, if the parent changes size, so will the control.

Now that we are starting to use formulas, we need to start working with data and manipulating it so that we can provide the correct data in the required format regardless of whether it's textual, numeric, or another data type.

Interacting with text

The most common type of data that you will be working with is text, also commonly known as a string. Textual data can take the format of a combination of alphanumeric characters. There are several basic functions that we can use to work with textual data.

First of all, if we wish to cast a value (convert numbers, dates, and time to text), then we can use the `Text` function:

```
Text(<the value you wish to cast here>)
```

If you are inserting input into your app that contains tags, for example, HTML or XML, then you may wish to use PlainText (shown in *Figure 6.5: Demonstration of HTML being removed from a string*) to strip out all of the tags so that you are then able to work with a plaintext value:

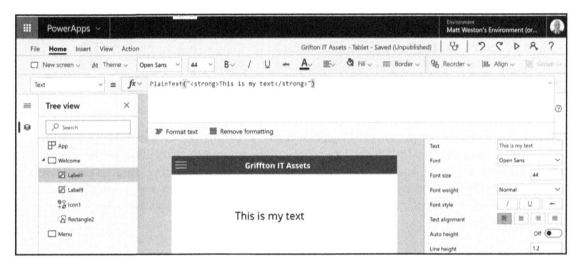

Figure 6.5: Demonstration of HTML being removed from a string

Once you are working with a string of text, especially if you've had to convert it from another data type, you can then start to use the other functions that are available to you. The most common actions that you will tend to use with strings are those that provide the ability to isolate portions of it.

When displaying text on the screen, there are several functions that you may wish to use to improve the readability of your text or to perform some last-minute transformation. Commonly, you may replace text or ensure that it utilizes the correct case when shown on the screen.

Now, let's look at available text functions.

Replace and substitute

If I want to replace elements of a string, then two functions are available to me through PowerApps. The first is Replace, which differs slightly from the Replace functions that you may be familiar with from other programming languages. When you use Replace, you need to provide a numerical start point for the replacement, and the numerical length of the characters you are going to replace.

In the following example, I'm going to replace `IT` with `Computer`. To do this, I need to count the number of characters from the beginning of the string to the start of what I want to replace, which will be `I`. In the following example, that would be `10` characters from the start. I then need the number of additional characters that I'm going to replace, that is, `2`. This will give me an output of `Griffton Computer Assets`:

```
Replace("Griffton IT Assets",10,2,"Computer")
```

In your PowerApps Studio, it will look as follows:

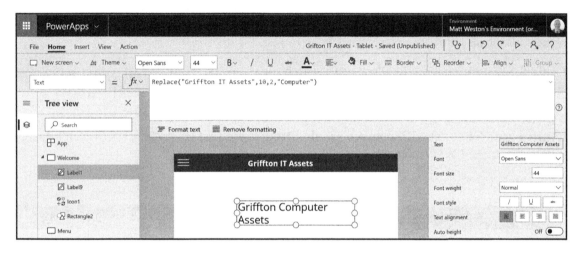

Figure 6.6: Example of Replace being used in a formula

The second method is to use `Substitute`, which works much more like the `Replace` functionality in other languages. You provide the input string, the string that you want to match and replace, and then the text that you wish to be displayed instead.

```
Substitute("Griffton IT Assets", "IT", "Computer")
```

While `Substitute` is the simpler function to use, it is also the least accurate as it will replace all instances of the string that are found. Therefore, if `IT` occurs more than once, it will be replaced by `Computer` every time.

It is important to note that the matching that takes place in `Substitute` is case-sensitive.

In this example, we have explicitly told the formula which part of the string I want to transform; however, often, we don't have the luxury of having a string start and end in exactly the same place every time. Therefore, we need to be able to dynamically isolate a string.

Searching and matching

When we are working with strings, it is common for us to search for specific elements or occurrences of characters. PowerApps provides us with several ways that we can search within a string of text. Some functions will return a character position whereas others will return a Boolean value if the string has been found.

Using the `Find` function will allow us to search for a specific string of text within another string. This will return the numeric value of the index where the matched string is found.

The following formula will search for the `IT` string in `Griffton IT Assets` and will return a value of `10`. The 10th character in the string is the first character of `IT` as can be seen in *Figure 6.7: The Find function being used to locate a word*.

```
Find("IT","Griffton IT Assets")
```

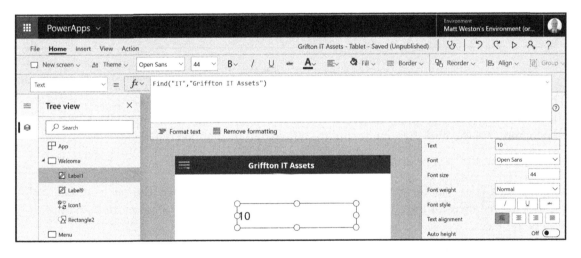

Figure 6.7: The Find function being used to locate a word

The `Find` function can be combined with the `Replace` function from the previous section to dynamically find the start index rather than you having to type it in yourself.

`StartsWith` and `EndsWith` both examine a string of text to see whether the match occurs at the beginning or end. This function will simply return a `true` or `false` value based on whether it finds a match or not. The same formula is then demonstrated, in PowerApps, in *Figure 6.8: Screenshot of the StartsWith function being used*:

```
StartsWith("Griffton IT Assets","Griffton")
EndsWith("Griffton IT Assets","ts")
```

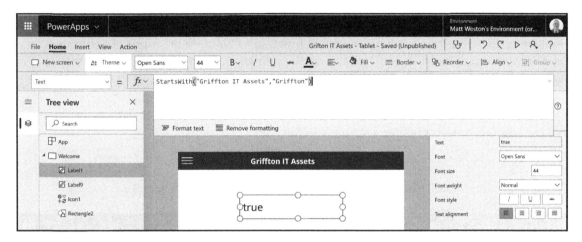

Figure 6.8: Screenshot of the StartsWith function being used

 Unlike other functions, `StartsWith` and `EndsWith` are not case-sensitive when performing a match.

So far, we have been able to identify and interact with strings by using known text. But there are often times, especially in validation, where we need to use data patterns.

Regular expressions

If the built-in methods of matching within a string are not advanced enough, we can use more in-depth methods of matching such as **Regular Expressions** (**RegEx**). Regular expressions are commonly used throughout development to test for or to identify patterns within strings rather than looking for specific matches.

Regular expressions are always considered to be a bit of a dark art, with some developers loving them and others hating them. They can have a steep learning curve to begin with, but once you are used to them, they become an extremely important part of your toolkit. Luckily, there are many resources on the web which can assist you in writing your own or provide pre-built expressions.

Once you have written your regular expression, you can use it within your formula by using the `IsMatch` function. `IsMatch` will take in the string that you're looking to match, and the regular expression that it's going to use to validate the pattern, and then return a Boolean result. Commonly, I have used this function to validate the input of fields such as postcodes or email addresses. If we take email as an example, a basic regular expression would look like this:

```
^\w+@[a-zA-Z_]+?\.[a-zA-Z]{2,3}$
```

We can use this to test whether a string is in the correct format:

```
IsMatch("matt@grifftonit.com","^\w+@[a-zA-Z_]+?\.[a-zA-Z]{2,3}$")
```

As the preceding email address is in the correct format, it will return `true`:

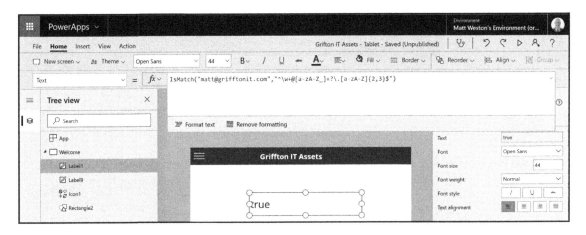

Figure 6.9: Using regular expressions to validate a string

A good source of pre-built regular expressions can be found at `http://www.regexlib.com/`.

Much of what we do in app development starts with transforming data to the correct format. This should always be taken into consideration before trying to write formulas, so you understand the data that is being retrieved and how you need to manipulate it. It is just as important to be able to interact with numbers in the same way.

Using numbers

The second most common type of data that you will be working with in your PowerApp is numerical data. Just like text, there are numerous mathematical functions that we can call upon within our app. PowerApps also supports basic mathematical operators:

- + (Add)
- - (Subtract)
- * (Multiply)
- / (Divide)

Mathematical formulas can be built from either static numbers or by using inputs from other controls that are on the screen. Assuming that the input is a number from your control, the formula will calculate a value. For example, you may wish to calculate the center point of the X axis of the screen that you're working on; therefore, I could take the `Width` attribute of the screen and divide it by 2:

```
"Centre point is: "& Parent.Width/2
```

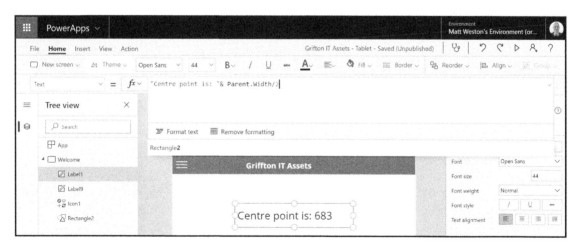

Figure 6.10: Performing division within a formula

Quite often when doing math, particularly when using division, we may not always have a rounded number to work with. Therefore, we can use the Rounding function to transform the value.

Rounding

There will be many times when a value is returned with a decimal value but the behavior that you wish your app to display is a rounded value. Three functions will allow you to round your value in various ways.

Round

Round is quite a generic function that will simply round a number up or down depending on what it is closest to. You will need to provide the function with the number and the number of decimal points that you want it to display:

```
Round(68.5,0)
```

As an example, I am going to round to the closest integer; therefore, I would provide the number of decimal places set to 0. In this scenario, if the value were 68.2, the displayed value would be 68. If the value were 68.5, the displayed value would be 69.

RoundUp and RoundDown

RoundUp works in a very similar way to that of Round, in that you can provide it with a value and the number of decimal points that you wish to display. However, it will always round up to the higher value regardless of whether it's in the lower half of the value. For example, 68.2 will be rounded up to 69, as shown in *Figure 6.11: Formula being used to demonstrate rounding*.

```
RoundUp(68.2,0)
```

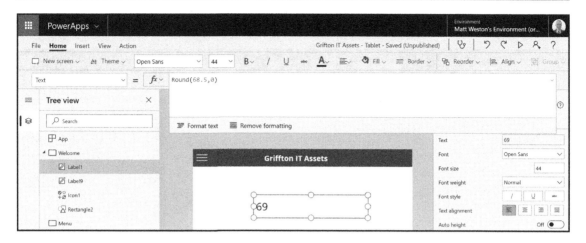

Figure 6.11: Formula being used to demonstrate rounding

`RoundDown` is the opposite and will simply return the lower value instead:

```
RoundDown(68.2,0)
```

Here, `68.2` will be rounded down to `68`.

There will be times where more complicated mathematical functions will be required, therefore there are several other numerical functions that can be explored to meet all levels of complexity.

Other numerical functions

There are numerous other numerical functions that you can begin to explore and that will help you to build the functionality you require throughout your app. Such examples include the following:

- `Abs`: The absolute positive value of a number, for example, `Abs(-10)`, will result in 10, as shown in *Figure 6.12: Demonstrating the absolute function*.
- `Power`: The value of a number raised to a specific power; for example, `Power(10,3)`, will equate 10 x 10 x 10, which equals 1,000.

- Sqrt: The square root of a value; for example, Sqrt(169), will return 13.

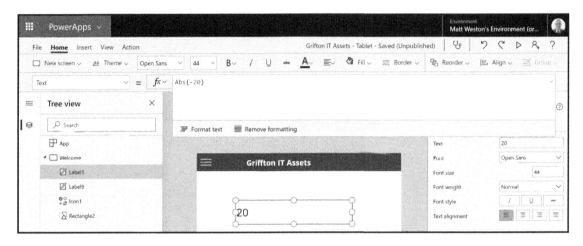

Figure 6.12: Demonstrating the absolute function

As well as arithmetical type functions, PowerApps also has several functions based on trigonometry. The functions associated with this type of mathematics are as follows:

- **Cos (Cosine) / Acos (Arc-cosine)**
- **Cot (Cotangent) / Acot (Arc-cotangent)**
- **Sin (Sine) / Asin (Arc-sine)**
- **Tan (Tangent) / Atan (Arc-tangent)**

The inputs for these functions are values representing the number of radians of an angle; the result of the calculation is returned.

Two functions will convert values between degrees and radians:

- **Degrees**: Accepts several radians to display, which will then be converted into degrees
- **Radians**: Accepts several degrees to display as radians; for example, 180 degrees will be converted into 3.14159265 radians

Now, let's move on to functionalities.

Working with dates

PowerApps provides many functions to help us with dates in several different ways. The most basic functions start with how to actually get the current date or date-time. The date or time is displayed when the function is called. So, if you use either the Now or Today functions on a screen deep within your app, you won't get the date-time stamp until the user navigates to that screen.

The first function is Now(), which will return the current date and time. This function, unlike most we have already seen in this chapter, has an empty argument list, therefore you just need to call the function to get the result:

```
Now()
```

This function will return a value that is formatted in the ShortDateTime24 format. We will explore date formatting later in this section:

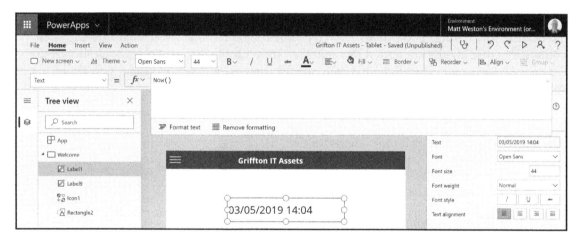

Figure 6.13: Getting the current date and time

The second function, Today, will simply return the current date in ShortDate format:

```
Today()
```

Again, there are no arguments related to this function. Let's look at how to format dates.

Formatting dates

When we are working with dates and times, they may not always be in the format that we want, especially if you've used the `Today` or `Now` functions, which only return short formats. Just like if you work with dates in other development languages, there are several predefined formats that we can work with. The thing to remember is that dates are treated as strings so we, first of all, need to use the `Text` function, which we saw earlier:

```
Text(Now(), DateTimeFormat.LongDate)
```

Using the preceding example, if today's date is 05/02/2019, the result would be 02 May 2019.

As well as selecting date formats, you can also provide a locale to the format so that it is representative of a region. This takes the form of standard ISO codes; for example, the British way of formatting a date would be associated with the `en-GB` locale:

```
Text(Now(), DateTimeFormat.ShortDate, "en-GB")
```

There are also more flexible ways in which you can format dates if you don't wish to use the built-in formatting. You can also specify your own date time formats; for example, if you wish to display the shortened day name along with the day and month, as shown in *Figure 6.14: Using date formatting to display specific parts of the date time string*, you could supply the following format to the function:

```
Text(Now(),  "ddd dd mm")
```

Alternative strings you could use are as follows:

- `dddd`: Full name of the day, for example, Monday
- `ddd`: Short name of the day, for example, Mon
- `mm`: If this is the first instance of `mm`, it will display the short month
- `mmm`: Full name of the month, for example, May
- `yy`: Short year
- `yyyy`: Long year
- `hh`: Hours of the time
- `mm`: If this is the second instance of `mm`, it will display the minutes of the time
- `ss`: Seconds of the time

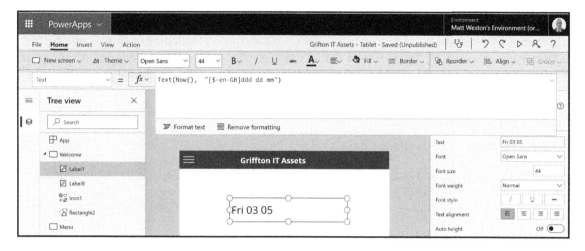

Figure 6.14: Using date formatting to display specific parts of the date time string

TIP

If you wish to display just the minutes, you won't be able to use the format string we used in the preceding as the first instance of mm will only display the month. In this case, consider using the Minute function.

Since we know how to format dates, let's check how to calculate them.

Calculating dates

As well as just being able to display dates, we are also able to do some basic calculations on them. This is especially useful if you're trying to display projected dates or if you're trying to illustrate how much time has elapsed.

The first function we will look at here is how to calculate the difference between two dates using the DateDiff function. DateDiff takes several arguments to define how it's going to behave, the obvious ones being two dates, the start date and then the end date, but also the unit of time that is going to be used as the output. So, if I want to calculate how many days are left in the current year, I can use the following:

```
DateDiff(Now(),Date(Year(Now()), 12, 31),"Days")
```

The second function is `DateAdd`, which will calculate a date based on a numerical difference. The reason that I've not specifically said that it will calculate a date in the future is because, if you supply the function with a negative figure, it will return a date in the past. You need to provide the function with three arguments: the start date, a value for the time that you wish to add, and the unit of time.

In my first example, the returned value will be 10 days in the future:

```
DateAdd(Today(),10,Days)
```

Conversely, in my second example, demonstrated in *Figure 6.15: Calculating 10 days in the past*, the returned value will be 10 days in the past:

```
DateAdd(Today(),-10,Days)
```

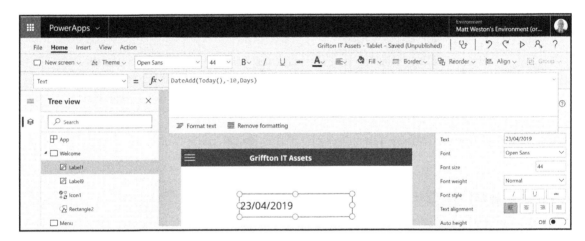

Figure 6.15: Calculating 10 days in the past

So, now that we have interacted with dates, we can now change elements on the screen based on the date. Whether it is hiding and showing information based on a date calculation or changing colors, we can start to add some depth to the app by using these calculations.

As we start to build out our formulas, we will commonly need to branch our logic to handle different outcomes based on a value. This type of logic is known as a **condition**.

Using conditions

Conditions are ways of carrying out a calculation to provide a true or false outcome. They are used to provide branches in logic, so if one condition is met, then action A will ensue. If not, then something else will happen.

If

The most common and useful condition is the `If` function, which takes in three arguments:

- The test
- What to do if the test returns `true`
- What to do if the test returns `false`

In the following example, you will see that we can also combine the outputs of other functions into our condition to return a different output:

```
If(Text(Today(),"dddd") = "Saturday","Weekend :)","Weekday :(")
```

Figure 6.16: An example of an If function being used to change the output of a label

There will be occasions where your condition will depend on multiple inputs being compared to provide the evaluation. Multiple conditions will always be either AND or OR in nature and can be defined using this syntax:

- AND / `&&`
- OR / `||`

In my first example, I only returned Saturday as a day on the weekend whereas Sunday should also be part of the weekend. Therefore, I will provide two evaluations and separate them with an OR (||) operator:

```
If(Text(Today(),"dddd") = "Saturday" || Text(Today(),"dddd") =
"Sunday","Weekend :)","Weekday :(")
```

The preceding example illustrates that all conditions that are used in the If statement should be able to resolve to either true or false. While you can combine multiple conditions together, the overall result will only ever be either true or false.

Switch

If there are multiple outputs from a condition, then you may wish to use a switch statement rather than combining multiple If statements. A Switch statement allows you to declare multiple condition outcomes and will always follow the pattern value followed by the result. For example, for the days of the week, I could use a Switch statement where the value would be Monday and the result would be Weekday:

```
Switch(Text(Today(),"dddd"),"Thursday","Weekday","Friday","Weekday","Saturd
ay","Weekend","Sunday","Weekend")
```

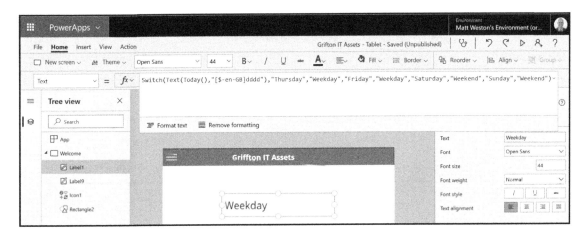

Figure 6.17: A switch statement demonstrating several different logic paths

I hope you now have a good idea about how to deal with the dates; now, let's check the functionalities for variables.

Variables

Variables are a fundamental part of any development approach, regardless of whether you are using PowerApps or you are developing using a programming language. They are used to store temporary copies of data so that they can be consumed by other areas of your app.

All variables are defined by boundaries from which they can be accessed; that is, we can create variables that can only be accessed within a single screen or that can be accessed throughout the app. This is known as scope.

Global variables

Global variables are scoped so that they can be accessed from anywhere within your app. Global variables are extremely versatile as you can store any type of data within it; that is, you can store tables of data as well as simple strings and numbers.

To define a global variable, we use the `Set` function and provide it with the variable name and value. In the following example, I will create a global variable called `varMyVariable` and assign it a string value of `My Global Variable`:

```
Set(varMyVariable,"My Global Variable")
```

Once the variable has been created, I can refer to it simply by the variable name; I don't need to use a function to retrieve the value.

 When naming global variables, consider prefixing them with `var`, for example, `varMyVariable`, so that you can easily identify that this is global.

Context variables

Context variables are those that are scoped to a screen rather than being globally available throughout the app. This does not mean that other screens are unable to use the variable as it can be passed in a controlled manner to other screens during navigation.

Unlike global variables where the function name is quite obvious, setting context variables uses the less obvious UpdateContext function. The syntax around this function is also slightly more complicated as the variable is treated like an array. Therefore, if I want to set a context variable called ctx_MyVariable to a value of 2, I would use this syntax:

```
UpdateContext({ ctx_MyVariable: "Me Context"})
```

The variable is created the first time that this function is called and will be subsequently updated the next time it is used.

As previously mentioned, context variables can be passed to other screens if they're needed elsewhere. One optional argument for the Navigate function is the ability to pass a variable. So, if I wanted to move to a screen called Welcome and pass the MyVariable context variable, I would use the following function:

```
Navigate(Welcome,ScreenTransition.Fade,{MyVariable: 2})
```

 When naming your context variables, consider prefixing your variable with ctx_, for example, ctx_MyVariable, so that you can easily identify that this is a context variable.

Let's check out how to review variables.

Reviewing variables

The final point we need to mention here is the ability to review your variables without having to call them into a control on the page. You have a variables list that can be viewed within the app and that will allow us to look at what variables have been created and what values have been assigned to them.

To review this screen, click on the **File** menu within PowerApps Studio. Variables appear right at the bottom of the left-hand navigation, and when you click, you will be presented with your variables:

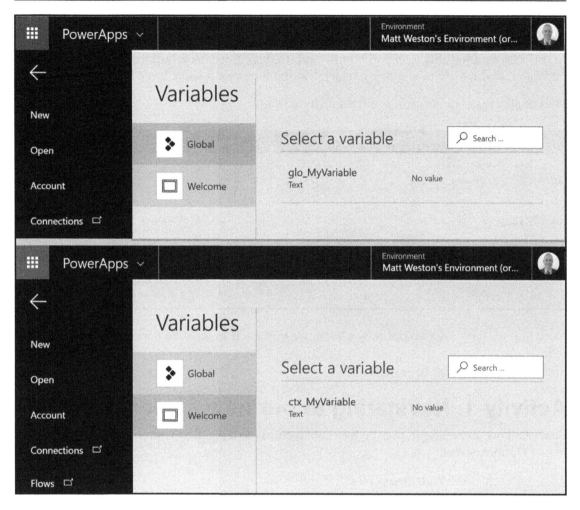

Figure 6.18: Variables being displayed in the Variables screen. The top shows Global Variables,
the bottom shows a context variable for the screen called Welcome.

If you are storing more complex data types within a variable (for example, a table), you can
also expand that table to see what is being stored within.

Lab 5

In this lab, we are going to expand on the app that we have been building through *Lab 1* and *Lab 2*, and we are now going to start fleshing it out with some basic functionality.

First of all, create a new screen and name it Options:

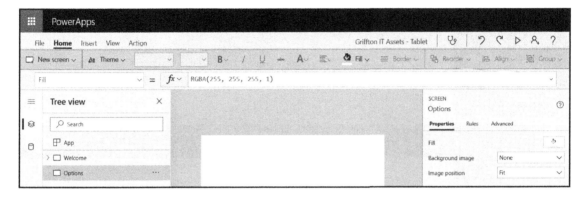

Now that we have created our new screen, we will need to provide users with a way to get to it.

Activity 1: Navigating to our new screen

First of all, we are going to use the navigate formula to transition from our welcome screen to our Options screen:

1. Select the **Welcome** screen.
2. Select the **Enter** button that we placed in the center of the screen:

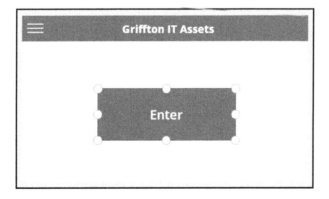

3. Change the **Properties** drop-down menu to display **OnSelect**:

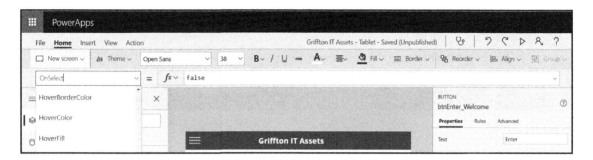

4. Enter the following formula:

```
Navigate(Options,ScreenTransition.Fade)
```

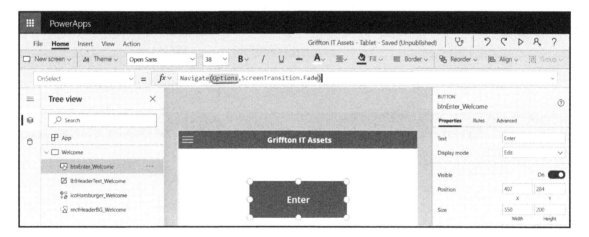

5. Test your formula by holding down the *Alt* key and clicking on your button. Notice that it has taken you to your **Options** page.
6. Return to the **Welcome** screen by clicking in the screen explorer.

Activity 2: Using math to position a control

We are now going to add some additional controls onto the **Welcome** page to display some more information:

1. Insert a **LABEL** onto the screen and name it `lblDateBar`:

2. Select the **X** property, from the **Properties** drop-down menu, and set it to 0:

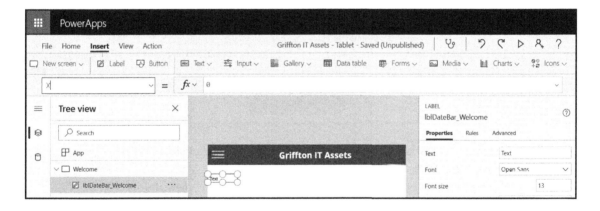

3. Select the **Y** property of `lblDateBar` and dynamically set the `Y` position, so that the date bar sits just below the header, by entering this formula:

```
rectHeaderBG.Y + rectHeaderBG.Height
```

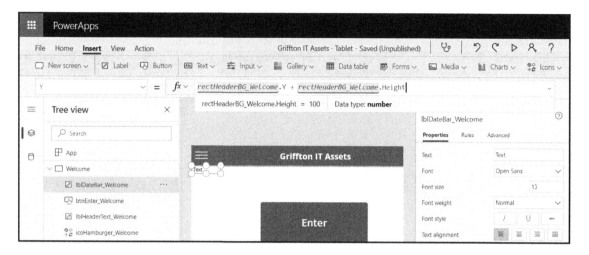

4. Select the `Width` property and dynamically make it the same width as the screen by entering this formula:

```
Parent.Width
```

5. Set the following additional properties on `lblDateBar`:
   1. **Height**: 75
   2. **Size**: 18
   3. **Align**: `Align.Right`
   4. **Font weight**: `FontWeight.Bold`

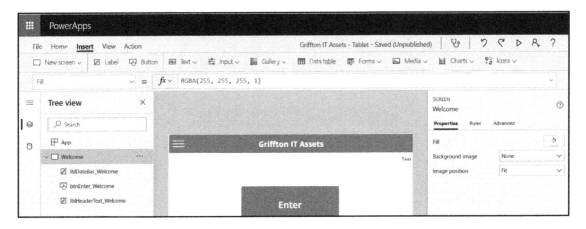

6. Select the `Text` property and enter the following:

```
Text(Now(),"dddd dd mmm yyyy")
```

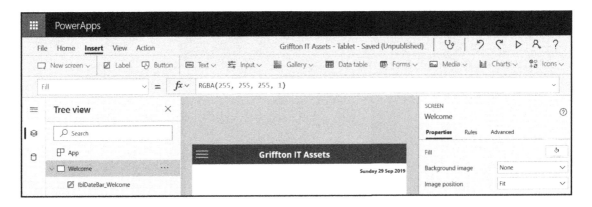

We have just used a formula to add some dynamic content to our app. We will now build some conditions into the app too.

Activity 3: Using conditions to change control behavior

We will now add a checkbox onto the **Welcome** screen. This will ask the user to confirm that they accept the terms and conditions and wish to proceed into the app; until they tick that box, the **Enter** button will be disabled:

1. Insert a **CHECK BOX** onto the **Welcome** screen and name it `cbAcceptTCs`:

2. Position the checkbox dynamically by setting the following properties:
   1. Set the **Y** property by taking the **Y** value of the **Enter** button, adding the height, and then adding a further `40` pixels with the following formula, `btnEnter_Welcome.Y + btnEnter_Welcome.Height + 40`:

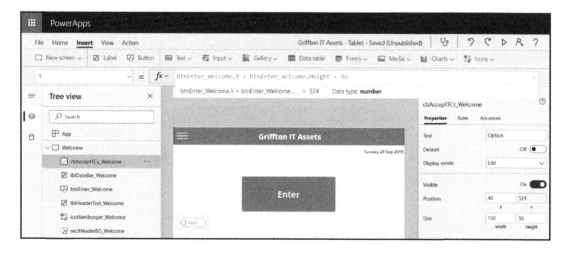

2. Set the **X** property so that the checkbox is the same as the button by using the following formula, `(Parent.Width - cbAcceptTCs_Welcome.Width)/2`:

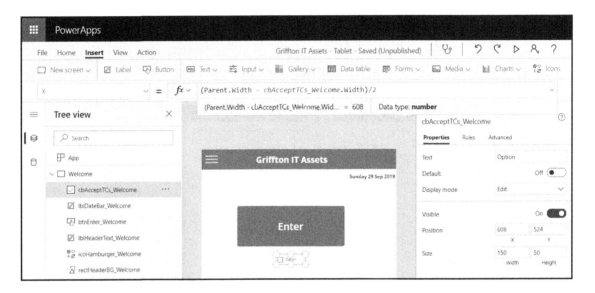

3. Set the **Width** of the checkbox control to `275`.

3. Enter the following into the text property, `I agree to the Griffton T&Cs`:

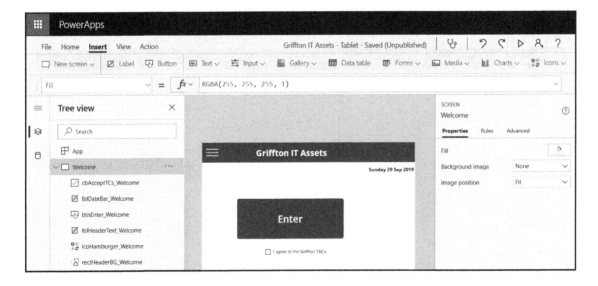

4. Select `btnEnter` and select the **DisplayMode** property.
5. Enter the following formula to only enable the control if the checkbox is ticked, `If(cbAcceptTCs.Value = true, DisplayMode.Edit, DisplayMode.Disabled):`

Now, press the play button in the top-right corner of your screen to observe your app. Notice that the date bar is displaying today's date, including the day. Also, you will notice that your **Enter** button is grayed out and will not do anything when clicked. Place a tick in the checkbox below and see how the **Enter** button activates and will now allow you to click it to navigate to the next screen:

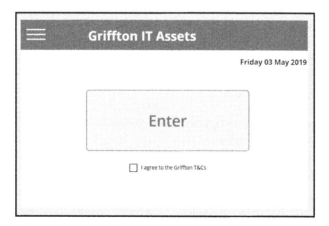

We have now used formulas in several different ways, firstly to enable us to navigate between screens, but also to affect positioning and behavior.

Summary

Throughout this chapter, we have started to delve into formulas and look at how they can be used to add functionality to our PowerApps. Formulas have been described as looking and feeling like formulas in Microsoft Excel; therefore skills used in creating spreadsheets can easily be transferred to PowerApps.

Formulas are entered into the formula bar, which uses IntelliSense to guide us to the formula we wish to use; it also provides guidance about what arguments it requires. As an alternative to always typing, you can use the function browser to identify your formula and then double-click to place it into the formula bar.

PowerApps provides several built-in functions that allow you to interact with various data types. We focused on the most common examples, text, numbers, and dates, and explored what we can do to transform our data to ensure we are displaying it correctly. We spent some time looking at the mathematical functions that we can use to start making our app a little more intelligent.

Not all logic is linear; therefore, we introduced the ability to branch our logic based on input. There are two ways to branch: one is using the `If` function, which will evaluate an expression to either `true` or `false` and perform a function as a result. Alternatively, for more complex branching, we can use the `Switch` statement, which will allow us to have multiple branches of logic from the same logical test.

We looked at the two types of variable that can be stored within PowerApps, giving us a temporary copy of a piece of data for use elsewhere in the app. Global variables are scoped to the entire app, meaning that they can be easily used anywhere. Of the two types of variable, the syntax for global variables is somewhat easier to write. Context variables, on the other hand, are scoped to a single screen but can be passed to other screens as an argument of the `Navigate` function.

In the next chapter, we will be investigating how we can read and write data from data sources that are external to PowerApp.

Questions

1. In the following date format, `dd mm yyyy`, what does `mm` return?
2. If you see the following logical operator, `&&`, what does it mean?
3. If I had multiple outcomes from a single condition, what would be the best function to use?
4. What would I use to validate a string against a known pattern?
5. Cos, Sin, and Tan are examples of what type of function?
6. What would precede any comments that I am going to put into my formula?
7. What are the two results that can be returned from an `If` statement?
8. What type of variable would I use if it is only going to be used on one screen or manually passed to another?

Further reading

The full formula reference is provided and maintained by Microsoft and provides explanations and examples of how each one is used (`https://docs.microsoft.com/en-gb/powerapps/maker/canvas-apps/formula-reference`).

7
Working with Data

In the previous chapter, we started to build on our app even further by introducing and implementing some basic formulas. On their own, formulas will allow an app to take advantage of some of its basic functionality, but the real depth of apps comes from their consumption and interaction with data.

Data can be stored in a number of different ways, both internally and externally. We will explore external data sources in `Chapter 8`, *Introducing Connectors*, when we start to become intimate with connectors. In this chapter, we will look at how we can build data structures internally within the app and explore how we can use them while we're running our PowerApps.

In this chapter, we will cover the following topics:

- Creating and interacting with collections
- Displaying data as tables
- Using forms
- Lab 6

By the end of this chapter, you will have an understanding of collections and the important role that they can play within the development of your PowerApps. You will understand how we can retrieve data and then display and interact with it in a number of ways using the controls provided by PowerApps.

Technical requirements

To follow along with this chapter, you will need an active PowerApps subscription. This will be also helpful in the *Lab 6* section.

Creating and interacting with collections

Collections are one of the most common methods for storing data locally within your PowerApp, and once you start developing, you will find that they are extremely useful in a number of different ways. They can be built dynamically while you're running your app, as well as when your app loads. This means you could use it to retrieve data from a data source and store it locally so that it can be manipulated before being written back. In this chapter, we are going to use collections to build data that we can then interact with using our output controls, galleries, and tables.

A collection can be compared to a table, where you have a number of rows of data with each attribute being expressed as a column. Collections can store arrays of data within them, so they're slightly more complex than just a simple data table, but the premise is the same.

Filling collections

When you're filling in a collection, you can do two different things: you can either take a data source and push it straight to a collection – for example, you could push all of the contents of a list straight into a collection – or you can build the collection manually.

Generally, if you have options that you want to manage within your PowerApp, you would initialize your collection while your app is loading. An example of this would be your navigation.

To fill in your collection, you can use Collect or ClearCollect. Collect will append your data values to the collection, so if you run it multiple times, your collection will continue to enumerate the operations. ClearCollect, on the other hand, will clear down the collection before adding your values to it.

When providing the entries for a collection, you will generally do so in the form of a record or array of values. In the following example, we are going to create a collection called colNavigation that has two pieces of information associated with it: Title and Screen:

```
Collect(colNavigation,{Title: "Home", Screen: "Welcome"},{Title: "Search",
Screen: "Search"})
```

In my collection, the result of the preceding code is as follows:

Title	Screen
Home	Welcome
Search	Search

At any point, I can view the top five entries within my collection by going to **File** | **Collections**:

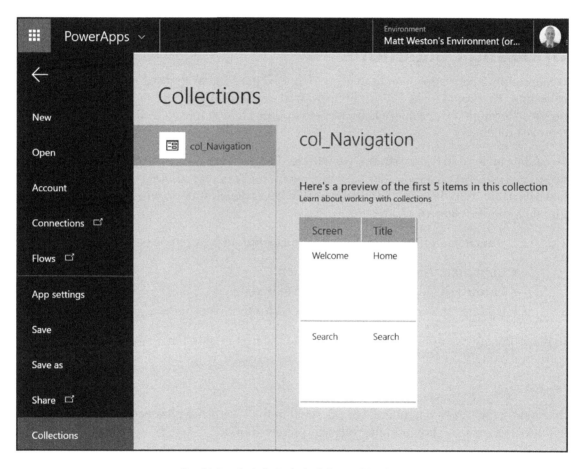

Figure 7.1: A populated collection showing the Screen and Title columns

This screen should always be checked to ensure that the correct data is being stored within your collection and that it is the first point of call for debugging data.

 Consider using a collection to store your navigation or branding configuration so that you can maintain consistency across each screen.

Now that we have created a collection, we need to modify the data stored within it.

Updating collections

While running your apps, you may need to update the content that's stored within the collection. This could be as a result of user input or just changing the state of data as you progress through the app. Let's learn how to update an item in a collection and then remove an item.

To update an item in the collection, we will need to use the `Patch` function (https://docs. microsoft.com/en-us/powerapps/maker/canvas-apps/functions/function-patch). This takes its name from the verb that's used in REST API development, where `Patch` means to update a specific element of a record.

The `Patch` function requires the following information in order to be effective:

- **Collection**: The name of the collection
- **Record**: The identifier of the record to update
- **Update**: The changes that are required for that record

In the following example, I am going to update the first item in the `colNavigation` collection using the `First` function to define the record to be updated:

```
Patch(colNavigation, First(colNavigation), {Title: "Welcome"})
```

By running the `Patch` command, we can see that the `Title` field has been changed from `Home` to `Welcome`, as shown in the following screenshot:

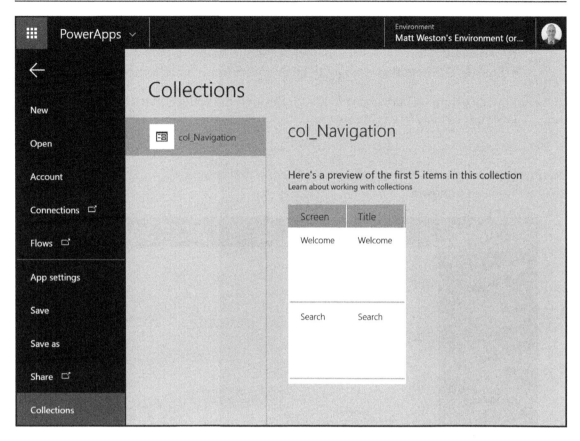

Figure 7.2: The navigation collection with the updated Welcome title

As well as being able to update records, `Patch` can also be used to create new records. The syntax is principally the same; the only difference is that rather than defining the record to be updated within the collection, we use the `Defaults` keyword to create a blank record and then perform an update on it. For example, the following formula will create a new item in my navigation collection:

```
Patch(colNavigation,Defaults(colNavigation),{Title:"Options",Screen:Options
})
```

Collections are designed to allow for the addition and removal of items while the app is running. They also allow updates. We can remove specific items from the collection using the `Remove` function.

`Remove` requires the following information:

- **Collection**: The data source that we want to remove an item from
- **Source**: The item that is going to be removed from the collection

In the following example, I am going to search through the collection to find the `Search` keyword in the `Title` column:

```
Remove(col_Navigation, Search(col_Navigation, "Search", "Title"))
```

By running this formula, the record in the collection that contains `Search` in the `Title` column has been removed:

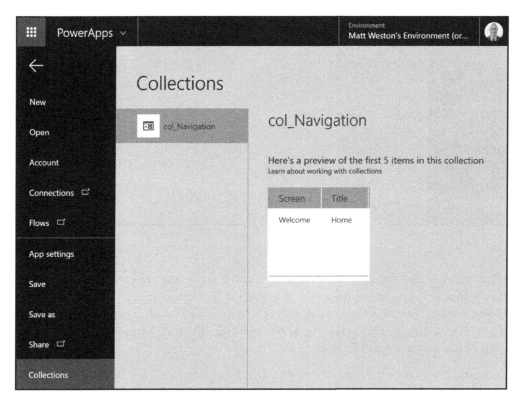

Figure 7.3: The navigation collection showing that a record has been removed

In this section, we have demonstrated how to display and interact with our data through the use of the **Gallery** control. However, there will be times where you'll need a much simpler way of presenting data, and that can be achieved through a data table.

Displaying data as tables

Once you have data within a data source, you need to display it to the app user. There are a number of controls that can be placed onto the canvas that allow you to quickly and easily represent and interact with data.

Displaying data in a gallery

We learned about **Gallery** controls in `Chapter 5`, *Exploring Controls*, while we were investigating the main controls that are used within PowerApps. Galleries are similar to data tables in that they don't actually store data within themselves. They act as an interactive control with an underlying data source. The key time to use a gallery is if you wish to apply a little more design creativity and freedom since you are able to add a number of different controls. Now, let's connect a gallery to a data source and examine the resulting behavior.

There are two ways to connect a gallery to a data source:

- The first way is from within the **Properties** pane of the gallery, which will display all the data sources that are available within your PowerApp. As you add connectors and draw in data from other sources, they will also be listed here:

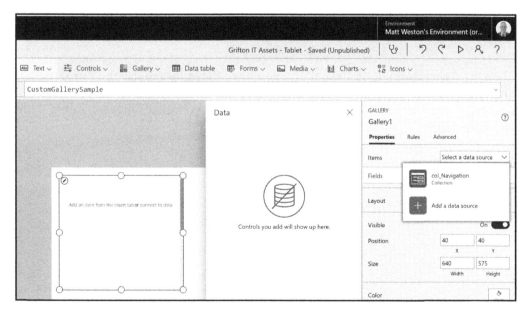

Figure 7.4: A gallery placed onto the canvas

While this is the simplest way of adding a data source, it is also the least flexible as you are unable to add filters or other logic in the **Properties** pane.

- The second way is to modify the **Items** property of the gallery. Within the formula bar, you can reference the data source by name:

Figure 7.5: Setting the Items property to bind the gallery to a data source

Once a gallery is on the page and is connected to a data source, we can modify what is displayed and how it is presented on the screen. In my example, I am going to take a blank gallery and add a label to it.

 Ensure that you have the gallery selected while inserting another control; otherwise, it will be placed on the canvas rather than within the gallery.

Once you have a control within the gallery, you have the ability to use the **Properties** pane to assign a field to the control. In my example, I have bound my gallery to the colNavigation collection, which we defined earlier. Therefore, I can select either **Title** or **Screen** as the value:

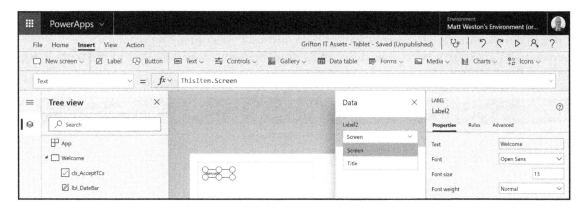

Figure 7.6: Using the ThisItem reference to display information from a data source

Again, I can use the formula bar to achieve the same effect. Once a gallery is bound to a data source, we can use the `ThisItem` keyword to refer to the specific row within the data source. In the preceding screenshot, I used the following statement to display the screen from the navigation collection:

```
ThisItem.Screen
```

There are times when data can be stored in a more rigid tabular structure, which is where we would consider using a **Data table** control.

Displaying data in a data table

The most common way of displaying any type of data is in a table. PowerApps has a **Data table** control available that allows us to show the rows of data with the relevant headers. Just like a gallery, you have full control over what fields are displayed.

Similar to a gallery, you can use the **Properties** pane to select the data source from all of the ones that are connected to your PowerApp, including collections. The reason we're selecting a data source is because data tables don't actually store data within them; they act as an output control:

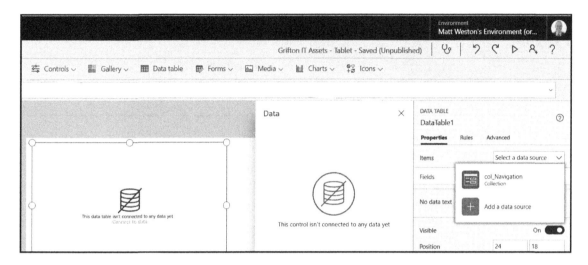

Figure 7.7: Adding a Data table control to the canvas

Each field that you select will be immediately placed in the data table. You can easily change the order of the columns by dragging and dropping them with the field selector, as shown in the following screenshot:

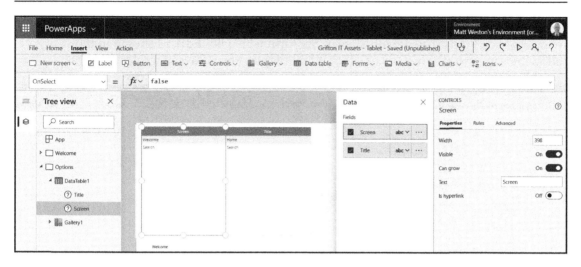

Figure 7.8: Selecting the fields

Data tables are much more rigid in terms of design than the gallery, where we can only change the order of the columns and change the basics around the heading style. The unfortunate thing is that, as far as custom styling goes, there is no option to create alternating colors for the rows or add highlights to columns. The only color change that you can customize is the **OnSelect** color, which shows which row in the table you have clicked or tapped on.

The two methods of displaying data, that is, galleries and data tables, are both designed to be primary ways of displaying data. However, it is conceivable that, within your app, you will need to display data within a form, which allows us to govern the way that we interact with the data source. In the next section, we'll learn about using forms.

Using forms

Forms provide us with a native way to quickly create, view, and edit forms so that we can modify the data within our data source. The setup of a form is very similar to that of a gallery or a data table, whereby we put the control on the page and select the data source. The form will automatically render the fields on the canvas for you. The main difference, however, is that forms can only be connected to an external data source; for example, a list within SharePoint.

When a form is placed on the canvas and connected to a data source, it will automatically render the key fields. The default state of the form is usually **Edit**, as shown in the following screenshot, which means that it will display the values of a selected item:

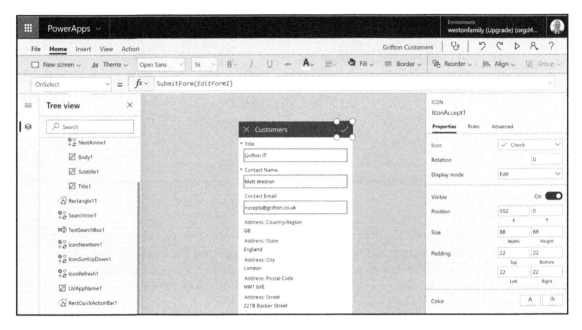

Figure 7.9: A rendered form, as displayed in the app that was generated from SharePoint

The form control is intelligent enough to understand the data type of the field and render the form controls. For example, if the data type is complex, such as from a lookup field in SharePoint, the form will be rendered with a combobox control automatically.

Alternatively, forms can also be placed into new or view mode. View mode will display the form in a read-only state, as follows:

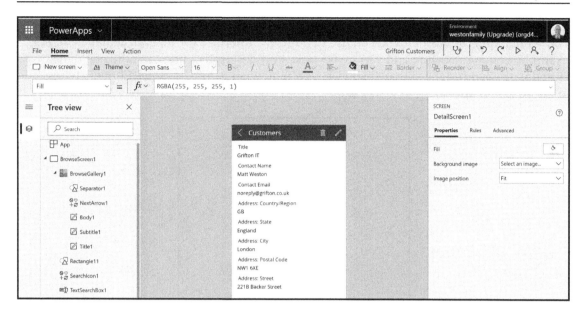

Figure 7.10: The form control in view mode

Consider using the view form as a way of displaying the full details of a record.

The new form will take these fields and display them as empty fields so that the user can fill them in and then submit that data back to the data source.

If we consider the app that we generated from SharePoint in `Chapter 3`, *Creating Apps from SharePoint*, then this is a perfect example of a number of forms that are bound to a data source. We can see that there are a number of controls in use—there is a gallery to display the list of items from SharePoint, which is linked to a view form. Then, we have the edit form, which is also used for the new form. If the form is in edit mode, then we need to provide it with details of the item we need to update so that we can retrieve the data and then write back any changes. If we change the form type property to new, then we will have a blank form that allows us to create a new item.

Each field, when represented in the form, is created as a data card. A data card provides you with a mini canvas that you can use to build the interface for that particular field. For example, you may wish to add a more bespoke and descriptive title than the one that's stored within your data source. Likewise, you may wish to add some additional styling to make your app appealing to your users:

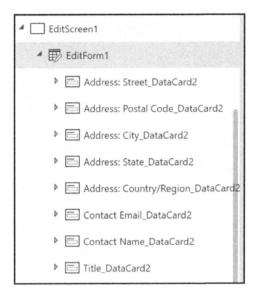

Figure 7.11: The makeup of a form control, where each field has a data card

Consider building validation and help into your data cards to make the user experience as rich as possible.

Once your new and edit forms have been configured, you need to submit the data through the relevant connector to the data source. If you are familiar with standard development practices, then you will know that this usually involves writing code to tell the form where to submit the data to.

By the very nature of giving the form a data source, all of the wiring has been done for you. Therefore, the only thing you need to do, for both update and create, is submit the form. This is achieved by a very simple function that will perform the necessary actions by understanding what mode the form is in:

```
SubmitForm(frmNew)
```

Add a button or an icon either to a custom card or elsewhere on the canvas to initiate `SubmitForm`. This will give your users a clear understanding of how to save their changes.

Lab 6

In this lab, we are going to build on what we have already created in PowerApps by adding navigation and branding. Both navigation and branding will be managed globally, so we will store the values in collections that can be accessed from each page and then display them on our canvas.

Activity 1: Creating the collections

Let's learn how to create collections:

1. Begin by opening our **Griffton IT Assets** PowerApp, which we created in the previous labs:

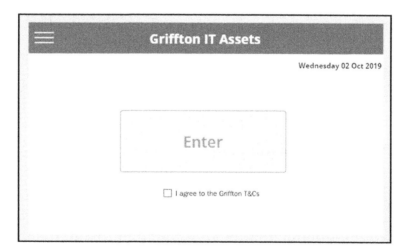

2. Create three new blank screens called **Search**, **New Asset**, and **View Assets**:

3. Now that we have created a number of different screens to navigate between, we will create a collection to store the navigation items. Click on **App** in the screen explorer and select the **OnStart** property:

4. Now, let's create a collection as follows:

```
ClearCollect(
 colNavigation,
 {
 Title: "Home",
 Screen: 'Welcome',
 Transition: ScreenTransition.Fade
 },
 {
 Title: "Search",
 Screen: 'Search',
```

```
Transition: ScreenTransition.Fade
},
{
Title: "New Asset",
Screen: 'New Asset',
Transition: ScreenTransition.Fade
},
{
Title: "View Assets",
Screen: 'View Assets',
Transition: ScreenTransition.Fade
}
);
```

5. Add this function to the **OnStart** property:

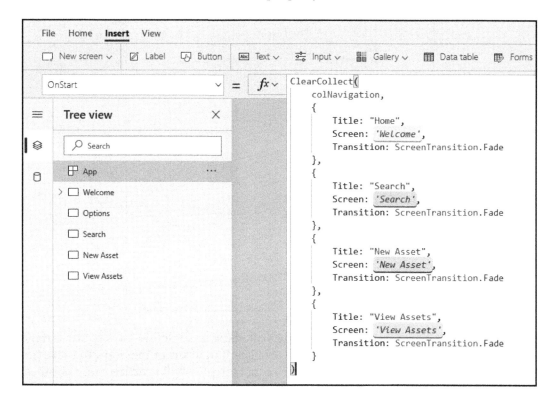

6. In the **App OnStart** event, create a second collection for colors. This collection will contain all of the colors we want to apply to the app. Create the `colColors` collection, as follows:

```
// Branding
ClearCollect(colColors,
    {Name: "Primary", Color: RGBA(102,153,0,1)},
    {Name: "Secondary", Color: RGBA(153,0,102,1)},
    {Name: "Screen", Color: RGBA(240,240,245,1)},
    {Name: "Text", Color: RGBA(0,0,0,1)}
)
```

Your code should look as follows:

```
        },
        {
            Title: "New Asset",
            Screen: 'New Asset',
            Transition: ScreenTransition.Fade
        },
        {

            Title: "View Assets",
            Screen: 'View Assets',
            Transition: ScreenTransition.Fade
        }
);

// Branding
ClearCollect(colColors,
    {Name: "Primary", Color: RGBA(102,153,0,1)},
    {Name: "Secondary", Color: RGBA(153,0,102,1)},
    {Name: "Screen", Color: RGBA(240,240,245,1)},
    {Name: "Text", Color: RGBA(0,0,0,1)}
)
    ≡ Format text      ≡ Remove formatting
```

7. Now, let's add a third collection that will allow us to define the key attribute for our headers to ensure that they are consistent in terms of the branding on every screen and also in terms of their position. Here, we will practice using another function by using a lookup field to select a color from our `colColors` collection:

```
// Styles
ClearCollect(colStyles,
    {Name: "Header", Color: LookUp(colColors,Name="Primary").Color,
X:0, Y:0},
```

```
        {Name: "Menu", Color: LookUp(colColors,Name="Secondary").Color,
    X: 20, Y:15},
        {Name: "ScreenTitle", Color:
    LookUp(colColors,Name="Secondary").Color, X: 500, Y: 25},
        {Name: "Navigation", X: 0, Y: 100, Width:250}
    )
```

8. Click on the ellipsis (**...**) next to the app and select **Run OnStart** to populate the collections:

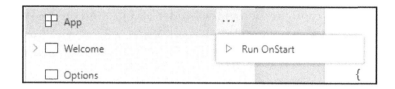

Now that we have created our collections and populated them, we just need to update our app so that we can start using them.

Activity 2: Applying branding

In this activity, we will take the values that we stored within our colors and styles collections and apply them to our header controls. Let's get started:

1. On the **Welcome** screen, select the background rectangle that's being used for the header and select the **Fill** property. Now, we will start to apply the styling that is stored in the colStyles collection. In the **Fill** property, enter the following formula, which will take the color defined in the colStyles collection. Here, the style is named Header:

```
LookUp(colStyles,Name="Header").Color
```

This is shown in the following screenshot:

2. Set the height, width, and **X** and **Y** properties for the header in the same way:

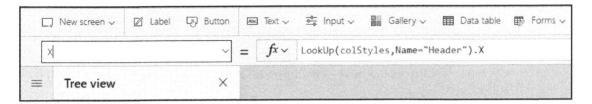

3. Copy the same configuration to the header background on the **Welcome** screen.
4. Complete *step 1* to *step 3* for the color and **X** and **Y** properties for the hamburger menu and add the header by selecting the relevant style name from the collection:

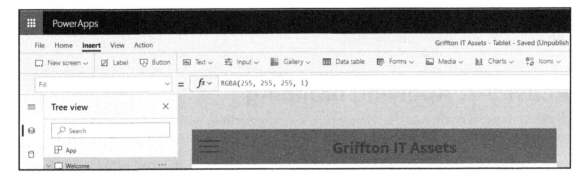

Now that we have added basic styling to our **Welcome** screen, we will add some navigation functionality.

Activity 3: Adding navigation

In this activity, we will use a gallery to display the navigation down the left-hand side of the screen, which will appear and disappear when the menu is selected. Let's get started:

1. On the **Welcome** screen, insert a **Gallery** control using the **Blank vertical gallery** layout and name it `galNavigation`:

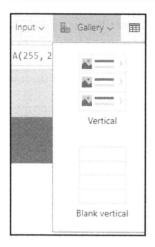

2. Apply the relevant styling from the styles collection to the X, Y, and Width properties: LookUp(colStyles,Name="Navigation").Width.

3. Select the **Items** property for the gallery and change the data source to colNavigation, which we created in the *Activity 1 – creating the collections* section:

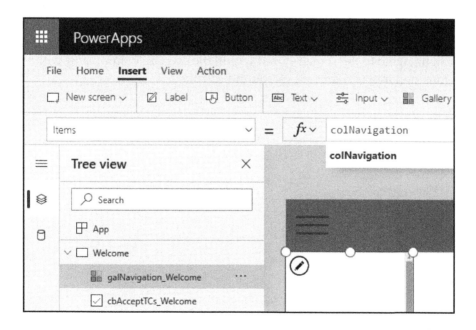

4. In the gallery, click on the area that says **Add an item from the insert tab** and add a label. Notice that it has automatically taken the first column in the collection, that is, Title.

5. Position the label within the gallery and then reduce the size of the gallery card:

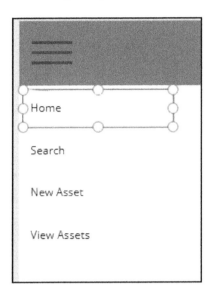

6. Select the **OnSelect** property of your gallery and modify the function so that you can navigate to the screen stored within the Screen column and with the transition in the Transition column:

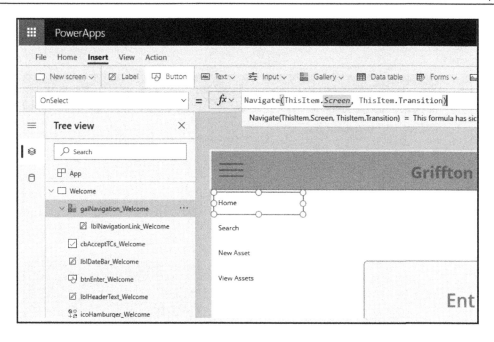

7. Finally, we will add the ability to hide and show the menu when the hamburger is selected. Return to the app and select the **OnStart** property. Add `Set(varShowMenu,false)` to the `OnStart` function:

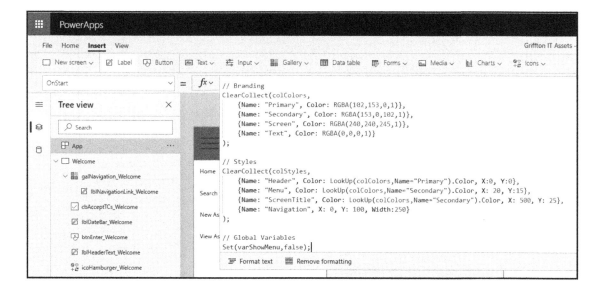

8. Click on **Gallery** and select the **Visible** property. Set the property to
   `varShowMenu`:

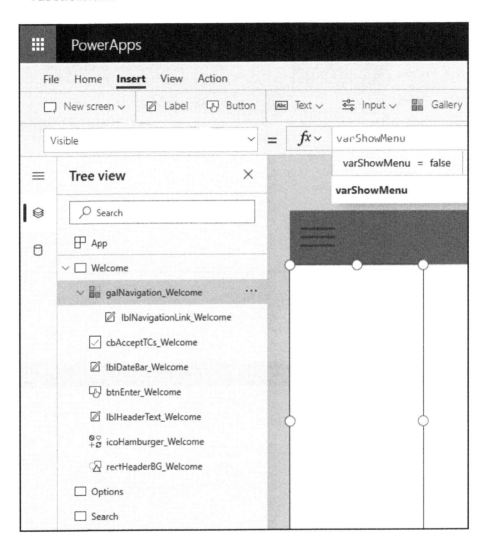

Notice that our navigation is no longer visible.

9. Select the hamburger icon in the header, select the **OnSelect** property, and add `Set(varShowMenu, !varShowMenu)`, which will toggle the value each time it is clicked:

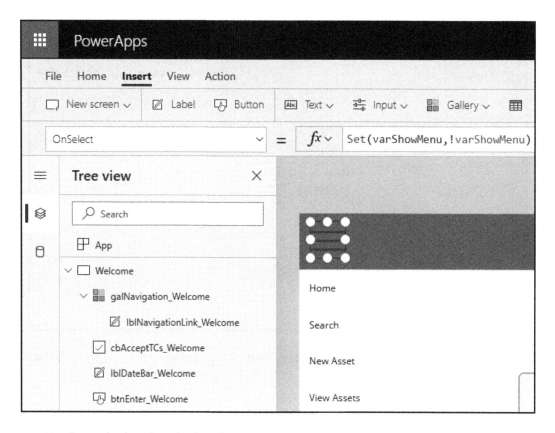

10. Copy the header, the hamburger icon, the screen title, and menu from the welcome screen and paste it into every other screen. Note that all the controls are immediately placed in the correct place since they take their styling information from the collection.

Now you can save, test, and publish your app, all while navigating around the app. All of this functionality is driven from the collections:

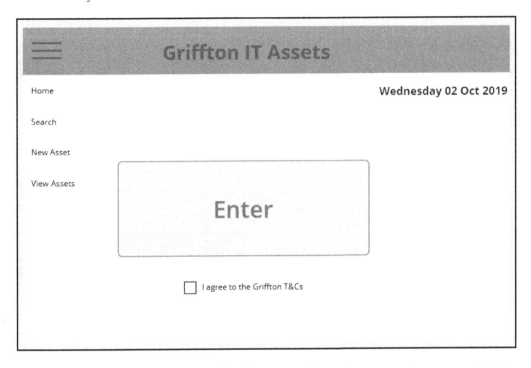

In the next lab, we will add additional **Gallery** controls so that we can interact with data from an external data source.

Summary

In this chapter, we introduced some key structures and ways to interact with data. We primarily used collections as a means of storing data locally within the app and looked at how to interact with the data stored within them.

Once data is stored in the app, we can start to represent it on the canvas using different types of controls. We can use the **Gallery** control to create flexible methods that display relevant data by adding controls and functionality from within the confines of a data card.

The second topic that we looked at in this chapter was all about using the data table, which makes it extremely simple for us to display and read data. However, it is also very inflexible since we can only make styling changes to the table headers and to selected rows.

Then, we learned how to interact with our data by viewing items from the data source, as well as how to edit and create new items. This is achieved by using the form control and placing it into the relevant form mode. We can also easily submit changes by using the `SubmitForm` function, which will perform the relevant action. This is also based on the form mode attribute.

In the next chapter, we'll learn about connectors so that we can begin to interact with other data sources.

Questions

1. What two formulas that are available within PowerApps can you use to populate a collection with data?
2. Which control offers the quickest way to create an edit form for an item of data?
3. Which control allows you to define a flexible, repetitive design for each record or data?
4. Which formula should you use to update a record in a data source or collection?
5. Which formula should you use to submit a form control back to the data source?

Introducing Connectors 8

In the previous chapter, we started working with data in our PowerApp. However, all the data was stored locally in the PowerApp. Being able to use/access internal storage is the key to having a performant PowerApp; however, to make a truly powerful app, we need to be able to interact with data that's stored in an external data source. The mechanisms that unlock this data and make it available in PowerApps are known as connectors.

Connectors are one of the most important elements of PowerApp development as they allow the app to consume data and services from a huge number of sources. When we talk about development, we talk about the ability to reuse code so that we don't have to develop the same thing every single time. Using connectors effectively allows us to achieve this, but in a way that is very easy to use by both developers and non-developers.

In this chapter, we will cover the following topics:

- Understanding standard connectors
- Understanding premium connectors
- Understanding custom connectors
- Lab 7

We will also look at how we can unlock the power of our own data sources by using APIs and custom connectors to make them resurface within PowerApps.

By the end of this chapter, you will understand what connectors are and what the differences are between standard and premium connectors. You will also be able to create your own custom connector that you can use within your PowerApps.

Technical requirements

To follow along with this chapter and to complete the lab, you will need an active PowerApps subscription. You will also need to have either OneDrive or OneDrive for Business as a medium for storing data.

Understanding standard connectors

Standard connectors are connectors that are freely available for use with every level of licensing within PowerApps. They are available across the entire Microsoft Power Platform, so they can be easily utilized in Power Automate and Logic Apps, as well as anything we create in PowerApps.

Standard connectors cover the most commonly used data sources, such as SharePoint, OneDrive, and even some third-party data sources such as Google Drive. You can establish connections with these data sources either from within your PowerApp while editing, or outside the PowerApp from the data menu. Once the connections list is open, click on **Connections | New connection** at the top of the page to begin the connection selection process:

Figure 8.1: New connection list

Once you've started this process, you have the ability to select a connection to any data source in the list, such as SharePoint or the Common Data Service, which we will explore in `Chapter 15`, *Introducing Model-Driven Apps*.

There are over 250 connectors within PowerApps that, when presented to us, are in alphabetical order. However, this list is constantly growing, with the list expected to exceed 350 connectors in the latter half of 2019. Therefore, we need to be able to search, or accurately filter the list, to find an appropriate connector.

Standard connectors encompass many of the Office 365 services that are available to the Microsoft Power Platform, as well as very limited access to the services provided by Microsoft Azure. As part of the licensing changes that were introduced on the 1st October 2019, Azure services such as Azure automation were changed from being standard to premium. Interactions with Office 365 services such as Excel, SharePoint, Microsoft Forms, and so on are all still part of the standard connector package. You should also be aware that there are a large number of connectors available that allow you to connect to non-Microsoft services, including competitor services such as Google Drive, Gmail, and so on.

Regardless of whether we're adding the connection through the PowerApps portal or through the app itself, we have the ability to perform some basic text filtering on the list to find the connector that we want. Until you enter a search term, for example, **Planner**, this is labelled on the screen as **Search**:

Figure 8.2: Filtering the connectors list by typing Planner into the search box

The reason why I describe this as a filter rather than a search is because it takes the text that you enter into the search box and filters the connector titles using that text.

Once you have found the connector you want, for example, **Office 365 Outlook,** click the + icon. You will be told how to establish the data connection:

Figure 8.3: The dialogue box that's displayed when you create a connection for the first time

If the connection requires you to authenticate, then you will be asked to provide the required username and password. If you are authenticating against another application in Office 365, then you will be subjected to the normal security checks, including multi-factor authentication (if that has been configured within your organization). Likewise, if you authenticate against another service provider, such as Google, then you will need to log in using your Google credentials.

Once your connection has been established, it will appear in the list of connections that's displayed in the **Data** menu of the PowerApps home screen:

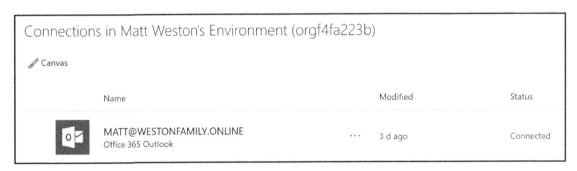

Figure 8.4: Available connectors in my environment

Establishing a connection will provide data either in the form of a table or in the form of actions. A table is actually a body of JSON that's returned from a web service and translated for use by PowerApps.

There are some connections that will only offer tables of data and others that will only offer actions.

Now that we have a table of data, we need to be able to work with it in our PowerApp.

Interacting with tables of data

When we work with tables that have been returned from a connector, we need to be able to do one of two things: either store it locally or display it on the canvas. Previously, we looked at using collections to store data locally within the app. The same method can be used to copy the data from the data source into a locally stored collection.

When retrieving data through the connection, we can simply use the name of the data source. For example, if I create a connection to SharePoint and to a list called `Assets`, my data source will simply be called `Assets`.

Therefore, using the `Collect` function, I can store the contents of the list locally within the app:

```
Collect(colAssets, Assets)
```

 The simplest data source that you can connect to is a table stored within Excel. For this to work, the Excel workbook must be stored in cloud storage such as OneDrive or SharePoint.

Connectors will have at least one action, which allows you to do something with the data source. Let's have a look at how we can do this within PowerApps.

Interacting with actions

If the connector you use allows you to call an action, then it's known as a function of the data source. If, for example, I wish to retrieve the user picture from Office 365, I can create a connection to Office 365 users. From there, I can call the `UserPhoto` action to return the image's URL.

When calling an action, the formula will always start with the name of the data source, followed by the name of the action. If actions require any additional arguments, the help text above the formula bar will provide any necessary information:

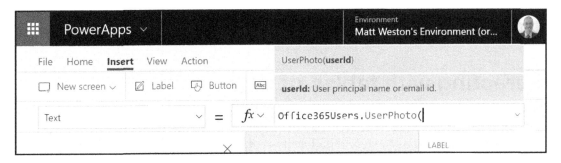

Figure 8.5: An example of a formula using a connector

Therefore, if I entered the following formula, I could retrieve and display the picture of the user (who is logged in):

```
Office365Users.UserPhoto(User().Email)
```

Every connector will have a number of actions associated with it. These actions can be found by typing the name of the connector into the formula bar, followed by a full stop (.). This will launch IntelliSense and allow us to select an action from the list of actions that are available from that connector.

Now that we have looked at standard connectors, we'll have a look at premium connectors.

Understanding premium connectors

Premium connectors are those that are only available if you subscribe to PowerApps Plan 1 or 2. Premium connectors are still created and supported by Microsoft; therefore, they will work out of the box without any further configuration. Such premium connectors also include external applications such as Salesforce, DocuSign, Survey Monkey, Amazon, and so on. What you should always keep in mind, however, is that you will need to hold a subscription with the service provider, as well as have PowerApps Plan 1 or 2 in order to fully utilize them.

In the **New connection** list, all the premium connectors are identified by the **Premium** stamp. Unlike Microsoft Power Automate, there is no simple way to filter standard or premium connectors:

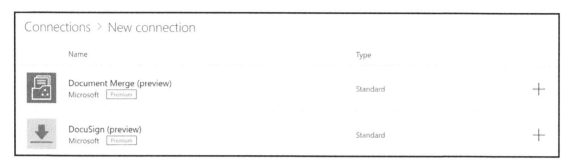

Figure 8.6: Premium connectors

While there are a large number of connectors available in PowerApps, there will be a time where a service doesn't have a connector available for us to use. Therefore, we need to create our own in the form of custom connectors.

Introducing custom connectors

Custom connectors can offer PowerApps developers a great number of options when it comes to connecting to data. Custom connectors can be used to create a connection to a data source that hasn't been served by either the standard or premium connectors. Alternatively, they can also be used to extend the functionality of a built-in connector by connecting to further REST endpoints. As an example, we could extend the actions that are available to the SharePoint connector by connecting to REST endpoints that are not made available through standard connectors, for example, the ability to break permissions inheritance.

There are several ways we can create custom connectors, depending on the preference of the developer:

- From a blank template
- From the URL of an OpenAPI file
- From a Postman collection

To find custom connectors, we must navigate to the main PowerApps screen and select **Data** from the left-hand navigation. When selecting custom connectors, you will see all of the custom connectors that you have access to within your organization. You will also have the ability to create a new connector, update and delete an existing connector, or download a connector to your desktop.

Creating a custom connector from scratch

Creating a new custom connector from scratch is extremely easy thanks to the step by step wizard that's been built by Microsoft. To start the wizard, select **Create from blank** from the **New custom connector** menu. This can be found at the top right corner of the screen:

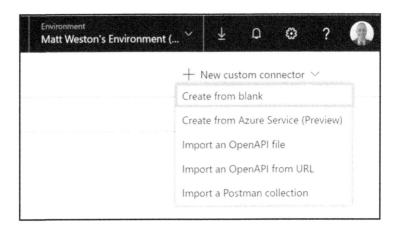

Figure 8.7: New connector menu options

When the **Create a custom connector** dialogue pops up, give the connector a name. This should be a friendly name that makes it clear what the connector is for, as this is what will be visible in the browser.

Once you have named your custom connector, you will begin stepping through a number of screens that walk you through the setup process:

- **General**: Where you're going to connect to
- **Security**: How you're going to authenticate
- **Definition**: What you're going to do once you've connected
- **Test**: Confirm that your configuration is working:

Figure 8.8: Custom connector wizard tabs

The first tab you will be presented with is the **General** tab, which will collect high-level information about the connector. Let's take a look at this tab.

The General tab

The **General** tab collects information from you about any required inputs, so that it can build the identity of the connector. It allows you to define the icon that's used to represent it when it's accessed across the Microsoft Power Platform, as well as the **Icon background color** and **Description**:

 When uploading your icon, ensure that it will be displayed easily when viewed on a black background. In some cases, images with a transparent background will be displayed on a black background instead.

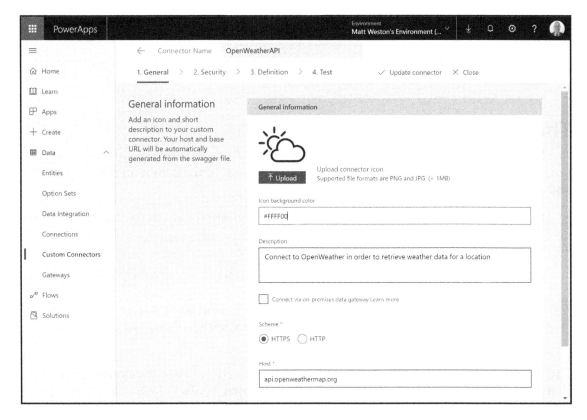

Figure 8.9: The General tab of the custom connector wizard

If you require a simple color picker, consider using the one at the following link: `https://www.w3schools.com/colors/colors_picker.asp`.

Once you have defined the look and feel of your connector, you should always consider giving the connector a short description to make it clear to your users what they can do with it.

The most important part of this first tab is the basic connection information. This tells the users what they need in order to connect to your service, and tells them whether the connection is secure (HTTPS) or not. You also need to provide the host, which is the URL of the service that you are connecting to.

Once we have defined where the service is, we need to define how we're going to authenticate it. We can do this in the **Security** tab.

The Security tab

The **Security** tab will allow you to configure the method you're using to authenticate the target REST API and will support all of the following (that is, the common) methods of authenticating:

- **No authentication**: The connector will not prompt for any type of authentication.
- **Basic authentication**: This requires the user to enter a username and password to establish the connection.
- **API key**: This requires the user to provide a unique key to establish the connection.
- **OAuth 2.0**: This requires the user to provide a client ID and secret so that they can authenticate against an OAuth data source such as Azure AD, Facebook, Google, and so on.

The options shown in the following screenshot show that the authentication type will change, depending on what's selected from the dropdown, and will help you define what the user will see when they create the connection:

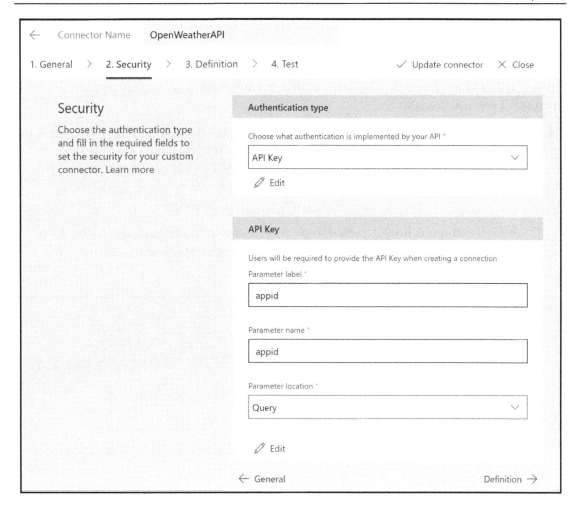

Figure 8.10: The security tab

 While using an API key, the parameter name and location must match with what the API expects. For example, if the API requires `appid` in the query string, that is how the authentication should be configured.

Now that we have defined how the connector is going to authenticate against the service, we need to define how it's going to call it.

The Definition tab

The definition element of a custom connector allows you to define the actions that can be performed through the API. This could be the retrieval of data or an update action. When creating the definition, you also have the ability to create a trigger that can be used in Microsoft Power Automate.

On the left-hand side of the screen, you will find the actions list and will have the option to create a new action by selecting the **New action** button. This will create a new action definition in the center space of the screen that you define by filling in the required form fields. You are required to fill in the following information:

- **Summary**: This is the name of the operation.
- **Description**: A brief description of the action to provide guidance to the user.
- **Operation ID**: The name of the operation that will be referenced through the formula bar:

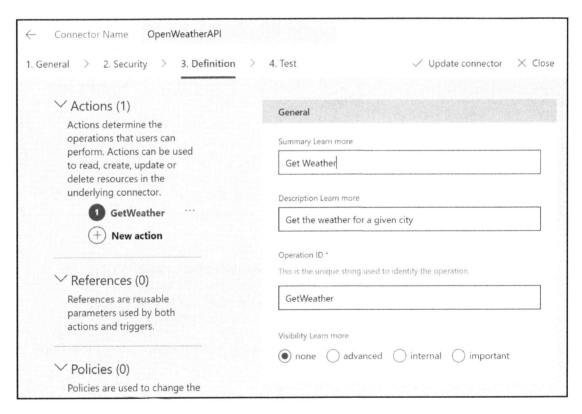

Figure 8.11: The Definition tab

Once this general information has been entered, the next step is to create a connection to the REST endpoint. One of the most effective ways of being able to define this is to take the URL of the API, including any query string parameters, and use the **Import from sample** function. This is the most simple way – since you define the **Verb** – to enter the full **URL** and any JSON that's required in the **Headers** and **Body**. Then, press **Import**:

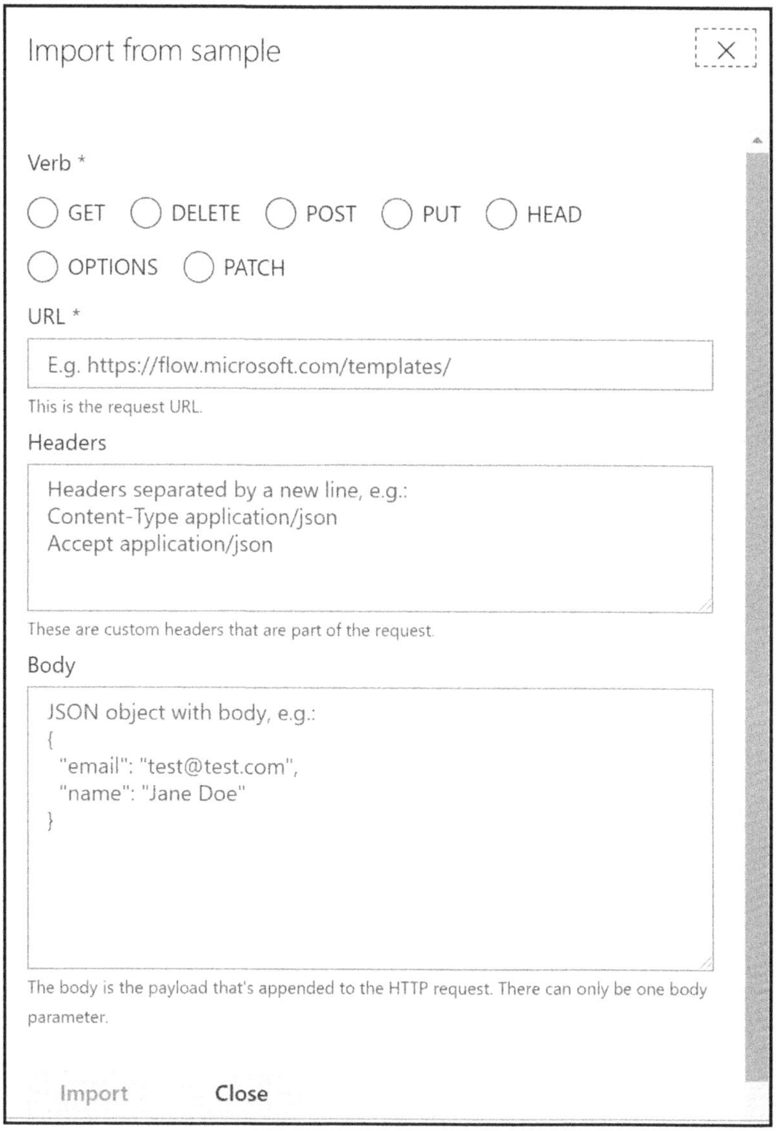

Figure 8.12: Import from sample blade

Then, the import process will create a visual representation of the request, automatically strip the query string parameters from the URL, and place them under the **Query** heading.

In this example, I needed to provide a query string parameter called q. If I click on that query item, I can further configure the behavior of the action by defining default values, descriptions, and whether the parameter is mandatory or not:

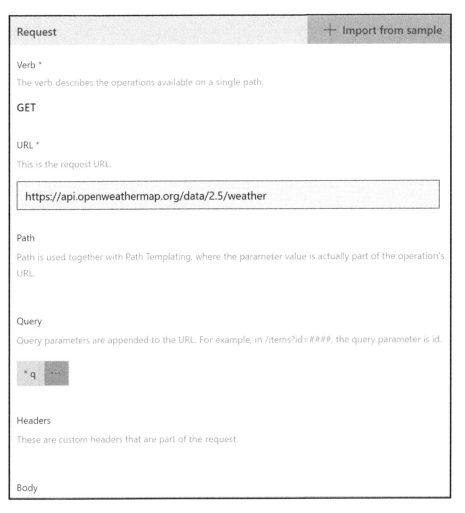

Figure 8.13: Request definition generated from the sample

There are also visibility options available to the parameter:

- **none**: This actually means no definition; therefore, it will take the default value, that is, **important.**
- **advanced**: The parameter will appear in a selection of advanced options that refer to its use in Microsoft Power Automate, rather than PowerApps.
- **internal**: The parameter will be passed to the API; however, it will be hidden from the end user.
- **important**: The parameter will be passed to the API and will be available to the end user so that they can pass a value:

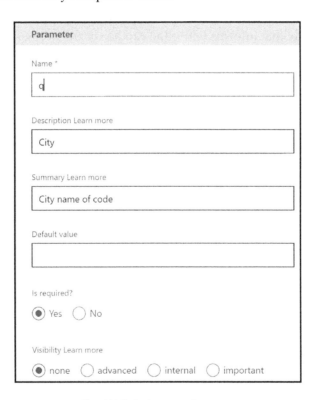

Figure 8.14: Configuring a query string parameter

If your parameter is a static value, consider setting the default value and changing its visibility to **internal** to ensure that the correct value is always passed to the REST endpoint.

Once we've finished configuring our custom connector, it is important to test it before we push it out to our users. We can do this in the **Test** tab.

The Test tab

Once you have at least one action and the configuration has been validated, you can test the connector from within this wizard. This is extremely useful to ensure that you are going to get the correct response from the API before you allow your users to start using it.

If your connector requires you to pass query string parameters, you will be prompted to supply those to ensure that the call to the API has everything it needs. What will be returned is a status code that informs you if the call has been successful or not, as well as a response body:

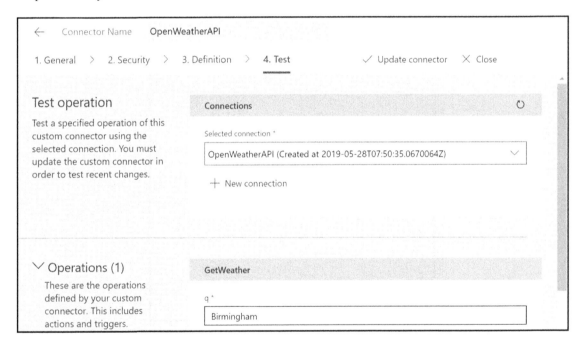

Figure 8.15: The Test tab

Once the connector has been created, it can be added as a data source in PowerApps and used just like any built-in connector. There may be occasions, however, where we will be provided with an OpenAPI file for this. If this happens, we need to import this file directly into PowerApps.

Importing an OpenAPI file

As an alternative to creating a connector manually, you can import an OpenAPI file that may have been supplied to you by a third-party service provider or that you may have written yourself. The OpenAPI file can either be imported from your local filesystem or, if it exists on the internet, imported from a URL. Follow these steps to get started:

1. As part of the import process, the JSON of the file will be validated and then imported. The result will be the same as when we created the connector from scratch, whereby any authentication will be defined, as well as the actions and required parameters.

2. If you have created your own OpenAPI file, then it is likely that you have it stored somewhere that's locally accessible to your machine. To upload it to the Microsoft Power Platform, click on the **New custom connector** menu and select **Import an OpenAPI file**:

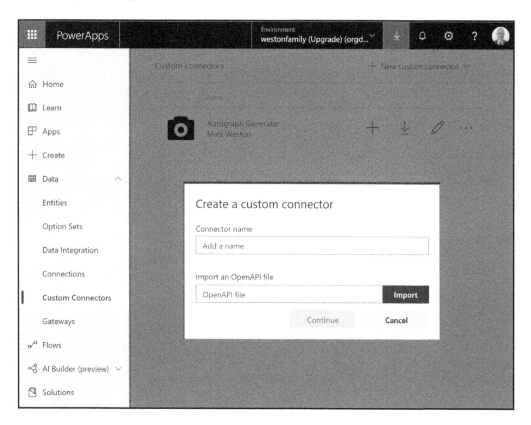

Figure 8.16: Importing the OpenAPI file

3. Once you see the **Create a custom connector** dialog box, give your connector a name and then select the **Import** button. This will open a file explorer box so that you can select the file from your local machine.

4. Once the file has been uploaded, assuming that it is a valid OpenAPI file, it will open the custom connector screen to allow you to modify the configurable settings.

If you wish to implement more complex types of data, for example, binary files, you may wish to write your own OpenAPI file. Alternatively, you could create one using the in-built Create Connector wizard (which we used to create a connector from scratch), download it, edit it, and then reimport it.

Creating a connector from within Postman

Postman is a free tool that is extremely useful for testing interactivity with web-based APIs. One of the key features of Postman is that it allows you to create a Postman collection, which means that we can define and save all of our API calls within Postman.

Once a collection has been saved, we can import this file, which will be processed and once again create the defined connector and any actions that are associated with the connector. As an example, this could be a collection that connects to a weather API and would contain actions such as *Get Weather for Today*.

The steps to export a collection from Postman is relatively simple:

1. To export a collection from Postman, you need to open the Postman application and click on the ellipsis next to your chosen collection before selecting **Export**:

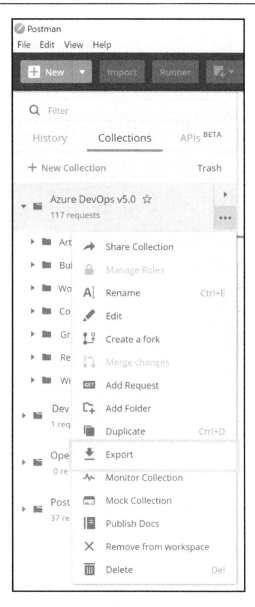

Figure 8.17: Exporting from Postman

2. When you export, you need to ensure that your collection is exported using the **Collection v1** schema. While this may be marked as deprecated in the latest versions of Postman, you will still be able to select it:

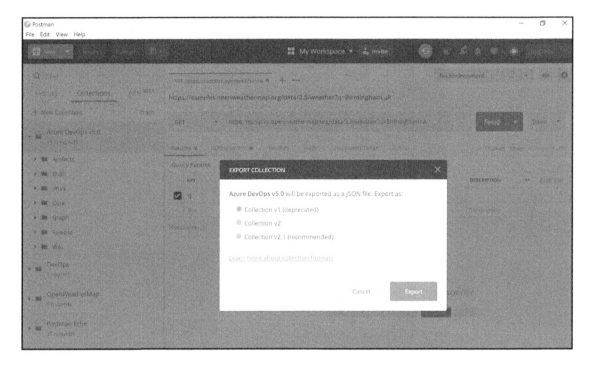

Figure 8.18: Selecting the collection type

3. From this point, we can select the **New custom connector** menu and select **Import a Postman collection**. Then, we can select the file we wish to export using the file explorer in exactly the same way that we did when we imported an OpenAPI file:

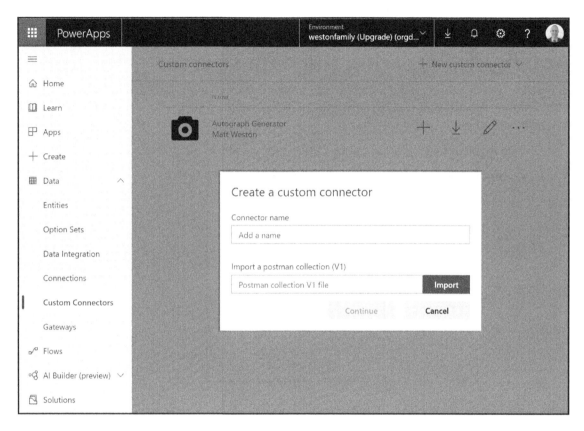

Figure 8.19: Importing the Postman collection

Once the file has been imported, we will able to modify the configurable elements of the custom connector.

Lab 7

In this lab, we are going to establish a connection to a data source that isn't local to our PowerApp. For simplicity, the data source will be an Excel spreadsheet that will need to be stored within cloud storage such as OneDrive.

Activity 1: Preparing the data source

Before we use a connector, the first thing that we need to do is prepare a data source. To demonstrate this, we will use Microsoft Excel and store the data source within OneDrive. Let's get started:

1. Create an Excel workbook and save it to OneDrive as `Assets.xlsx`.

2. Right-click the tab at the bottom of the screen named `Sheet1`:

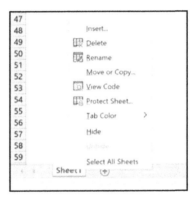

3. Select **Rename** and change the name of the tab to `Categories`:

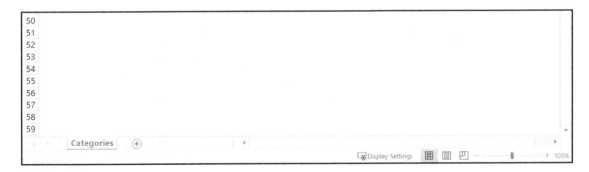

4. On the `Categories` tab, add some data, as follows:

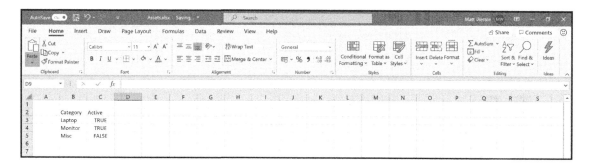

5. Ensure that you have a cell containing data selected, for example, the `Category` cell, and select **Format as Table** from the **Styles** group in the ribbon. Select any formatting you like:

6. Select the cell range that corresponds to your data, leave **My table has headers** ticked, and then click **OK**:

7. With the table still highlighted, select **Table Design** from the ribbon:

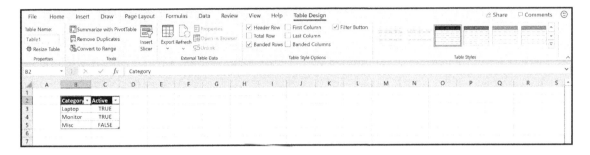

8. Under **Table Name** on the far left of the ribbon, change the table's name from Table 1 to categories.
9. Close Microsoft Excel.

Now that we have prepared our Excel spreadsheet for use within PowerApps, we can use this data within an app.

Activity 2: Adding the data source to the app

Now that we have a data source, we are going to modify our app so that we can start utilizing the data contained within our Excel workbook. Let's get started:

1. Open the PowerApp that we have been building throughout the labs in this book.
2. Once your app is open in PowerApps Studio, click on the **View** menu:

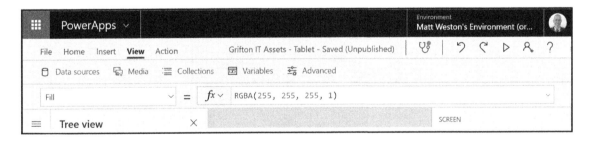

3. Select **Data sources**:

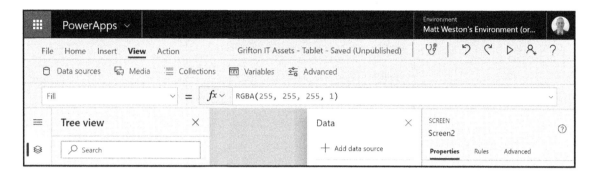

4. When the data blade appears, click on **Add data source** and select **+ New connection**:

5. Either search for, or browse to, **OneDrive** (or **OneDrive for Business**, if that's what you're using) and select it:

6. On the OneDrive description screen, click **Create**:

7. Navigate through your OneDrive structure and select **Assets.xlsx**:

8. Now, we need to tell the app which table we are going to take our data from. Choose the **Categories** table and select **Connect**:

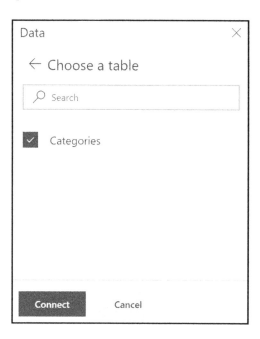

9. Open the **Options** screen from the tree view in the left-hand blade.
10. On this screen, click on the **Insert** menu:

11. From the **Insert** menu, select **Gallery** and insert a **Blank horizontal** gallery:

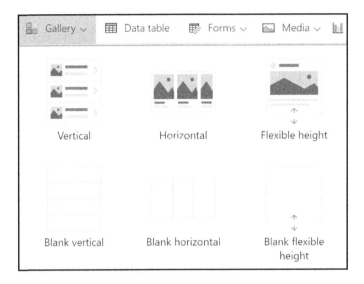

12. Right-click the control within the tree view and rename this control `galCategories`.

13. From the **Properties** pane, change the **Data source** and select **Categories**:

14. With `galCategories` selected (it is important to have the gallery selected so that the control is created inside it), return to the **Insert** menu.

15. Select **Label**.

16. Change the **Text** property of the label so that it displays the category name by entering `ThisItem.Category`:

17. We only want to show the active categories. We can do this by filtering the entries from the data source that are set to be **Active**. Select the **Items** property of the **Gallery** control:

18. Change the `Items` formula to the `Filter` formula and ensure that only categories where `Active` is `True` are returned.
Change `Categories` to `Filter(Categories, Active="True")`:

Notice that only two of the three categories are being displayed.

19. Apply the same branding to the label that we applied to the header background. Ensure that the text can be read by changing the font color and center aligning it.

Now that we have created our first interaction with the data source, we will add another one which will show us our assets.

Activity 3: Adding a list of assets

In this activity, we will create the list of assets within the Excel workbook, and then display the assets within the app. We will also create some basic interactions between our categories and our assets.

1. Open your Excel workbook once more and create a new table called `Assets` with the following data:

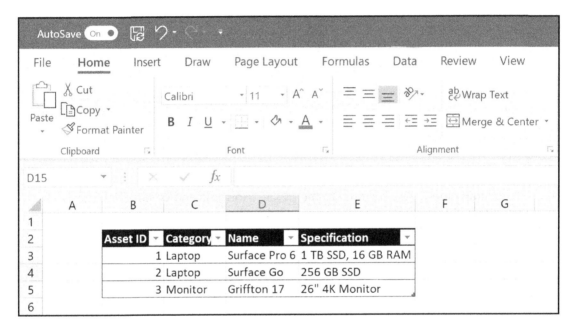

2. Repeat the steps from activity 2 to connect the `Assets` table to the app.
3. Place a **Blank vertical** gallery onto the **Options** screen and name it `galAssets`.
4. Select the **Assets** data source:

5. Add labels to the gallery to display the **Assets and the Specifications fields**:

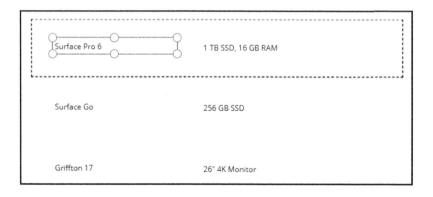

6. We will now configure the filters, created in Activity 2, so that our list of assets will change. Select the Label control which we added to galCategories.

7. Change the **OnSelect** property of the label so that it sets a context variable to the selected category: `UpdateContext({ctxSelectedCategory:ThisItem.Category}):`

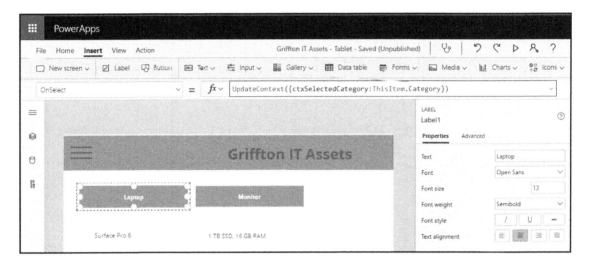

8. Modify the **Items** property of `galAssets` so that it filters based on the context variable, that is, `Filter(Assets, Category = ctxSelectedCategory):`

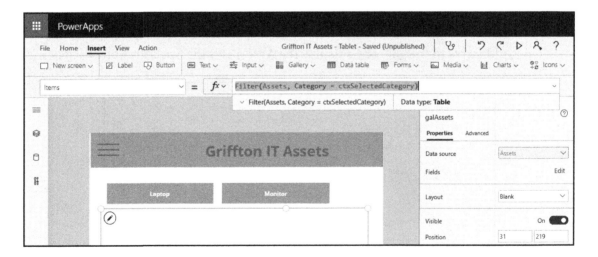

9. Run the app and click each category in turn. Notice how the data that's displayed in the assets list changes:

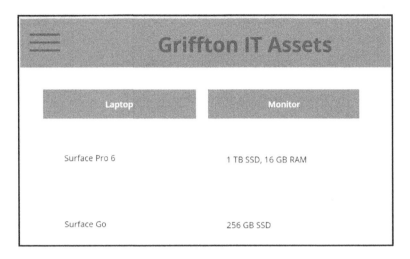

In this lab, we have created our first connection to data stored outside of our PowerApp by connecting to an Excel spreadsheet. Now, we can start to improve the UI by adding additional icons and changing the display properties.

Summary

In this chapter, we have opened the door to hundreds of additional data sources that live externally to our PowerApp. This is truly where the power of a connected app can be established, as you can retrieve data from multiple sources, as well as write data back (depending on the connection).

In this chapter, we looked at the built-in connectors that are provided by Microsoft so that we can connect to over 250 different sources of data. We have also broken down these connectors into two distinct groups: standard connectors, which are available with a standard Office 365 license, and premium connectors, which require us to have a minimum of PowerApps Plan 1 before we can use them. Many of these premium connectors will require you to have licenses with the service provider so that you can use them.

As well as being able to use built-in connectors, we have the ability to create our own so that we can connect to any data source that has an API. These are known as custom connectors. These connectors can be created using an in-built wizard that guides us through a step-by-step process regarding how to create and then define the relevant actions.

Alternatively, we can also populate the description of the connector by importing an OpenAPI file from either a URL or from the local filesystem, or by importing a collection from Postman. While custom connectors are extremely useful, they are only available with PowerApps Plan 1 and above.

In the next chapter, we'll learn how to use GPS in PowerApps.

Questions

1. There are two types of built-in connector. What are they?
2. True or False: Custom connectors can be created from a URL to an OData file.
3. True or False: I can use an Excel workbook stored on a filesystem as a data source.
4. True or False: Azure AD can be used as an authentication method when defining a custom connector.
5. What is the name of the free tool that can be used to test an API?

Further reading

Take a look at the following resources to find out more about the topics that were covered in this chapter:

- Microsoft documentation for custom connectors: `https://docs.microsoft.com/en-gb/powerapps/maker/canvas-apps/register-custom-api`
- Creating Postman collections: `https://learning.getpostman.com/docs/postman/collections/creating_collections/`
- API testing with Postman: `https://www.packtpub.com/gb/application-development/api-testing-postman-video`

3
Section 3: Extending the Capabilities of Your PowerApp

Within this section, we are going to start to dive deeper into the functionality that PowerApps allows us to use for the creation of our apps.

In the first chapter within this section, we will look at the first area where our PowerApps can access data by using the capabilities of the local device. We will explore the options that we have to not only capture and track geographic location but also how we can output that data back into our app.

Next, we will again explore more integrations with the device, by learning how to use the camera. We will be using the camera to not only capture images, but also to capture data from barcodes and QR codes, and then using that data within our apps.

In Chapter 11, *Securing Your PowerApps*, we will look at how we can add levels of security into our app, to provide different experiences for users based on either roles defined within an app or by using Azure Active Directory groups.

Chapter 12, *Working Offline*, will look at how we can start to add some robustness to our apps by giving them the ability to continue functioning even without an active network connection.

Microsoft Flow is introduced in Chapter 13, *Using Power Automate with PowerApps*, where we investigate how one of the other areas of the Power Platform can be leveraged within our app to add additional processing power.

We will expand beyond Flow within Chapter 14, *Using Azure with PowerApps*, and look at how we can call on other services within Microsoft Azure to allow us to satisfy the requirements for our apps.

This section includes the following chapters:

- Chapter 9, *Using GPS in PowerApps*
- Chapter 10, *Working with Images and Barcodes*
- Chapter 11, *Securing Your PowerApps*
- Chapter 12, *Working Offline*
- Chapter 13, *Using Power Automate with PowerApps*
- Chapter 14, *Using Azure with PowerApps*

Using GPS in PowerApps

9

In this chapter, we are going to learn how to generate some basic mapping data using the GPS functionality of the mobile device that is serving our app. Mapping data is one of the most basic, yet most powerful, forms of data that can be used and exploited.

This chapter differs from the previous chapters, where we used connectors to interact with data sources to retrieve and use data. Now, we are going to be using the native capabilities of PowerApps and the device itself to generate our data.

In this chapter, we will cover the following topics:

- Placing maps into your apps
- Capturing geographic position
- Lab 8

Throughout this chapter, we will look at the types of data that we can capture from PowerApps and how we can use that data to enrich our apps even further.

Technical requirements

To follow along with the lab in this chapter, you will need to have completed the labs in the previous chapters. It is recommended that you use a mobile device for testing purposes.

To be able to use APIs from Bing, you will need to have a valid Microsoft account (Live, Outlook, MSN). Likewise, for Google Maps, you will need to have a valid Google account.

Placing maps into your apps

Maps can be used to show contextual information to your users, thereby allowing you to represent location data in a meaningful way. Two of the most popular mapping technologies that we can use are Bing and Google Maps, both of which can be leveraged within our PowerApp. Both mapping technologies provide a free service that can also be used for commercial purposes, which adds to their popularity.

Leveraging Bing maps

Bing maps provide a static map API that you can access with a free API key. Simply navigate to `https://www.bingmapsportal.com` and get the basic map key. You will need to register and sign in using a Microsoft account so that you can access the Bing Maps Dev Center:

 To register for a Microsoft account, please visit the following Microsoft guide: `https://support.microsoft.com/en-us/help/4026324/microsoft-account-how-to-create`.

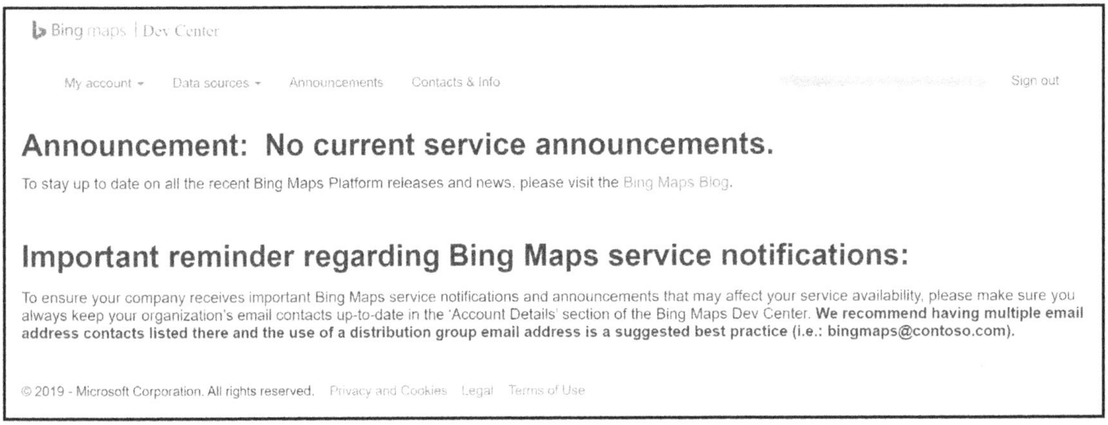

b Bing maps | Dev Center

My account ▾   Data sources ▾   Announcements   Contacts & Info   Sign out

Announcement: No current service announcements.

To stay up to date on all the recent Bing Maps Platform releases and news, please visit the Bing Maps Blog.

Important reminder regarding Bing Maps service notifications:

To ensure your company receives important Bing Maps service notifications and announcements that may affect your service availability, please make sure you always keep your organization's email contacts up-to-date in the 'Account Details' section of the Bing Maps Dev Center. **We recommend having multiple email address contacts listed there and the use of a distribution group email address is a suggested best practice (i.e.: bingmaps@contoso.com).**

© 2019 - Microsoft Corporation. All rights reserved.   Privacy and Cookies   Legal   Terms of Use

Figure 9.1: Bing Maps Dev Center

The ability to generate a key can be found under the **My account** menu by clicking on **My keys**. This will allow you to generate new keys or view your existing keys:

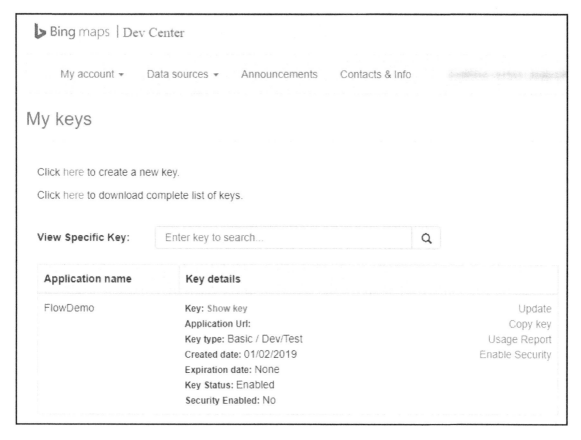

Figure 9.2: My keys

Once you have generated a key, keep the window open or copy the key to the clipboard so that you can use it once you've returned to PowerApps.

In PowerApps, we will use an image control to display the map, and we will simply provide the URL of the web service as the **Image** property:

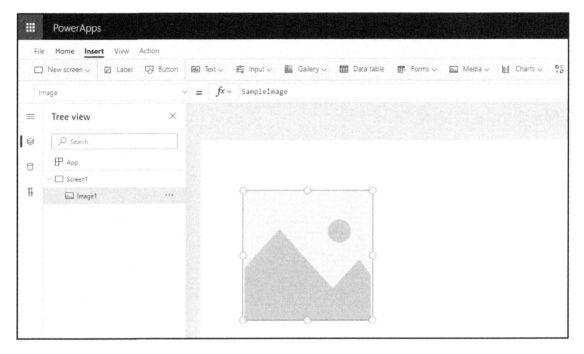

Figure 9.3: Image control on the canvas

When we place an image control on the canvas, we simply need to put the full URL, plus the relevant query string parameters, into the formula bar. Assuming that the call was successful, a map will be returned. The Bing Maps web service will process the web request based on the parameters that are supplied and will return a graphic displaying the relevant information:

```
https://dev.virtualearth.net/REST/v1/Imagery/Map/Road/Routes?wp.0=Dudley,UK
;64;1&wp.1=Dudley,UK;66;2&key={api key}
```

In the preceding example, the API returns a road map showing the routes for Dudley in the United Kingdom and adds a pin to the center of the map. The important parts of this API are related to the location name and country code. The actual output of the API can be seen in the following screenshot, whereby the map has been generated for Dudley in the United Kingdom:

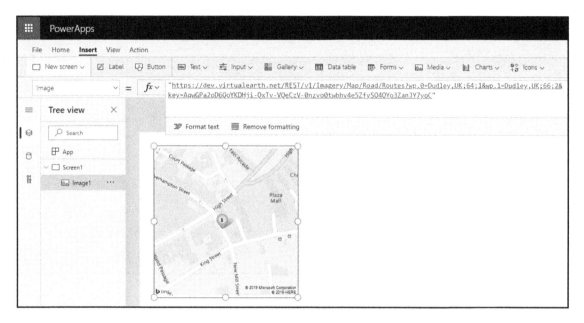

Figure 9.4: Bing Maps API being called by an image control

Rather than statically putting the mapping parameters directly into the URL, we can replace them with inputs from other controls within the PowerApp. For example, we could use dropdowns so that we can select the mapping type, and the coordinates could be entered in text boxes. In the following screenshot, the map type has been set from the `ddMapType` dropdown and the location has been taken from the `txtLocation` text box:

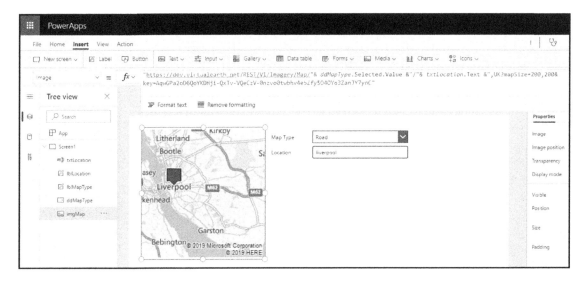

Figure 9.5: Bing Maps being displayed based on data provided by other controls

If you don't want to use Bing, you can use Google Maps.

Leveraging Google Maps

Just like Bing Maps, Google also provides a static map API that we can call in the same way in order to return mapping information from Google. Again, you will need to register for a Google account in order to use the API. Go to `https://developers.google.com/maps/documentation/maps-static/intro` to do so.

To get an API key, select the **Get an API Key and Signature** link from the left-hand menu and then follow the onscreen instructions:

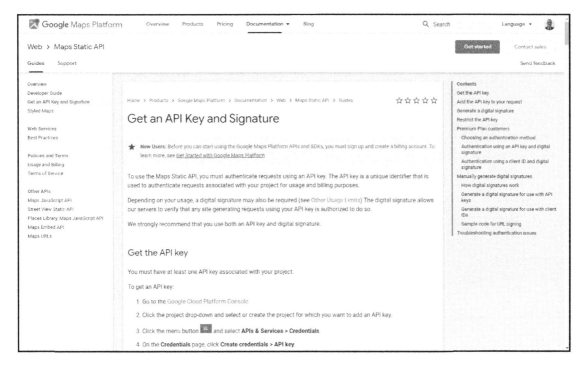

Figure 9.6: Getting an API key from Google Maps

We put the Google map on the canvas in exactly the same way as we would with a Bing map. First, however, we need to add an image to the page and then supply the API call to the **Image** property:

```
https://maps.googleapis.com/maps/api/staticmap?center=Brooklyn+Bridge,New+Y
ork,NY&zoom=13&size=600x600&maptype=roadmap&key={API Key}
```

This example will result in an image of New York with the center point at Brooklyn Bridge:

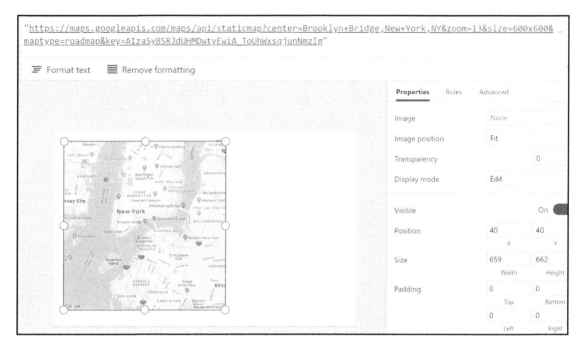

Figure 9.7: A Google map being displayed on the canvas

In both examples, we have supplied a location name in order to find the area that we want, but both APIs also support latitude and longitude data:

```
https://maps.googleapis.com/maps/api/staticmap?center=51.477222,0&s
ize=400x400&key={API Key}
```

The preceding code will show a part of London based on the coordinates provided:

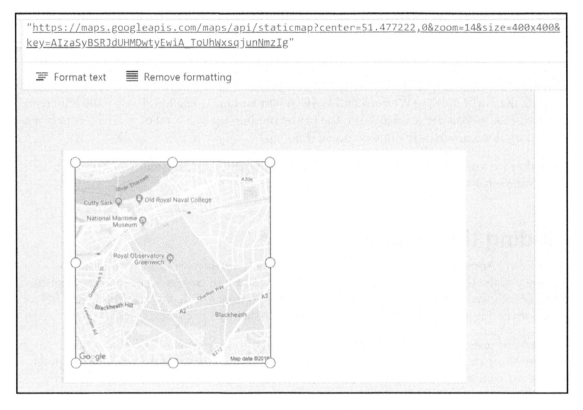

Figure 9.8: Showing a map based on latitude and longitude

This approach to selecting a location will become more important as we start to use the mobile device's native GPS capability.

Capturing geographic position

PowerApps has the fantastic ability to integrate with the location services that are provided by a mobile device using GPS or cellular information. With this service, we can determine the position of the device using latitude and longitude, as well as the direction the device is facing.

We determine the GPS location using the position that's relative to two imaginary lines running around the Earth. The first is the equator, which signifies 0° latitude, and gives us the division between the Northern and Southern hemispheres. The latitude value increases as you progress further north and decreases as you go further south, to a maximum value of 90. Therefore, the north pole has +90° latitude, and the south pole has -90° latitude.

The second imaginary line is at 0° longitude and is known as the prime meridian. This line dissects the Earth into the Western and Eastern hemispheres. The longitude values increase and decrease as you move away from the prime median up to a total of +/- 180°, which is a secondary line known as the international dateline.

Now that we understand how latitude and longitude works, let's use PowerApps to determine our location based on these values.

Finding the location

With PowerApps, we can use a very simple formula to retrieve existing locations. The accuracy of the GPS, however, can vary immensely and will be less accurate if the user has only recently switched on their GPS since not enough time will have passed for the GPS to lock onto enough satellites to provide an accurate reading.

PowerApps uses objects called signals, which are values that can change at any time without the user directly interacting with the app. Any formula that utilizes these signals will be recalculated as the values change. For this reason, you should consider capturing the GPS location and freezing it.

To demonstrate how to capture the latitude and longitude, we will capture the basic location data and display it in a label. We will modify the **OnSelect** property of the button to capture the location. The reason we're placing it into a collection is to make it simple to see what has been captured. You don't necessarily need to do this when you're creating your app:

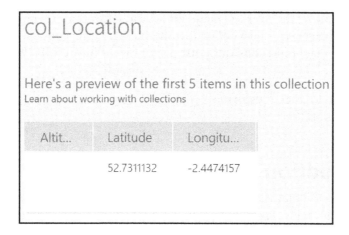

Figure 9.9: Location information being captured within the PowerApp

Note that, from the one call, three items have been captured: the latitude, the longitude, and the altitude of the device. We can output these properties into a label or any alternative control to display them to the user:

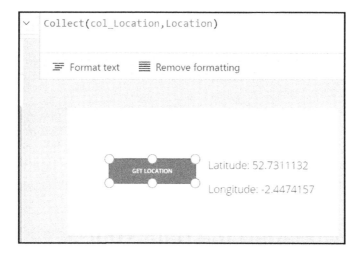

Figure 9.10: Capturing the location of the device and sorting it within a collection

If you don't see any data being populated here when you run this in PowerApps studio, ensure that your operating system has allowed the use of location services.

It's good practice to allow the user to enable and disable location tracking through the app. Apps that use location services and GPS naturally have a higher power consumption than those that don't, so you should consider your use of location carefully. To enable GPS, use `Enable(Location)`. Use `Disable(Location)` to disable it.

As well as being able to track the current location of a user, mobile devices also have the ability to track direction.

Finding direction

As well as being able to determine a location, we can provide additional context regarding which way the user is facing, especially if you're capturing location data about a photograph.

PowerApps has a function named `Compass` that allows us to capture the direction the user is facing in degrees. The number of degrees will range from 0 to 360. To utilize this in your app, you will need to call the heading property of the compass:

```
Compass.Heading
```

You can use this heading to determine the direction; that is, North is 0 or 360 degrees, East is 90 degrees, South is 180 degrees, and West is 270 degrees.

Lab 8

Within this lab, we are going to add elements of GPS connectivity to our app. To follow along with this lab, you will need to have completed the previous labs, where we have been building our asset app. You will also need a mobile device to fully test the functionality we are about to develop.

Activity 1: Updating the data source

The first thing that we need to do is update our data source so that we can capture and store some location data:

1. Open the Excel spreadsheet that we used previously to store our assets and add another column called `Location`:

Asset ID	Category	Name	Specification	__PowerAppsId__	Location
1	Laptop	Surface Pro 6	1 TB SSD, 16 GB RAM	6D7XU_WlkLc	
2	Laptop	Surface Go	256 GB SSD	V3rYVKzuAVg	
3	Monitor	Griffton 17	26" 4K Monitor	jljJ2J-BMqg	

2. Add the following coordinates to the `Location` fields for the three items in the table: 40.804000, -74.464460.

3. Save and close the spreadsheet and return to PowerApps.

Now that we have updated our data source, we will add more functionality to the app so that we can use the location functions.

Activity 2: Creating a new asset

In this activity, we will update our PowerApp so that we can take advantage of the GPS functionality of the mobile device:

1. Open the PowerApp that we have been building throughout this book:

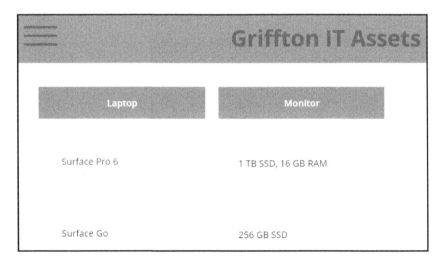

2. Open the **New Asset** screen from the screens list on the left-hand side of the PowerApps Studio.

3. Add an **Edit** form to the screen by going to the **Insert** menu, **Forms**, and then selecting **Edit**:

4. Rename the form to `frmNewAsset`.

5. Once the form is on the screen, ensure that you have **frmNewAsset** selected and set **Assets** as the data source:

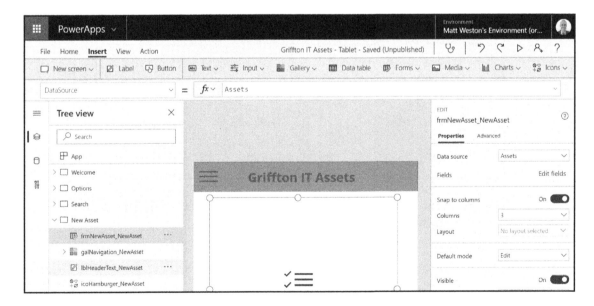

6. Select **Edit fields** and add the following fields:

- Asset ID
- Name
- Specification
- Category
- Location

This is shown in the following screenshot:

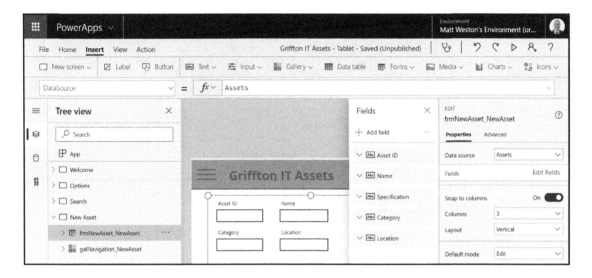

7. In the **Properties** blade for `frmNewAsset`, change the number of columns from 3 to 1:

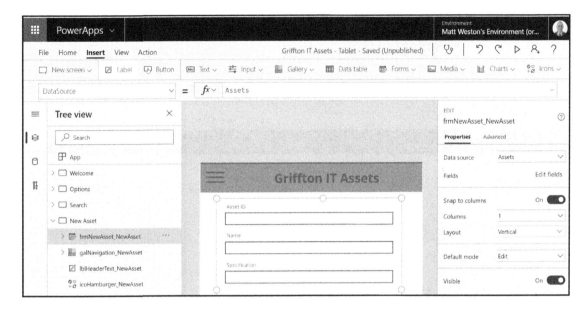

8. Change **Default mode** from **Edit** to **New**:

9. Select the screen and change the **OnVisible** property
   to `Set(varLocation,Concatenate(Text(Location.Latitude),",",Text(`
   `Location.Longitude)):`

10. Select the text box associated with `Location`.
11. Unlock the advanced properties by clicking the **Advanced** tab and selecting the padlock:

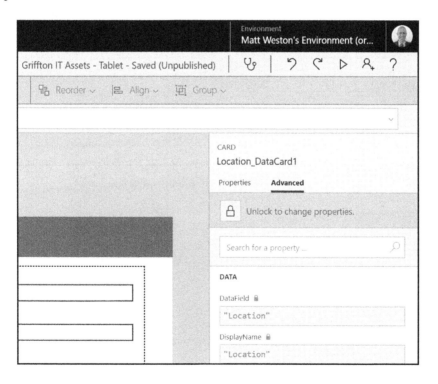

12. Select the text box in the **Location** field and change the **Default** property to `varLocation`:

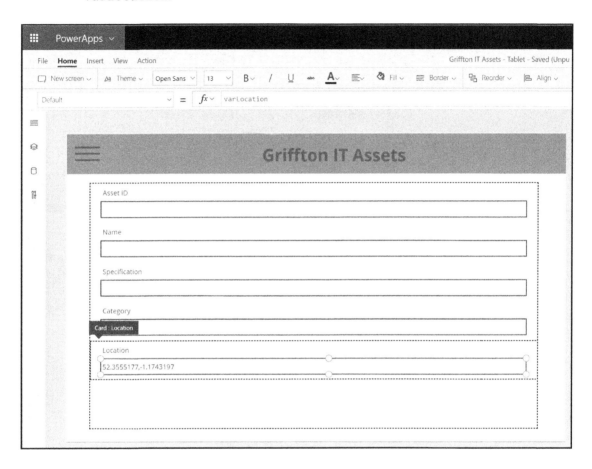

13. Add a custom card to the form by going back to the field select and clicking on the ellipsis at the top of the blade:

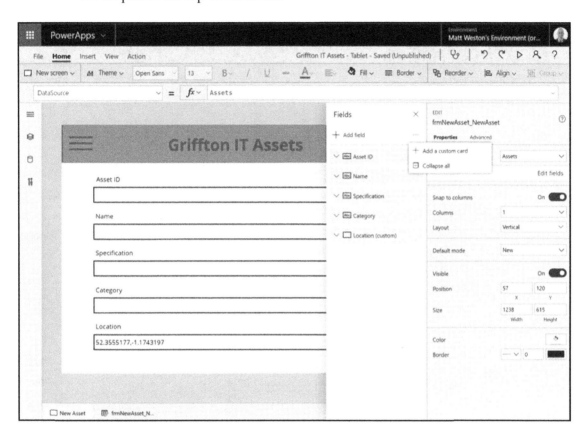

14. In the custom card, place a **Check** icon and change the **OnSelect** property to `SubmitForm(frmNewAsset);Navigate(Search,Fade)`. This will submit the form data to the data source:

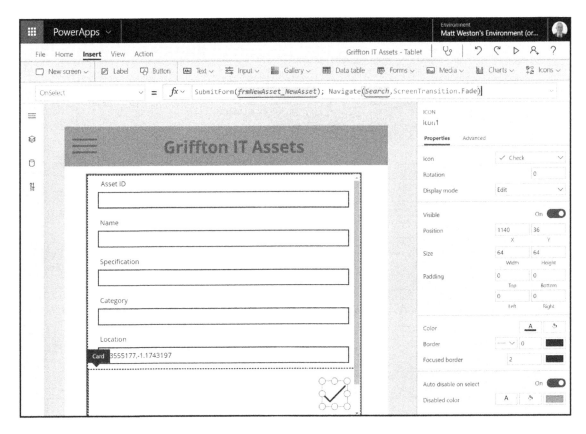

15. Complete the form and submit a new asset to the spreadsheet.

Now that we are writing geographic data back to our data source, let's update our app so that we can display this data using a mapping API.

Activity 3: Displaying a map

Now, we will continue to build out our app by adding a map to the view form, which will display the geographic location of where the asset was added to the register. This example will be based on the Bing Maps API, so ensure that you have signed up to `https://www.bingmapsportal.com`.

Let's get started:

1. Select the **View Assets** screen:

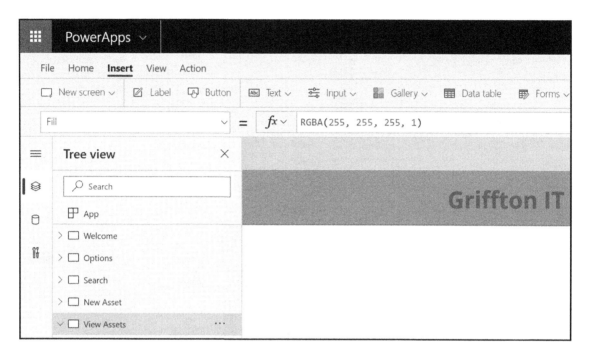

2. Place a display form on the screen and select **Assets** as the data source:

3. Using **Edit fields**, add all of the fields except for the location.

4. Change the number of columns to 1:

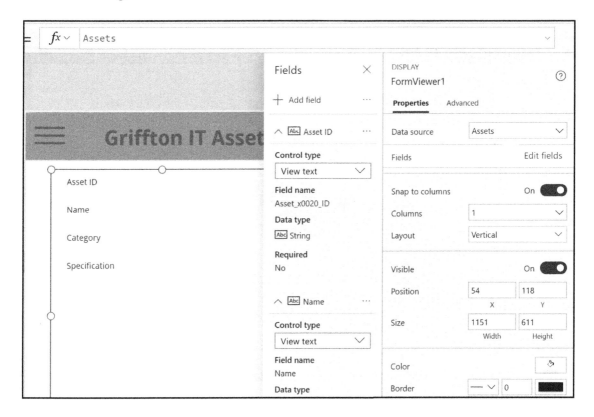

5. Now that we have our fields, let's add a custom card that holds our map. Click on the ellipsis and add a custom card to the form:

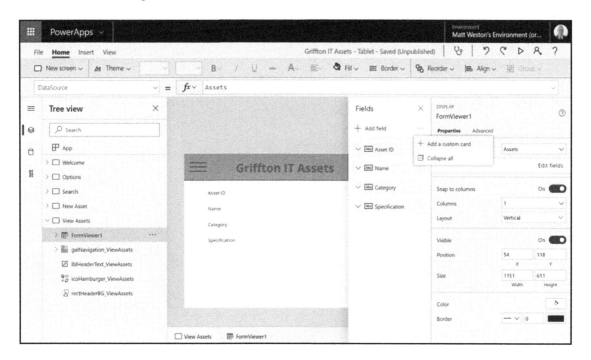

6. Click on the custom card and place an image control inside it:

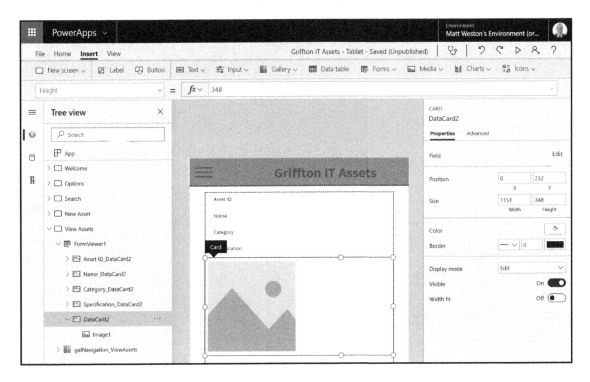

7. Set the image to the Bing Maps API URL:

```
"https://dev.virtualearth.net/REST/v1/Imagery/Map/AerialWithLab
els?pp="& ThisItem.Location &";;"& ThisItem.'Asset ID'
&"&key={Your API Key}".
```

This will take the **Location** field and use that to place a pin on the map. It will also put the asset ID into the pin:

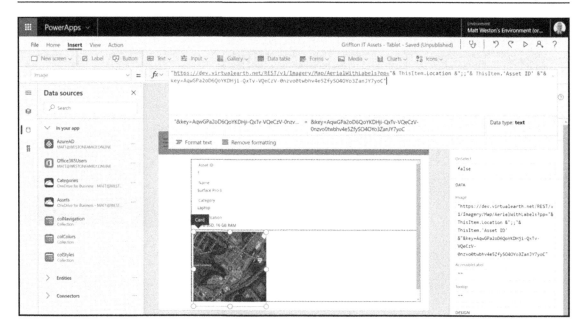

Now that we have prepared our details page, we will complete this section by allowing our users to navigate to the form to create a new entry and to also view the existing entries.

Activity 4: Adding navigation

Part of the functionality of this app is allowing our users to be able to add new assets and then view the details of them afterward. Now, let's update the various areas of navigation to make this possible:

1. From the screen list, go back to the **Options** screen:

2. Select the `galAssets` gallery control and add a **Right** icon:

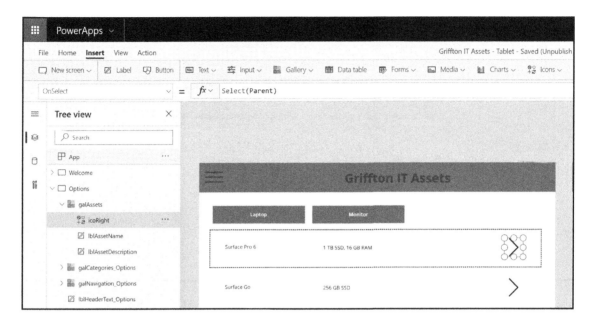

3. Change **OnSelect** to `Select(Parent);Navigate('View Assets',ScreenTransition.Fade)`.

Now, run your app and click on the right arrow to see your asset information and a map being displayed. Then, click on your hamburger menu and add a new item from the new screen so that the value of your current location will be placed in the data source:

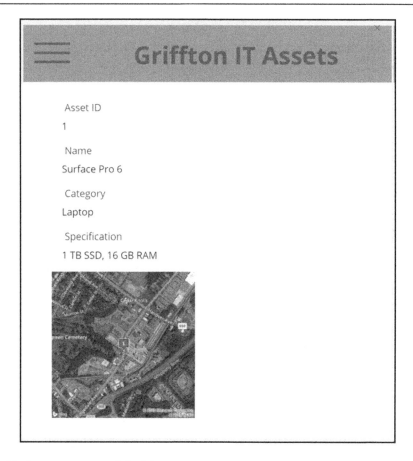

Save and publish your app and feel free to test it on your mobile device.

Summary

In this chapter, we looked at the most common type of data visualization: mapping. Mapping helps you display data in a context that's easier to understand by your users than by simply displaying latitude and longitude information on the screen. Specifically, we focused on how to display mapping data using the APIs provided by Bing Maps and Google Maps since they both offer free APIs for you to use within your apps.

PowerApps provides signals that allow us to track the GPS location of the device, as well as the direction that it's facing. The key thing to remember with signals is that their values constantly change. Therefore, if you wish to use signal values, then you should capture them.

Remember that location services are extremely power-intensive, so only use GPS when you need to in order to avoid unnecessary battery drain. This should be done by calling the disable function.

In the next chapter, we will learn how barcodes and QR codes work in PowerApps.

Questions

1. Why should a signal be captured rather than used directly in a formula?
2. What three pieces of data will the location formula retrieve?
3. How is direction expressed when using a compass?
4. What function can I use to disable GPS?
5. Why would you not leave location services on permanently?

Further reading

Take a look at the following resources to find out more about the topics that were covered in this chapter:

- Bing Maps API documentation: https://www.microsoft.com/en-us/maps/documentation
- Google Maps documentation: https://developers.google.com/maps/documentation/

10
Working with Images and Barcodes

In the previous chapter, we started to capture more contextual information within our apps by utilizing the built-in GPS functions of a mobile device. In this chapter, we will expand on our exploitation of mobile device capabilities by capturing and using images, as well as being able to read/identify information from barcodes and **Quick Response** (**QR**) codes.

Both barcodes and QR codes are available on almost everything that we interact with on a day-to-day basis, whether that is on our food goods or our electronics and even for quickly locating apps. These unique identifiers can be utilized throughout our apps, allowing us to encode and read data using methods other than standard textual formats.

In this chapter, we will be covering the following topics:

- Understanding how to store images within PowerApps
- Using images with the camera control
- Using the **Add picture** control
- Understanding the barcode scanner

By the end of this chapter, you will be able to leverage the camera-based capabilities of a mobile device to take and store photos and to extract data from barcodes and QR codes.

Technical requirements

To follow along with this chapter you will need to have completed the previous labs.

In order to be able to use the camera controls, you will need a device with a camera. To use the barcode scanner, you will need a mobile device with the PowerApps app installed.

Understanding how to store images within PowerApps

Before we start to utilize the image controls within PowerApps, it is important to understand where we can actually store them. PowerApps can read and use images from a number of different storage types, including SharePoint. However, while saving the images, we can only natively save them to Excel, SQL Server, and the Common Data Service. While we can't directly save the images to SharePoint (and other more obvious image stores), there are ways in which we can utilize other areas of Office 365 to save images, which we will investigate in the next chapter.

If we are talking about the storage of static images, we are not expecting the user to be able to create, edit, or delete them; we can store images locally with the PowerApp itself.

But really, when we are considering how we want to use images within PowerApps, especially given that we are designing for a mobile device, the obvious way of using images is with the camera control.

Using images with the camera control

The camera control is one of the controls that directly interacts with the camera attached to the device. This could be a camera that is built into the device itself, for example, the camera in a phone, or it could be a wired camera that is attached to a desktop device. The camera control allows us to directly capture an image using that device and then do something with it in PowerApps.

The camera control can be inserted into the page from the **Insert | Media** menu, and when it appears on your page, it will immediately start to stream a feed from your camera:

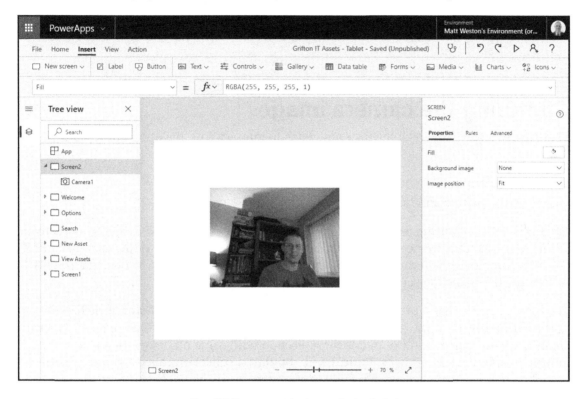

Figure 10.1: The camera control on the canvas showing a live feed

Within our app, we have the ability to select the camera that we want to take the feed from. The camera selection takes the form of a numerical value, with your primary camera being 0, and then subsequent cameras being numbered from there.

If we take Microsoft Surface as an example, the front-facing camera is camera 0, while the rear-facing is camera 1. The selection of the camera can then be something that is user-driven by using a combination of the other controls within PowerApps.

Once the user has the image lined up in the camera control, we need to be able to capture the image.

Capturing the camera image

There are two ways in which the user may wish to interact with the app in order to capture the image:

- By tapping the camera control
- By clicking another control elsewhere on the screen

The first way of capturing a picture is when a user taps or clicks on the image on the screen. For us to handle this, we need to modify the **OnSelect** event property of the camera control. For this example, we will capture the image and place each image into a collection so that we can use the collection screen to see what is being stored.

The camera control has a property available called Photo that, at the point of click, will capture the frame currently being displayed. Therefore, if I use the following formula, I can begin to capture images and populate the collection with some other key pieces of information. In the following example, I will populate a collection called MyPhotos each time the camera control is used. This will capture the Photo, the date and time the picture was taken, and the location it was taken in based on the GPS capabilities of the device:

```
Collect(
    MyPhotos,
    {
        Photograph: Camera1.Photo,
        DateTimeTaken: Now(),
        LocationTaken: Location
    }
)
```

The other aspects of the collection should look somewhat familiar. In this case, I am capturing the photograph, the date and time that it was taken, and the location information as well:

Figure 10.2: A collection storing images taken by the camera

Once the images are within a collection, we can use a gallery control to output them again. So, if we place a horizontal control on a page and select our collection, we can use an image control to display our pictures:

Figure 10.3: A gallery showing the images stored within a collection

In the following screenshot, I have left the textual representation of the image to illustrate how the image is actually saved. It is worth pointing out that the image format will differ, depending on the device the image is taken on. The preceding images were taken on a Microsoft Surface, which captures the image in a PNG format. iOS and Android generally capture in JPEG format. However, what provides a lot of value is the textual string that comes after the image type, which is a **base64** string encoding of the image:

Figure 10.4: An illustration of the base64 encoded string representing the image

As long as you remove the initial image type, for example, **data:image/png;base64**, from the image encoding, then you have something that is quite useful for not only displaying the image but also for passing into Microsoft Power Automate to create a file elsewhere. To remove the preceding code, we can use some of the textual functions that we discussed earlier in this book to remove a specific number of characters and isolate just the **base64** encoded string:

```
Mid(ThisItem.Photograph,Find(",", ThisItem.Photograph))
```

However, there are times that, as an app designer, we won't want our users to press the image to take the picture, and we would rather our users press a button to do that instead.

Capturing from an icon

The photo property that we used in the previous section will only capture the photo when it's called from the **OnSelect** event of the camera control. Calling the same property from any other control will always result in a null value being stored. Therefore, we have to approach this problem in a slightly different way.

There are two other properties to note about the camera control that we can use to capture an image from another control. Those properties are as follows:

- `Stream`: This is an image that is automatically updated based on the stream rate.
- `StreamRate`: This tells us how often to update the image stream. Consider `StreamRate` to be the equivalent of the shutter speed on a camera. The smallest value for this to work is 100, which equates to $1/10^{th}$ of a second.

These two properties are key for being able to configure our buttons on the screen. I will set `StreamRate` to `100` so that it spends the least amount of time capturing the image. Now, I can place an icon on the screen and assign the **OnSelect** event for that icon to capture the camera stream:

Figure 10.5: An icon on the page interacting with the camera control

The end result is the same in that I have an image that I can now use within my app or pass to a data store. As well as being able to capture images directly from the device, I can also provide the user with the ability to upload images manually.

Using the Add picture control

Using the **Add picture** control is the quickest and easiest way for images to be added to a PowerApp since it allows us to upload images from the local device. If this control is used and accessed using a desktop browser, then the local file explorer will be used to select the file, and if the control is used on a mobile device, then you will simply select the images from the local image store.

PowerApps supports all of the common image types, including the following:

- jpg
- jpeg
- png
- gif
- bmp
- tif
- tiff
- svg

The behavior of the **Add image** control is quite interesting as it actually creates a group of controls. It adds a button for the user to click on to upload an image and adds an image control, all within a control group, as shown in the following screenshot:

Figure 10.6: Control group containing an add media button and an image control

The camera on a device is versatile and can be used to capture data as well as images.

Understanding the barcode scanner

Barcodes come in a range of different sizes and types and even in different formats, since you could consider a QR code a **barcode**. Both types of graphics are designed to encode data into a graphic that scanners can then use to retrieve and process. Barcodes are used within our day-to-day lives; they are most commonly associated with shopping, with the goods being scanned and the scanning solution being able to immediately recognize what the goods are based on the code. The same applies to QR codes, which are now more commonly associated with web pages so that someone can scan the image and the associated page loads in the browser.

The **Barcode scanner** control supports the following barcodes:

- **UPC A**
- **UPC E**
- **EAN 8**
- **CODE 39**
- **CODE 128**
- **ITF**
- **PDF 417**

Some examples can be seen in the following image:

Figure 10.7: Examples of various barcodes

If we want to use this functionality with our app, we need to place a **Barcode scanner** control onto the page. This control can be found under the **Insert** group and the media menu. I should point out here that, in PowerApps, barcodes and QR codes are treated in exactly the same way—we use the same control and the same properties to capture the input. Therefore, as we work through the examples, you can use barcodes and QR codes interchangeably.

Notice that, when you place the **Barcode scanner** control on the page, all you are actually presented with is a button labeled **Scan**. The behavior that we will observe in the app is that when the scan button is pressed, the device camera will be activated and will start to look for barcodes or QR codes within the viewfinder.

The functionality of the barcode scanner is not available while using the browser. This will only work in the PowerApps app, which can be installed on iOS or Android.

When it detects a barcode or QR code, it will execute any formulas that have been entered into the **OnScan** event:

Figure 10.8: The Barcode scanner mode on a mobile device

Obviously, we are interested in capturing the information that's stored within a barcode or QR code, so we can either push the data into a store or into another control to be displayed. For this example, I am going to push the data into a label so that we can see what is retrieved by setting the **Text** property to the following:

```
BarcodeScanner1.Value
```

To illustrate what is returned, I have taken a photograph of a barcode and then scanned it using the barcode scanner:

Figure 10.9: The output of a barcode that has been scanned

Alternatively, I can scan a QR code and retrieve the data in exactly the same way. So, if I encode some information into a QR code (there are lots of websites for you to do this), then I can use my device camera to decode it and use the information within my app. In the following example, I have encoded a URL into the QR code and then read it using my PowerApp:

Figure 10.10: The output of a QR code that was scanned using the barcode scanner

There are times, however, when we actually want to give users the ability to import a picture from the local device, and that is where the **Add picture** control is used.

If you wish to feed the inputs from this control into a collection, then you can populate it by utilizing the **OnSelect** property.

Now that we've seen how to work with images and barcodes, let's conduct an experiment.

Lab 9

Within this lab, we are going to add two additional elements to our asset tracking app by capturing a picture of the asset and the barcode at the point of entry. The reason for using a barcode during this lab is because most products ship with at least one identifying barcode on them, making testing the solution much simpler.

Activity 1: Updating the data source

First of all, we need to update our data source to be able to receive the two new pieces of data:

1. Open the Excel spreadsheet, `Assets.xlsx`, which we have been using as our asset store throughout the previous labs.
2. Add a column with the title `Asset Photo[image]`.
3. Add a column with the title `Asset Barcode`:

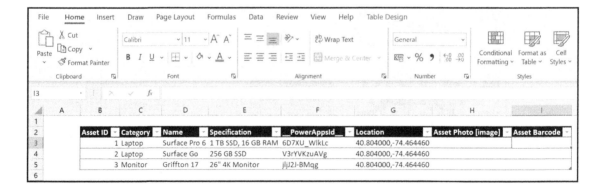

4. Save and close the spreadsheet.

Now that we have prepared our data source, let's update our app so that we can feed data into it.

Activity 2: Updating the PowerApp to capture a photo

Now, we are going to add two new data cards to the input form in the asset management app in order to capture a picture of the asset and the barcode:

1. Open the **Griffton Assets – Tablet** app.
2. Select the screen we called **New Asset**:

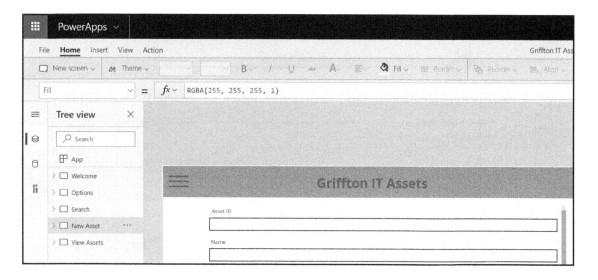

3. Select **frmNewAsset**, which is the form control that we are currently using to input the basic details of the asset:

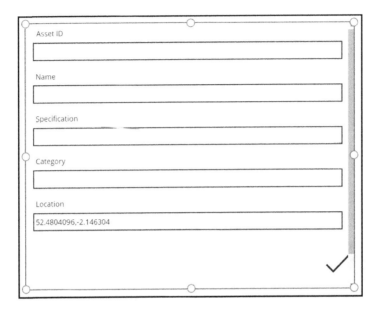

4. In the **Properties** pane, on the right-hand side of the page, click **Edit fields**:

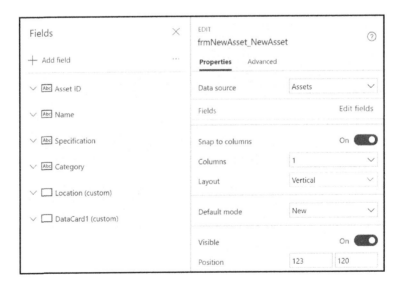

5. In the **Fields** blade, click **Add field**.

6. Select **Asset Barcode** and **Asset Photo**:

7. Reorder the fields so that the save icon is at the bottom of the form:

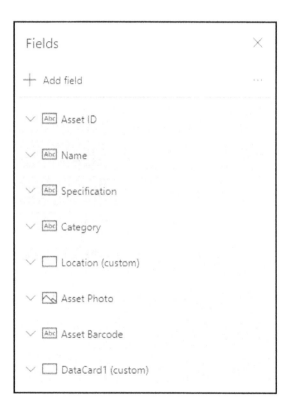

8. Click into the **Asset Photo** field; notice that, by default, it has an **Image upload** control. Unlock the data card in the **Advanced** properties and then delete this control. The app will then show errors, but we will deal with this shortly.

9. Insert a **Camera** control into the data card and name it `camAssetPhoto`:

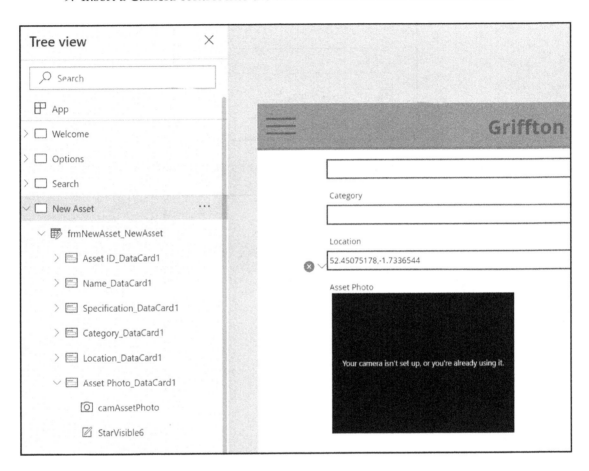

10. Within the **Asset Photo** data card, an image control will be present. This control is showing errors because it had a reference to the **Add Picture** control. Let's fix this. Rename the control to `imgAssetPhoto`, and then change the image to `If(IsBlank(camAssetPhoto.Photo), Parent.Default, camAssetPhoto.Photo)`:

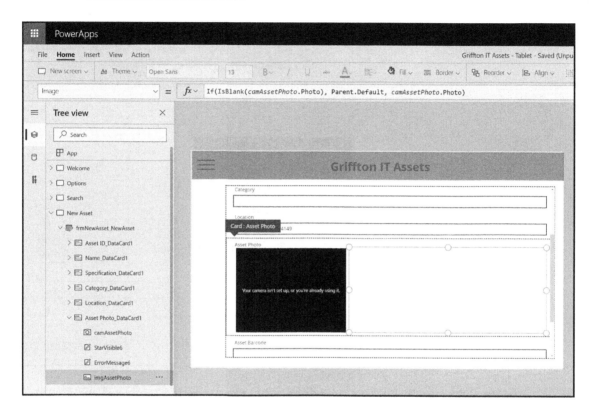

11. Fix the final errors by moving and sizing the image control so that it fills the area to the right of the camera control.

Now that we have a picture of the asset, let's capture the barcode information and store that against the asset as well.

Activity 3: Updating the app to scan and store barcode data

We will finish our new form off by adding the ability to scan the barcode:

1. Click into the data card for the **Asset Barcode**:

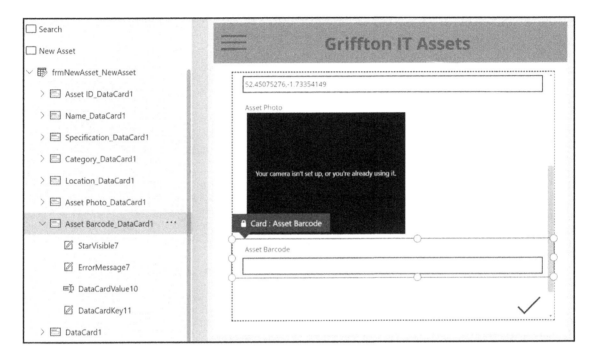

2. Unlock the card by clicking on **Advanced** in the properties pane and clicking the padlock.
3. Reduce the width of the **Asset Barcode** text box and insert a **Barcode scanner** control from the **Insert** menu:

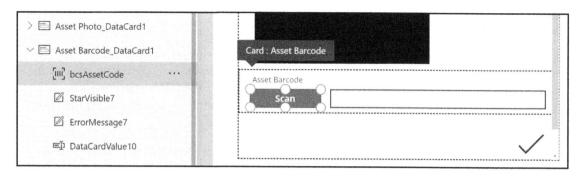

4. Select the text box and change the default value to reference the barcode scanner by setting it to `bcsAssetCode.Value`:

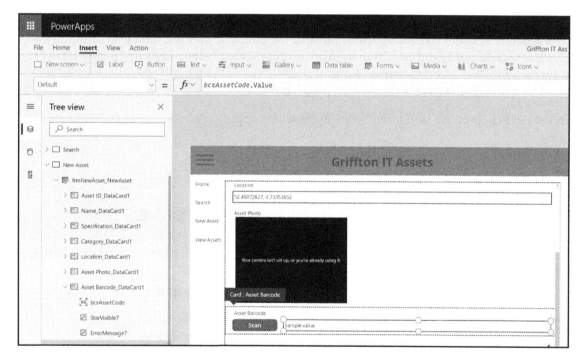

5. Save your app and publish it.

Due to the barcode scanner only working on a mobile device, use the PowerApps app to launch the app and then test the ability to create a new asset by saving the picture and the scanned barcode into the Excel spreadsheet.

Summary

In this chapter, we have investigated how we can start to leverage media controls to capture images that we use in our PowerApps, and highlighted the limitations around the storage, that is, we're only able to directly store media in Excel, SQL Server, or CDS. However, we can convert the images into a **base64** string that we can use within Microsoft Power Automate that we can store elsewhere.

We investigated the camera and the ability to capture images from the camera control so that we can use them within our app. We also looked at two ways of being able to capture the image, the first of which is by tapping the image itself, which captures the photo property of the control. The second way was by creating a separate button to take the picture, which uses the stream property instead. The thing we must remember when using the stream property is that we need to change `StreamRate` to a minimum value of 100.

The **Barcode scanner** control provides us with the ability to capture data from barcodes and quick response codes and use them within our app, which helps speed up the retrieval of information. The barcode scanner is one of the few controls that will only work when it's used on a mobile device; it doesn't work in a browser.

In the next chapter, we will learn how to secure our app.

Questions

1. True or false: I can upload a `.jfif` image into my PowerApp.
2. Which control would I use to be able to upload an image into an app?
3. If I wanted to use the `Camera1.Photo` formula, which control would I interact with?
4. If I wanted to use another control to interact with the camera, which camera property should I change?
5. What format is a captured image stored in?
6. True or false: Text within a QR code can be retrieved and used within an app.

11
Securing Your PowerApps

One of the most fundamental features of any system is the ability to secure the data that is being stored and processed. When developing any type of app, we should always keep security at the forefront of our mind, especially when our apps display or process any data. We need to ensure that the users have access to only the information that they are authorized to see, and that their levels of access are not higher than what they need to be able to perform their duties.

In previous chapters, we investigated retrieving and displaying data from data sources. We will now start to look at how security at the data source affects our app and how we can implement some levels of security within the PowerApp to govern what people can and cannot do.

App developers often make the mistake of simply hiding data in the app and assuming that this makes the data secure. This is certainly not the case as the underlying data source could be accessed in other ways, not just through PowerApps. This is often referred to as *security through obscurity*. So when designing your app, consideration should be given to three specific layers of user access—app, screen, and data source.

It is imperative that all aspects of security should be considered when creating your app to ensure that data is presented to the correct users, and that the correct users interact with it.

In this chapter, we will be covering the following topics:

- Securing the app
- Securing data
- Applying in-app security

By the end of the chapter, you will have gained an understanding of the options for securing your data, and of how to apply basic security to aspects of your PowerApp. These considerations should always be taken into account before building your app.

Technical requirements

To follow along with this example, you will need to have completed the previous labs.

To be able to work through the examples relating to Active Directory, you will need to have access to your tenancy **Azure Active Directory** (**AAD**) to be able to view user and group objects.

Securing your PowerApp

When the app is first published, it will only be available to the creator; therefore, it is up to that person to give access to the app to those that need it. Consideration should always be given to who *needs* to use the app, especially if the app is built to handle sensitive data, such as personally identifiable information.

The process of giving people access to the app actually takes place within the app **Details** section, which is accessible from the PowerApps browse screen, as shown in *Figure 11.1*: *The app Details screen navigation*:

Figure 11.1: The app Details screen navigation

When you share the PowerApp, you have a number of options for selecting the users you wish to share with:

- The first is that you can name each person individually and assign them as a user or a co-owner. Users simply can access and use the app, whereas co-owners will also be able to access and edit the app.
- The second option is to invite AAD security groups, which will allow you to invite several users at once. Levels of access can be assigned to a security group in the same way that you can with individual users.

While security groups provide the ability to add multiple users, you lose direct visibility of who has been given access to your app from the PowerApps screen.

Finally, you have the ability to invite everyone to use your app (as shown in the following screenshot), which means that everyone within your organization will be able to see and access it. Regardless of who you choose to share your app with, you will also need to consider any data storage access that may apply to your app:

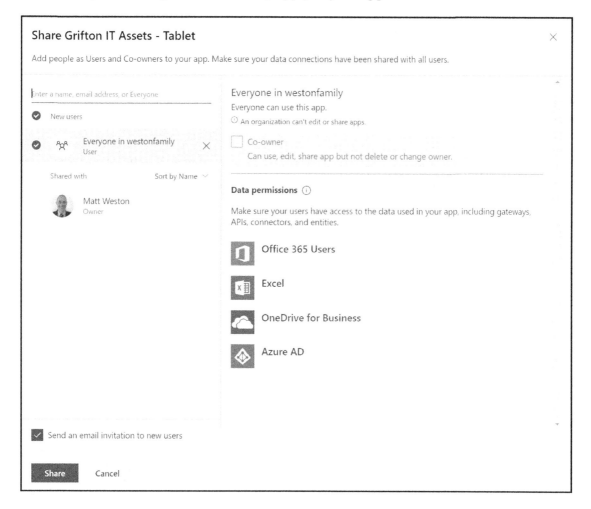

Figure 11.2: Options for sharing the app

When sharing the app with everyone, you will be unable to select the co-owner permission. This is to help protect the app by only giving edit access to explicit users within the organization.

Now that we know how to secure our app by specifying who can modify it, let's look at how to secure our data.

Securing your data

The key thing to understand with PowerApps is that the actual security of the data always lies in the data source rather than within the app itself. The ability of users to access data from various sources will depend on the connection that is established with the data source. PowerApps is purely designed to be a user-facing interface to access the data source, and therefore does not, by default, have any perception of the user and the rights they may have.

SQL Server, as an example, will use a username and password to authenticate and establish a connection with the data source. Any users using the app will automatically be able to access the data using the credentials that are stored within the connection.

Other data sources, such as SharePoint, require both the app creator and any subsequent users of the app to have explicit access to the underlying data source. So, for example, if your app user only has read access to a SharePoint list, yet your app allows them to perform an update on existing data, it will throw an error.

Exactly the same principle applies to any files, such as Excel files, that are stored in any type of cloud storage, for example, OneDrive. The file location would need to be shared with every user who needs to see the data through the app, which means that often, as an app owner, you may end up managing two independent sets of permissions to ensure that your users are not denied access.

Applying in-app security

As we build our apps, there are going to be screens that we only want our elevated users to access—for example, administration screens. To achieve this, we need to be able to distinguish users from each other and understand what roles they have available to them. One of the key ways of doing this within Office 365 is through the use of AAD security groups.

Storing access lists within the app

One of the simplest ways of being able to secure parts of your app is by using locally controlled access lists. This is a way that is usually favored by users who are producing less critical apps and want to maintain their own access control lists in a very simple way.

One way that is quite common is to store the user information within a collection that contains the username and the level of access you wish to give them. The advantage of this method is that it is completely within the control of the app owner to add and remove users from elevated rights; however, there is an admin overhead to changing the formula if new administrators are appointed.

In the following example, I am going to create two levels of users:

- `User`: These users have basic access to the app in order to carry out basic functions
- `Administrator`: These users have access to screens that are not available to standard users—for example settings screens

Ideally, I want my app to populate the control list at the point of the app being loaded, so I will populate a collection with my users:

```
Collect(col_Users,{User: "matt@grifftonit.com", Role: "Administrator"});
Collect(col_Users,{User: "laura@grifftonit.com", Role: "User"});
```

Once my collection is populated, I can query this collection throughout my app to determine whether various areas should be accessible to the logged-in user. The simplest way of doing this is to query the collection to see whether the user exists and to return their access level, as shown in *Figure 11.3: Screenshot of the formula to check user access level for a collection*:

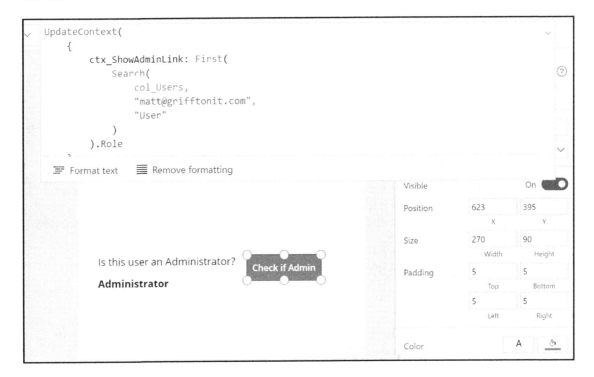

Figure 11.3: Screenshot of the formula to check user access level for a collection

In the preceding example, I am querying the role of the logged-in user, which can then be used to show or hide other components in my app.

It is not always feasible, however, to store lists of users within the app itself, especially if this involves large numbers of users or access lists that are updated often. In this case, you may consider using AAD to secure your apps.

Implementing security with AAD security groups

One of the most common ways of securing data, throughout the whole of Office 365, is through the use of AAD groups. AAD security groups effectively give centralized control over permissions to the AAD administrators. This is a group of people who are usually based within IT and help to govern the overall security of the organization. They will have the responsibility of adding people to these groups when people join the organization, and likewise, they will remove users who have left.

In order to access AAD, you need to access the Azure portal by navigating to `portal.azure.com`, and then select AAD from the left-hand navigation menu. You will be prompted to log in, so use the same username and password that you use to access PowerApps:

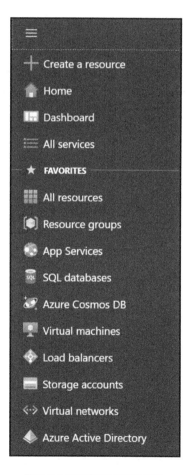

Figure 11.4: AAD left-hand navigation menu

AAD security groups are created within the Azure portal and assigned an owner. Members are then added to the group by searching for them and assigning them to the group, as shown in the following screenshot:

Figure 11.5: Adding a member to AAD

This will usually take a few seconds, and then you will get a notification to say that this has been successful. Once it has been confirmed, the new member will appear in the list of members, as shown in the following screenshot:

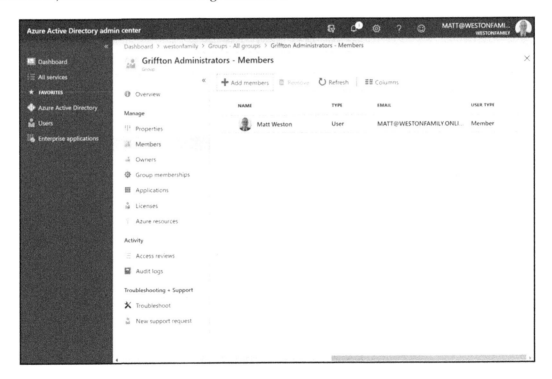

Figure 11.6: AAD group membership

Being an owner of a security group does not automatically make you a member.

Once we have completed our security group setup within AAD, we need to be able to leverage the security group through our PowerApp. We can do this by using the AAD connector, which will allow us to connect to and interact with AAD. This is effectively treated as a data source, and so we can add it to our app by going through the following steps:

1. Select the **View** menu from the top navigation bar.
2. Select **Data sources**:

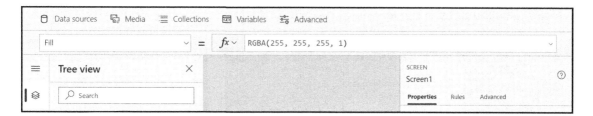

Figure 11.7: Data sources displayed on the top menu

3. If you do not see the AAD connector listed under **Connectors**, then scroll to the bottom and select **Show all connectors**. Once you see AAD, click on it, and select **Add a connection**:

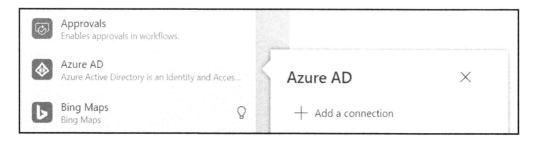

Figure 11.8: Selecting a connection

4. Now that you have added the connector to your PowerApp, you can start to use the actions that are associated with it.

In order to check whether a user belongs to a specific group, we can use the `CheckMemberGroups` function, for which we need to provide two pieces of information:

- **Unique principal name (UPN)** of the user
- Object IDs for the groups that we wish to check

The UPN can be found by utilizing the `User` function and selecting the `Email` property:

```
User().Email
```

This returns an email address; however, in most circumstances, the email address and the UPN are the same.

The really nice thing about the `CheckMemberGroups` function is that we can check several groups to see whether a member is a member. First of all, we need the object ID of a group, which can be found by going to your group within AAD and selecting **Properties**:

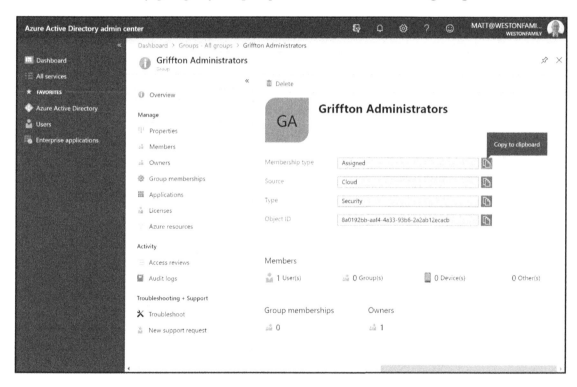

Figure 11.9: AAD group properties

When we use this object ID in our function, we need to provide it in a table format with a single column of `Value`. For example, let's look at the following code:

```
Table({Value:"8a0192bb-aaf4-4a33-93b6-2a2ab12ecacb"})
```

To complete the formula, we simply need to combine the two parts. The result will be returned from AAD as a table, so we will be unable to use a simple condition on the result to determine whether the user is present or not. Instead, we need to test whether the resulting table is empty by using the `IsEmpty()` formula.

In the following example, I am going to set a context variable to hold the result that I can then use to show or hide parts of my app:

```
If(IsEmpty(
 AzureAD.CheckMemberGroups(User().Email,Table({Value:"8a0192bb-
aaf4-4a33-93b6-2a2ab12ecacb"}))
 ),
 UpdateContext({ctx_ShowAdminLink:false}),
 UpdateContext({ctx_ShowAdminLink:true})
 )
```

If I wanted to use this to show an admin icon in my app, I could use the `ctx_ShowAdminLink` in the **Visible** property to only show whether a member of my administrator's group is logged in.

Lab 10

Within this lab, we are going to implement a basic access control list using a collection so that we can define our administrators. Administrators will be able to view a list of all admins.

Activity 1: Creating the collection

The first thing that we are going to do is create the list of administrators so that our app will respond in different ways to different users that log in:

1. Open your PowerApp.
2. In the **Tree view**, select **App**:

3. Ensure that you have the **OnStart** property selected.
4. Below the exiting formulas, start a new line and create a collection of users:

```
ClearCollect(colUsers,{User:
"user1@yourtenancy.onmicrosoft.com"},{User:
"user2@yourtenancy.onmicrosoft.com"})
```

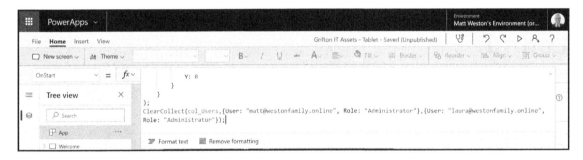

5. Click the ellipsis next to **App** and select **Run OnStart** to populate your collection:

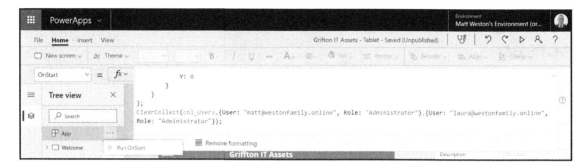

6. Confirm that your collection has been populated by going to the **Collections** screen:

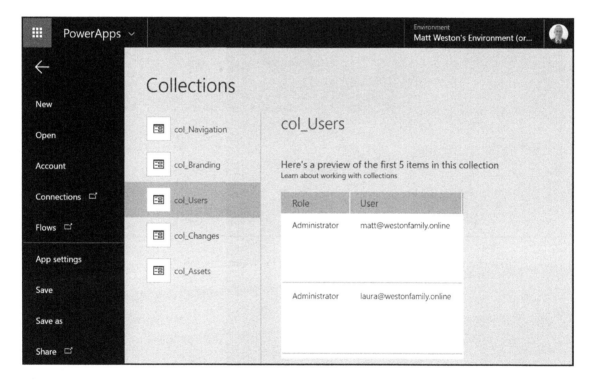

Now that we have created the underlying security structure, we can make the necessary changes to the rest of the app to display the administrators.

Activity 2: Creating the Administrators view screen

In order for our administrators to see the contents of the users collection, we need to create a view screen:

1. Insert a new screen named **Administrators** and copy across any branding that you want to be applied to the screen:

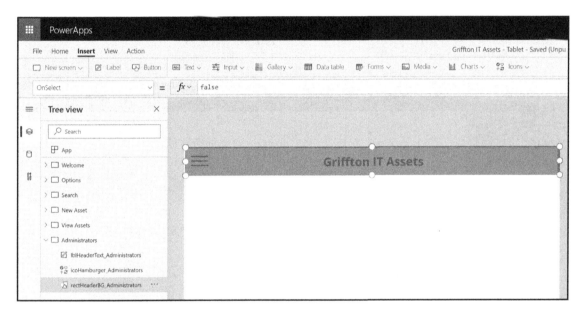

2. Insert a blank **Gallery** control onto your screen:

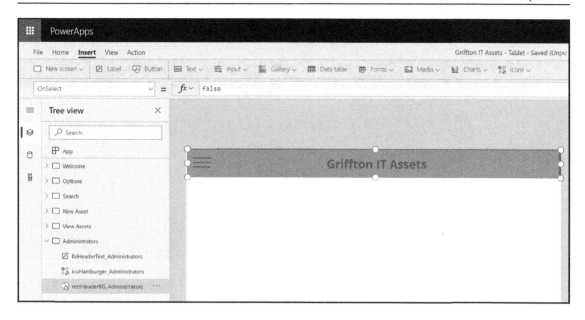

3. Set the data source as the user's collection: **colUsers**:

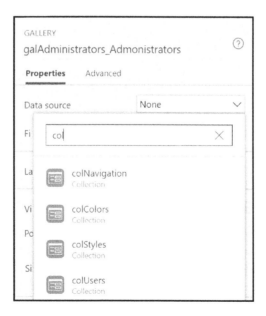

4. Insert a label control into the gallery:

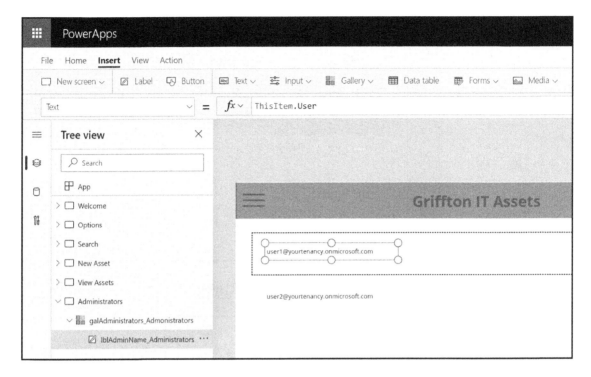

5. Assign the label to display the **User** property so that the username is displayed in the gallery.

Note that the users that you have defined within your collection are now displayed. Feel free to format these controls as you see fit.

Activity 3: Creating the link

Now that we have the constituent parts of the admin screens in place, we will create the link for our administrators to access it. The link will also check to see whether the logged-in user is part of the admin group and display the **Display Screen** link if they are found:

1. Navigate back to your **Options** screen.

2. Place the people icon from **Insert Icons** and place it on the right side of the header bar:

3. Change the **OnSelect** property
   to `Navigate(Administrators,ScreenTransition.Fade)`:

4. Change the **Visible** property to `!IsBlank(LookUp(colUsers,User =`
   `Lower(User().Email)).User)`:

Note that the icon will now show or be hidden depending on whether you are listed in the admin list. You can test this by adding and removing yourself from the collection and observing the behavior of the people icon.

Summary

In this chapter, we looked at one of the most important aspects of any app development—the ability to secure our app and its data. We covered the topic of security by looking at three areas in particular—securing the app, securing the data, and creating in-app security.

While securing the app, we saw how we have the ability to choose who we share the app with and to determine whether they are users of the app or co-owners. App owners are able to invite individual users, AAD security groups, or everyone within the organization. By inviting AAD security groups, you lose the ability to see who has access to the site within PowerApps.

While it does secure the data, PowerApps is still just a user interface for a data source, and therefore security should always be considered regarding the data source itself. There are some data sources, such as SQL Server, that have the username and password defined in the connection, and therefore these will be used for all users. Other data sources, such as SharePoint, will take the credentials of the PowerApps user and carry them through to access the data. This is done by taking the context of the logged-in user and carrying it through from PowerApps to the data source, and therefore access to the data source needs to be granted to each user.

While creating in-app security, there are always instances within an app where you will want to create the ability for elevated users to perform certain actions—for example, when authorizing an administrator role. We explored two possible ways of achieving this, firstly by storing the users within a collection, which means that it can be controlled by the app owner, and secondly by utilizing a broader scope of permission management by adopting the use of AAD security groups.

In the next chapter, we will investigate how we can take our PowerApps app offline in order to cater for situations where a network connection isn't always possible.

Questions

1. What is the name of the global store of users within Office 365?
2. True or false: The security of the data is managed purely through the PowerApp.
3. True or false: When using SharePoint as a data source, the user needs to have full control rights to the underlying SharePoint site.
4. Access lists can be added to the app and stored in what type of data storage?

12
Working Offline

In the previous chapters, we discovered how to use controls, connectors, and data sources to work with data. All of this, however, has been dependent on a network connection, Wi-Fi, or mobile to be able to push and pull data. Given that PowerApps is intended to be run from a mobile device, we all know that having a consistent data connection cannot always be guaranteed.

For us to mitigate potential issues with network dropouts, PowerApps allows us to cache data locally, which means that we can continue to work without interruption if we lose the connection to our data source. In this chapter, we will look at how we can achieve this and what steps we can take to ensure that a connection loss will not mean losing our app's ability to function. We will, therefore, look at the following topics:

- Detecting a connection state
- Storing data locally
- Allowing our app to work offline

By the end of this chapter, we will have looked at the key points of creating offline capability and how to ensure that your data source is updated once it is back online.

Technical requirements

To follow along with this chapter, it is recommended that you have completed the previous labs to build our example app. You will also need to have a mobile device with PowerApps installed to test the functionality we are exploring within this chapter.

Detecting a connection state

One of the key things for making your PowerApp available offline is the ability to detect whether a network is present or not. First of all, PowerApps can detect the presence of a connection signal using a function that can then be used within the logic of your app:

```
Connection.Connected
```

This function will return a Boolean value: `true` meaning it is connected and `false` meaning it is disconnected.

PowerApps also can determine whether the connection is based on the cellular connection of the device or whether it is using Wi-Fi. If the device is using a mobile network, then it is classed as a `Metered` connection:

```
Connection.Metered
```

Again, this returns a Boolean value: `true` for a metered network or `false` for an alternative connection.

Both of these connection states should be considered while developing your app, as you can change the behavior of the app depending on whether the app is online or offline, and you can change the behavior of the app depending on the type of connection that it is using. For example, if you are using the mobile network, you may choose to limit the images that are displayed to reduce the data being pulled by the app.

Now that we can make our app aware of the connection state, we need to start building in some functionality to allow us to react to these states.

Working with local data

One of the key abilities that we need to build into our app to allow us to go offline is to store data locally and then retrieve it again. This is achieved by using the functions of `SaveData` and `LoadData`.

It is key to understand what it means to you as a developer, and to your users, where your data is being stored when it is taken offline; therefore, we will now focus on the following:

- Saving data locally
- Loading data from the locally stored data file

Let's see how the first part goes.

Saving data locally

Before we can load data, we, first of all, need to save it by using the `SaveData` function. This will securely save our collection of data to an area that is local to the device being used. We are obviously in a world where data security is paramount. In the previous chapter, we discussed securing parts of our app so that users can't access data that they shouldn't and the same concept applies to our offline data.

PowerApps has excelled in this area because the `SaveData` function stores and encrypts data in a way that means that it is not accessible to other users or other PowerApps.

 If there is not enough space on the device to save the data file, the file will not be saved and you will be faced with a message informing you that not enough space is available to complete the operation.

The file is completely unique to the user and the app that has generated it, which means that different PowerApps on the same device can't share the same data file.

`SaveData` requires us to provide two pieces of information:

- The collection of data to save
- The filename given to the data file

The filename is expected as a string so always remember to put it within double quotes. So, for example, if I have a collection of data called `colAssets`, then my function will look like this:

```
SaveData(colAssets, "Assets")
```

This will then generate the `Assets` data file on the local device.

 Note that the first parameter is a collection; therefore, we need to ensure that our data is taken from the data source and stored within a collection.

The key consideration when storing your data offline is related to the amount of storage space that you have available on the device. The amount of space is dependent on the device, the operating system, the complexity of the app, and how much memory it is using. With this in mind, storing hundreds of megabytes of data could result in an out-of-space error, so always give thought to what data we are going to store locally on the device.

Now that we have our unique data file, we need to be able to retrieve that data to continue working.

Loading data from the local cache

For us to retrieve the data stored within the data file, we need to use the LoadData function. LoadData requires us to provide three parameters, the first two being exactly the same as SaveData:

- Firstly, we need to provide the target collection—the collection of data we're going to write to.
- Secondly, we need to provide the name of the data file.
- Thirdly, we need to provide a Boolean flag to determine whether the function will continue to run if it can't find the data file.

 The reason for doing this is because, potentially, at first load, the data file may not have been created; therefore, we would not want this to stop our app from running.

So, if I continue the example from SaveData where we are saving our assets, I would call the function like this:

```
LoadData(colAssets, "Assets", true)
```

Now we have retrieved the data from our data file and fed that data back into our colAssets collection. Additionally, we have looked at how we could take it offline. In the next section, we will consider the steps within our app that we need to follow to make it work.

Implementing offline capability

Now that we have discussed the component parts of building offline capability, we will look at the overall process to determine how and when each of the various functions should be used.

The process will look at how and when we interact with the master source of data, most notably with the on-start properties to ensure that we are loading the correct data at the point that the app is launched. We will then look at how we can work offline, followed by the handling of data when the app comes back online. To achieve this, we need to consider the following:

- Implementing the on-start process
- Working offline
- Synchronizing data between the online and offline data stores

The first element to consider is how we interact with the data and load the data from the correct place to start building the offline capability.

Implementing the on-start process

The most important part of working offline is that we need to start preparing for it from the point that the app loads. Users can open an app regardless of whether their device is online or not, so if we leave the offline capability elements for a later point in the app, we risk introducing issues. This isn't to say that you can't implement this functionality elsewhere, such as on the **OnVisible** event or even on an **OnSelect** event for a control:

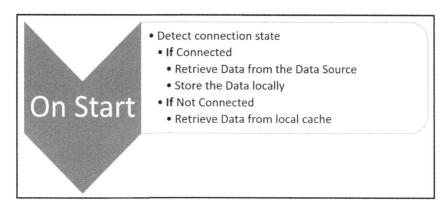

The first thing that we should check for is whether an internet connection is available by using the `Connection.Connected` function. As stated earlier, this will return `true` if the connection is available, so we can use a condition to branch our logic.

If the internet connection is available, then we can retrieve data from our data source and immediately store it within a collection. In Chapter 7, *Working with Data*, we discussed collections and so we know that, at this point, all of our data is stored within memory, resulting in the data only being available until the app is closed. Therefore, we need to save this collection to the local device using the SaveData function to build our offline cache.

If the internet connection is not available, then we should simply try to retrieve the data from the local data file and use that to populate our collection.

 The first load of data to build the offline cache will always require an internet connection to retrieve data.

The following code is an example of how we can implement the offline data storage within PowerApps:

```
If(Connection.Connected,
 ClearCollect(colAssets, 'Assets');
 SaveData(colAssets,"local_Assets"),
 LoadData(colAssets,"local_Assets", true)
);
```

At this point, if you are building the offline capability retrospectively, it is to ensure that you can change any data output controls, for example, galleries and data tables, so that they get their data from the collection rather than directly from the data source.

This will now allow our app to build the relevant collection and interact with the local cache if needed. However, we now need to consider the steps to allow our users to continue to work offline.

Working offline

Now that we have a data store available to us, we need to consider how we allow users to create and update data, not just view it. For us to be able to do this, we need to develop the capability to save changes back to our data source once an internet connection is reestablished. The offline process needs to be added to every piece of functionality that involves an interaction with the data source, for example, adding, updating, and deleting a new item:

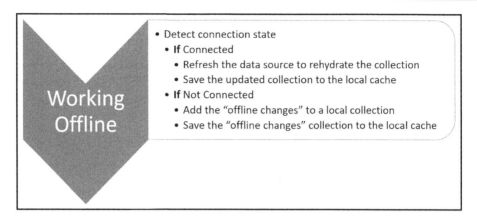

Once again, detecting the connection state is of paramount importance as that will determine how your app behaves in relation to saving data changes.

This time, if we have a connection, we can save our change directly to the data source; however, we then need to ensure that our local collection is updated to reflect the change we have just written back. Every time we update the main data source, we need to cascade that update through all levels of the offline capability to ensure that, regardless of whether we're online or offline, we still have the most up-to-date version of the data.

If the connection is not available, then we need to build a list of changes that we need to make when the connection returns. This is done by creating another collection to store our changes, which we will then sync back to our data source. To ensure that our offline changes are not lost, we should also save this collection to the local cache to provide resilience using the following code:

```
If(Connection.Connected,
    SubmitForm(EditForm1);
    Refresh('Assets');
    ClearCollect(colAssets,'Assets');
    SaveData(Assets,"local_Assets"),
    Collect(colAssetChanges,
        {Title:TitleDatacard.Text,Description:DescriptionDatacard.Text}
        );
    SaveData(colAssets, "local_AssetChanges")
);
```

In this example, if an asset is modified while the connection is available, the asset is updated within the data source and immediately updated by calling the Refresh function. The updated data is then cascaded down from the data source to the collection and then to the local cache.

If the connection is not available (refer to the preceding formula in bold), then we will save the update to the changes collection, and then save that to local storage for processing later.

Additions and deletions can be handled in a similar way, whereby each type of change has its own collection, that is, you have a collection of additions and a collection of deletions. Alternatively, you may wish to have a single collection that simply contains a status field to indicate the type of change it is expecting:

```
Collect(colChanges,{
    asset:{
        Title: TitleDatacard.Text,
        Description: DescriptionDatacard.Text
        },
    Change: "Update"}
)
```

This will then give us a collection that contains both the record that we want to update and the action that we need to carry out when we return to an online state.

Consider adding some metrics on to the screen for the user to see how many offline changes they have pending by counting the number of items in the collection.

Now that we have our changes being made offline, we need to consider how to synchronize these changes back to our data source.

Synchronizing online and offline data

Once our connection to the internet has been reestablished, it is vitally important that our offline changes are processed back to the data source and that my local collections are refreshed. There are two ways in which this is normally done, either by using a timer control to periodically check whether the connection is available or by implementing a button for a user to manually initiate the sync. The choice of approach purely comes down to how you want your app to behave.

In this example, I'm going to use a timer control as this is the approach that I use most often:

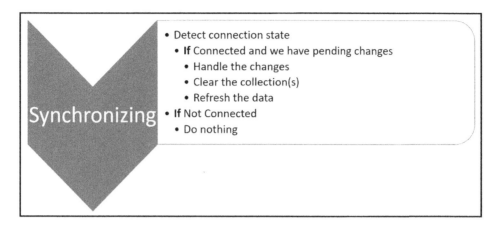

Stepping through this, I could use a timer that checks every minute to see whether the connection has been established. Again, this uses the `Connection.Connected` function to determine whether the connection's state has changed. We will also add an additional condition to this to ensure that we are only going to process if offline changes have been made.

Assuming that the connection has been reestablished, we will take the items that have changed and feed those changes back to the data source. It is imperative that, at the point of the changes being synchronized, we clear the collection holding the change as we don't want to risk processing it again.

Just like the other steps, we then need to get the latest data back from the data source by using `Refresh`, rehydrating the collection, and then saving to the local cache:

```
If(Connection.Connected && CountRows(colAssetsToBeAdded) > 0,
    Collect('Assets',colAssetsToBeAdded);
    Clear(colAssetsToBeAdded);
    SaveData(colAssetsToBeAdded,"local_AssetsToBeAdded");
    Refresh('Assets');
    ClearCollect(colAssets, 'Assets');
    SaveData(colAssets,"local_Assets"))
```

The preceding formula assumes that we have a collection specifically storing additions to the data source; therefore, the new items are simply added to the data source. This formula could then be repeated to handle updates and deletions in the same manner.

Lab 11

Within this lab, we will add the basic offline capabilities to the app that we have been developing throughout this book so far. We will add a connection indicator to give a visual representation of whether we are connected or not, and then we will add our data to an offline cache.

Activity 1: Adding a connection indicator

Let's follow these steps:

1. Open your app.
2. Navigate to the **Options** screen.
3. In the bottom-right corner of the screen, add a circle icon, resize it, and place a label next to it:

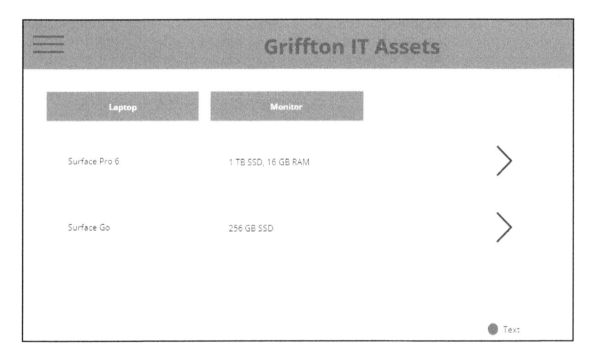

4. Add a timer control to the screen:

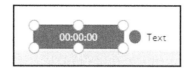

5. Change the **OnTimerEnd** property of the timer to the following, Set(varConnectionStatus,Connection.Connected):

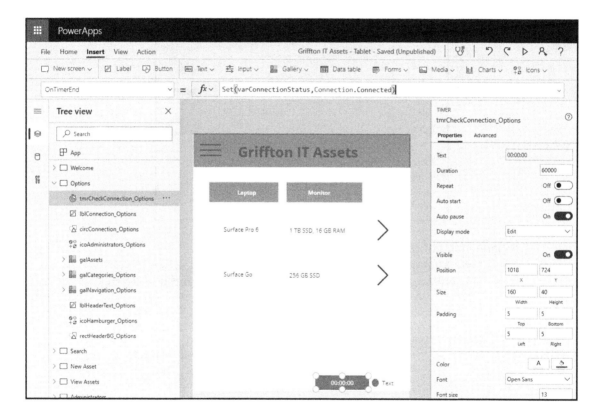

6. Change the **Repeat** property of the **TIMER** to **On**, **Auto start** to **On**, **Visible** to **Off**, and **Duration** to 5000 (5 seconds):

7. Change the **Fill** property of the circle icon to If(varConnectionStatus,RGBA(54, 176, 75, 1),RGBA(184, 0, 0, 1)). This will turn it green if the connection exists, or red if it doesn't:

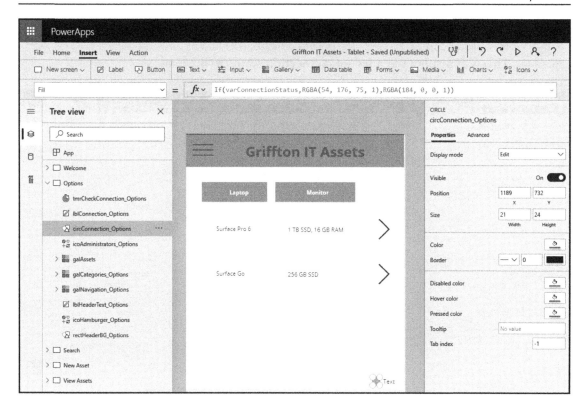

8. Change the **Text** property of the label
to If(varConnectionStatus,"Connected","Disconnected").
This will display the relevant connection status to the user:

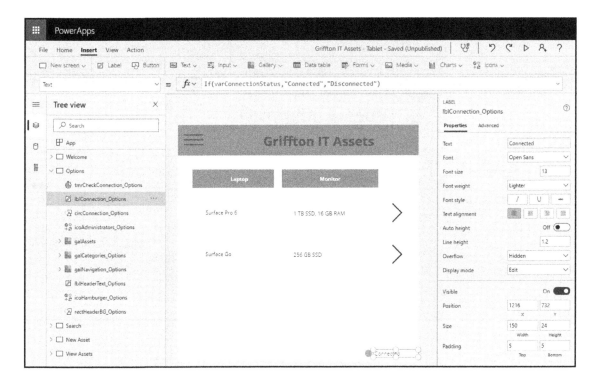

Now that we have a status indicator on the screen to detect the connection state, we should add a capability to the app to allow it to continue running if the app goes offline.

Activity 2: Adding data to an offline cache

We will now add the offline cache capability to our data so that we can take the basic data offline:

1. Click on **App** in the **Tree view** and select the **OnStart** property:

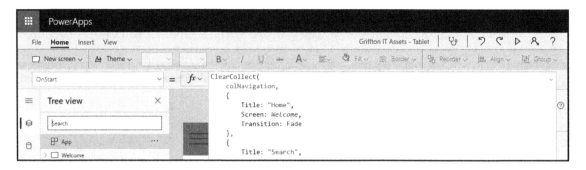

2. Beneath the existing formulas, add the following. Note that, in the ClearCollect formula, single quotes are used as we are dealing with a data source, whereas local_Assets is surrounded by double quotes since we are using a string:

```
If(Connection.Connected,
    ClearCollect(colAssets, 'Assets');
    SaveData(colAssets,"local_Assets")
);
LoadData(colAssets,"local_Assets", true);
```

This can be seen in the following screenshot:

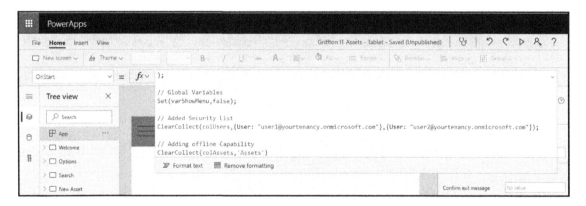

3. Run the **OnStart** formulas and review the outputs in the **Collections** screen. You will see that the contents of the data source are now stored within the collection:

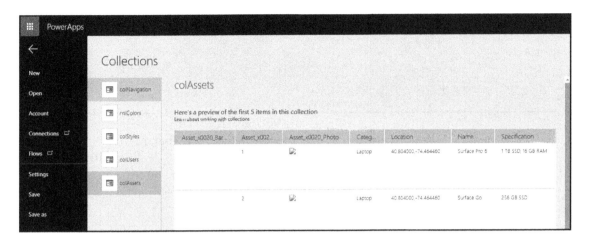

4. Select the **galAssets** gallery from the **Options** screen.
5. Change the **Items** property so that the data source connects to collection rather than directly connecting to the data source, Filter(colAssets, Category = ctxSelectedCategory):

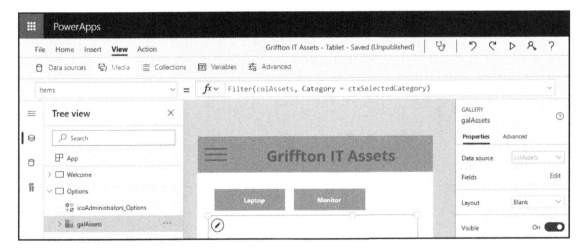

6. Change any other direct references to the data source to reference the collection.

Now that we have changed our controls to reference the collection, we need to ensure that we are reading and writing to and from the offline data store.

Activity 3: Tracking new additions while offline

We will now update our new asset form to allow it to write to the offline data store in the absence of a connection:

1. Navigate to your **New Asset** screen.
2. Rename each control contained within the form so that it has a friendlier name:
    - **Name field** = txtName.
    - **Specification** = txtSpecification.
    - **Category** = txtCategory.
    - **Location** = txtLocation:

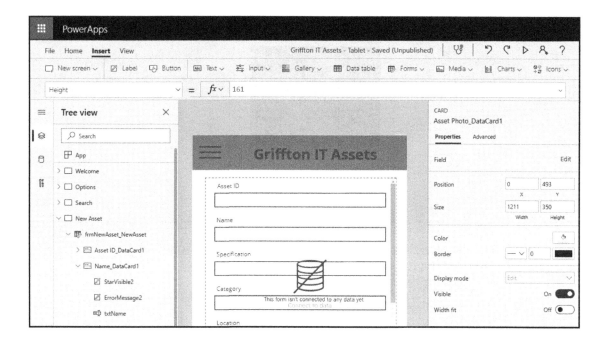

3. Select the **Check** button at the bottom of the form that we previously configured to submit the form:

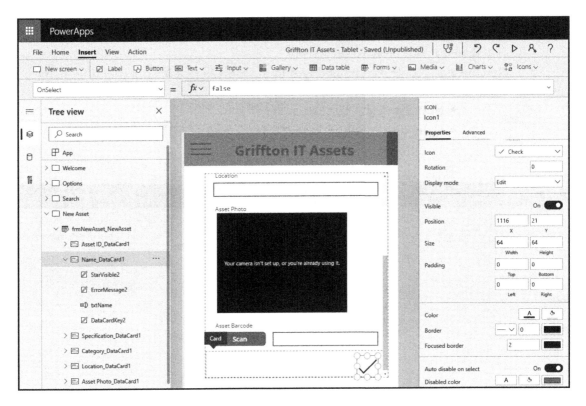

4. Update the **OnSelect** property of the check icon to the following:

```
If(Connection.Connected,
SubmitForm(frmNewAsset_NewAsset);
Refresh('Assets');
ClearCollect(colAssets,'Assets');
SaveData(Assets,"local_Assets"),
Collect(colAssetChanges,
{
Name: txtName.Text,
Specification: txtSpecification.Text,
Category: txtCategory.Text,
Location: txtLocation.Text,
Asset_x0020_Photo: imgAssetPhoto,
Asset_x0020_ID: txtID.Text,
Asset_x0020_Barcode: bcsAssetCode.Value
}
```

```
);
    SaveData(colAssets, "local_AssetChanges")
);
```

The following screenshot displays the preceding changes:

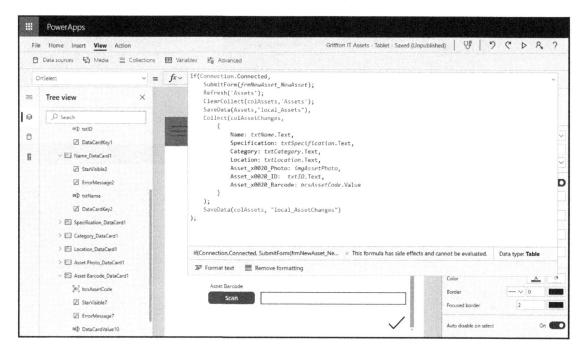

Finally, we need to synchronize the changes back to our data source once the connection has been reestablished.

Activity 4: Synchronizing changes

So far, we have made our assets list available offline; we have also created a list of changes that we need to synchronize back when the app is online, so we now need to write those changes back to the data source:

1. Return to the **Options** screen.
2. Select the timer we previously configured to check the connection state. We will need to select this from the controls **Tree view** as we change the **Visible** property to false, meaning that we can't see it on the screen.

3. Update the `OnTimerEnd` function to the following:

```
Set(varConnectionStatus,Connection.Connected);
// Write any assets created whilst offline
If(Connection.Connected && CountRows(colAssetChanges) > 0,
Collect('Assets',colAssetChanges);
Clear(colAssetChanges);
SaveData(colAssetChanges,"local_AssetChanges");
Refresh('Assets');
ClearCollect(colAssets, 'Assets');
SaveData(colAssets,"local_Assets")
)
```

The following screenshot shows the preceding change:

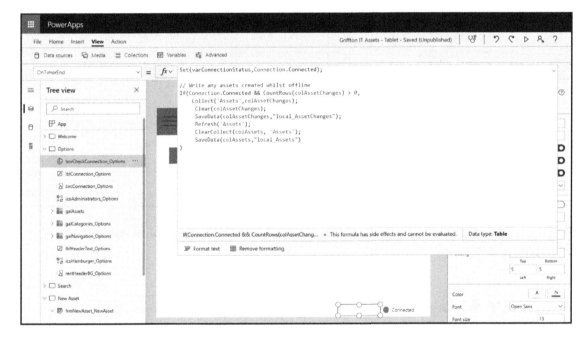

4. Save and publish your app.

Once the app has been published, switch to a mobile device to test it. Load the app, and then switch to airplane mode. Confirm that, when you switch back to the app, your indicator turns red after a short period and that you can still see your data.

Add a new entry into the assets list, and then switch airplane mode off. Notice that, after a short period of time, your change will be replicated in the data source.

Summary

Throughout this chapter, we have looked at how we can build an offline capability into your app to provide resilience for the inevitable event of a connection loss. We looked at how to detect whether the connection is available or not by using the `Connection.Connected` function to return a Boolean result based on the connection status.

Once we looked at how to detect the offline state, we then looked at how we could save our data locally to the device to ensure that our users could continue working without a live connection to the data source. To do that, we need to ensure that our data is replicated into a collection, a data source held within the memory of the app, and then replicated to the local device. The local data is encrypted and stored in a private area which is only accessible by the user and the app that created the file.

While we have a connection, it is extremely important to ensure that any changes to the data source are replicated down through the collection to the local cache.

If we are working offline, we need to store any updates to our data in collections, which would then be used to synchronize changes once the data connection is reestablished. These collections should also be stored locally to ensure that the changes are not lost if the app session is restarted.

Synchronization is usually achieved by using either the timer control or a manual synchronization button. Once the change has been successfully synchronized back to the data source, the entries in the changes collection must be removed to avoid any potential reprocessing.

In the next chapter, we will be using Microsoft Power Automate with PowerApps.

Questions

1. What function would I use to check whether an app is connected to the internet?
2. True or false: My PowerApp can detect whether the app is using a metered connection or not?
3. Which function is used to save the data from PowerApps to the local device?
4. Which function is used to load the data from the local device?
5. True or false: A data file from one PowerApp can be used in another on the same device?
6. True or false: Devices have an unlimited amount of space available to them to store local data?

13
Using Power Automate with PowerApps

PowerApps allows us to develop a huge amount of logic directly within an app, but this logic is limited to frontend processing rather than heavier processing. In the past, this would have been done with server-side code, but in PowerApps, we can offload this type of processing to Microsoft Power Automate, the Office 365-based automation platform.

 Microsoft Power Automate was previously known as Microsoft Flow and was changed in November 2019. While the application has changed names, the individual workflows are still known as Flows. Therefore, when we talk about the application, we refer to Power Automate, whereas when we discuss individual processes, we will refer to a Flow.

Using Power Automate alongside PowerApps allows you to unlock the door to almost limitless levels of functionality and interoperability with other services. It allows you to integrate not only with Microsoft Services, but with other third-party services as well, such as Adobe, Salesforce, and even Google.

In this chapter, we'll cover the following topics:

- Understanding Flows
- Creating Flows through the Azure portal
- Creating a Flow from within PowerApps
- Returning data from a Flow
- Using Power Automate to process data
- Lab 12

By the end of this chapter, you will be able to utilize Microsoft Power Automate to undertake some background processing for your app, including passing parameters from your PowerApp and also receiving a response, so that your app is able to respond to any output.

Technical requirements

To follow along with this chapter, you will need the following:

- A Microsoft Power Automate license, which can be attained by getting an Office 365/Dynamics 365 seeded license, a per-user license, or a per-app license
- A Bing maps API key (previously used in GPS)
- PowerApp so that you can implement Flow integration, either by creating one from scratch or by using the sample provided on GitHub (`https://github.com/PacktPublishing/Learn-Microsoft-PowerApps`)

Understanding Flows

Microsoft Power Automate is part of the Power Platform and serves as the automation platform within Office 365. Flow, unlike its predecessor applications, such as SharePoint Designer, is completely browser-based and also accessible through the Microsoft Power Automate mobile app, which is available for both iOS and Android devices. An overview of Flow is shown in the following screenshot:

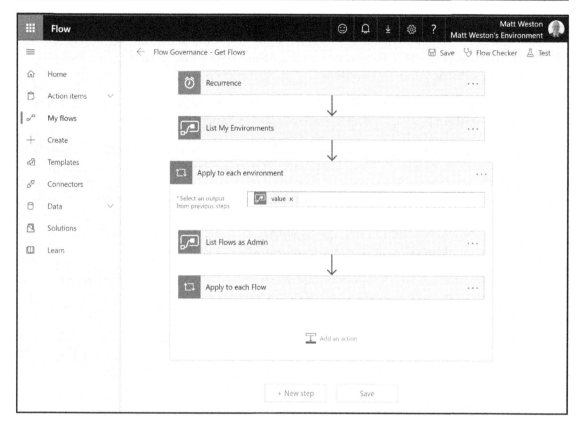

Figure 13.1: Microsoft Power Automate in a browser

PowerApps is built upon Azure Logic Apps, but the key difference is that it is accessible through the Office 365 portal (`portal.office.com`) and it targets business users rather than developers. Azure Logic Apps is accessible through the Azure portal (`portal.azure.com`) and are normally used by developers as there are more options with which to edit the underlying code compared to Flow.

Flow can be considered for three specific types of work:

- **Personal workflow**: Flow is intended to be used to help automate any mundane day to day tasks that eat into your productive time, such as sending email reminders.
- **Business Workflow**: Where businesses are inefficiently reliant on manual processes, Flow can be considered as an automated replacement that can be used to push documents to different parties for approval, for example.

- **Integration**: Most services don't talk to each other naturally, but when using the connectors that are available to Flow, you can establish communications between different systems. This allows you to process data from one service so that you can perform actions on another.

If you have an Office 365 license, then Flow is included with your subscription, but just like PowerApps, premium licenses are also available and enhance the existing functionality.

Flows are made up of two key components. The first key component is a trigger, which is the action or event that causes a Flow to execute. This could be an automated trigger that fires when an event takes place without direct interaction from a user; a recurrence trigger that fires on a scheduled basis; or a manual trigger that fires when a user interacts directly with the Flow. The second key component is an action, which makes up the logic of our workflow and allows us to build interactions with numerous data sources and employ normal development practices such as loops or branches in logic.

The manual trigger is the key component that we are most interested in as it allows us to trigger the Flow from within PowerApps, allowing us to pass data to it so that it can be processed.

There are two ways we can create a Flow that we can use with PowerApps: through the Flow portal and from PowerApps itself. Let's take a look at creating Flows through the Flow portal first.

Creating Flows through the Azure portal

To access Flow, we can either navigate directly to `https://flow.microsoft.com` or we can launch it from the Office 365 portal (`portal.office.com`), which allows us to select Power Automate from the list of available applications.

Once we have navigated to Flow, we have a variety of options available so that we can get started. These options are quite similar to those that are available for PowerApps since we can either start from a template, which has a number of preconfigured actions that we can then modify, or start from scratch, where we have a completely blank canvas on which to build the Flow as we see fit.

The first option we will look at is creating a Flow from one of the existing templates.

Creating a Flow from templates

If you are new to Power Automate, then there is a huge number of templates covering a vast array of scenarios, all of which can be accessed from the **Templates** menu option on the left-hand menu. These template Flows can also be used to get you started with building your logic if there is one close enough to your requirements. The following screenshot shows the screen that you go to in order to select your Flow templates:

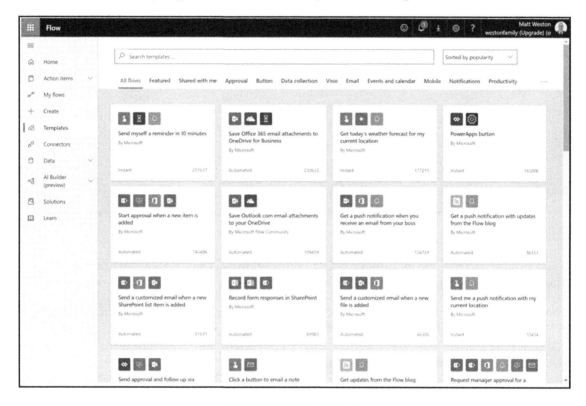

Figure 13.2: Flow Templates selection screen

If, for example, I select the **Send myself a reminder in 10 minutes template**, then this will generate a Flow that contains a manual trigger based on a Flow button, a **Delay** action, and a push notification action so that I can send a response to the Flow mobile app:

Figure 13.3: Send myself a reminder in 10 minutes Flow template

This template can then be modified, should you wish to add any further functionality. Alternatively, you can simply use it to see how this type of workflow can be configured.

Once you become familiar with Microsoft Power Automate, you will find yourself creating Flows from scratch, which means you have a blank canvas that you can build your logic from. Just like PowerApps, once we have investigated templates, we will want to create our own. To do this, we can create a template from scratch.

Creating Flows from scratch

When you are creating a Flow from scratch, the first thing you have to select is your trigger. While we can create recurring or automated triggers that can run on a data source, when we are working with PowerApps, we are more interested in an instant trigger. With PowerApps, we are specifically referring to the PowerApps trigger, which will allow us to create direct integration from our PowerApp to a Flow. Perform the following steps to learn how to do this:

1. To select a trigger, go to the **My flows** tab, and select the **New** button at the top of the screen. This will show the creation options that are available:

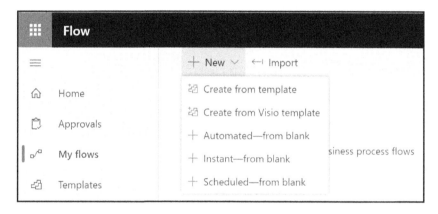

Figure 13.4: Creation menu showing the various options

2. When you select the **New** dropdown menu, you need to create an **Instant—from blank** Flow, which will give you the option to either start the automation from Flow (which will then be initiated from a Flow button) or from PowerApps (which will be initiated from an action call within a PowerApp), as shown in the following screenshot:

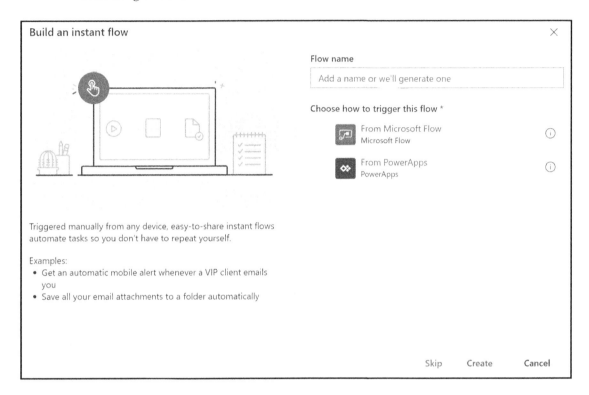

Figure 13.5: Instant trigger creation options

3. When the Flow is created, it will automatically place the PowerApp trigger on the canvas, as shown in the following screenshot. Now, we need to start building the logic that we want to perform. The logic comprises one or more actions that can run sequentially or in parallel:

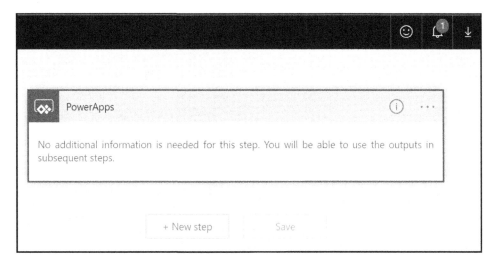

Figure 13.6: The PowerApps trigger. which has been placed on the Flow canvas

When placing an action into a Flow, you will want data to be passed from PowerApps to Flow, so you need to be able to tell Flow to ask for it when the trigger is called.

Requesting data from PowerApps

Whenever we work with actions in Power Automate, we have the ability to use **Dynamic content** to bring in values from the trigger or from other actions. **Dynamic content** appears in a toolbox within the Flow editor when we need to set a value in an action.

> **Dynamic content** can only be selected from the trigger or any actions that have been executed before the current action, so you should always consider how you structure your actions within Flow.

If you use the PowerApp trigger, then you have the option to use **Ask in PowerApps**, as shown in the following screenshot:

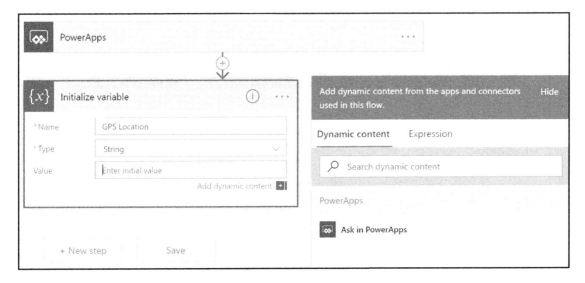

Figure 13.7: Using the Ask in PowerApps dynamic content within an Initialize variable action

This wires up the request, through the trigger, back to our PowerApp, so that when we call the Flow in PowerApps, we will have to provide it with a parameter.

 The name of the action using the **Ask in PowerApps Dynamic content**, is the name that's been assigned to the parameter. Always rename your action to what you want the parameter to be called, save the Flow, and then use **Dynamic content**.

Before we start configuring our PowerApp so that we can use the Flow, we should consider running some local tests to ensure that the logic we have built is going to provide us with the results that we want.

Testing your Flow

Microsoft Power Automate has built-in functionality that allows you to test your logic. You can find this by clicking on the **Test** button in the top right corner of the screen, as shown in the following screenshot:

Figure 13.8: Microsoft Power Automate Test button

Depending on the type of trigger that you have used, you will have different testing options available to you that allow you to debug effectively. If this is the first time you are running the Flow, then you will only be able to select **I'll perform the trigger action**. The behavior for initiating the Flow will depend on the type of trigger that has been employed. In the case of the PowerApps trigger, a blade will appear on the right-hand side of the screen that will ask us to provide inputs as they would appear from PowerApps.

For example, if our input is a string, then we will be asked to provide a string value. This is shown in the following screenshot:

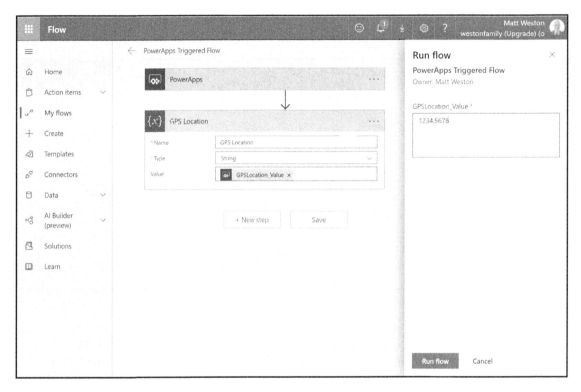

Figure 13.9: Providing test values

If we were using an automated trigger, then the behavior would differ since we would need to go to the data source and trigger the starting event from there by, for example, putting an item into a SharePoint list.

Once the Flow runs, it will allow you to check the state of each action, that is, whether it was successful, failed, was skipped, or anything else. You will also be able to see the inputs and outputs for each action to ensure that the data that is being passed is what you expect, which is a huge aid for debugging as you can quickly identify and rectify mistakes:

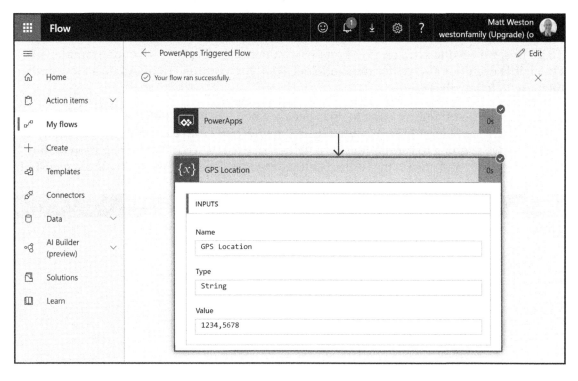

Figure 13.10: Flow successfully completed

The symbol against each action denotes the outcome:

- A green tick denotes success
- A yellow tick denotes success after a retry cycle
- A light gray cross denotes skipped
- A dark gray cross denotes canceled
- A red cross denotes an error

Once you have created and tested the Flow, you need to be able to call it from within PowerApps.

Calling a Flow within PowerApps

To do this, we need to have an event that we can use to trigger the Flow; for example, the **OnVisible** event for a screen or the **OnSelect** event for a button. To associate a Flow and then use it, follow these steps:

1. The first thing we need to do is decide where we want the Flow to be executed. Do we want it to be executed from the screen or from a control? In this example, we're going to execute the Flow from a button, so we will place a button on the screen and ensure that it has been selected, as shown in the following screenshot:

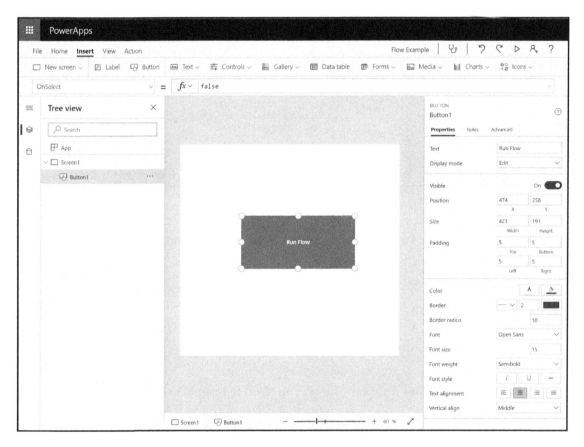

Figure 13.11: Placement of a button that will execute the Flow

2. With the desired control selected, we need to navigate to the **Action** menu and then select **Flows**. This will present a list of Flows that are either already associated with the control or available for association, as in the following screenshot:

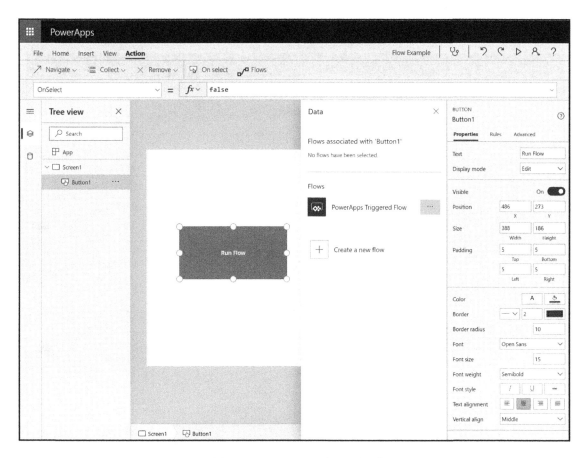

Figure 13.12: Showing Flows that are available for association with a control

3. To associate the Flow with the control, we simply need to click on the desired Flow within the **Flows** blade. PowerApps will show that it is being added. Once we've done this, it will set the screen's focus on the formula bar. If we have requested parameters from within Flow, this will show a validation error until we have provided the necessary information. This is shown in the following screenshot:

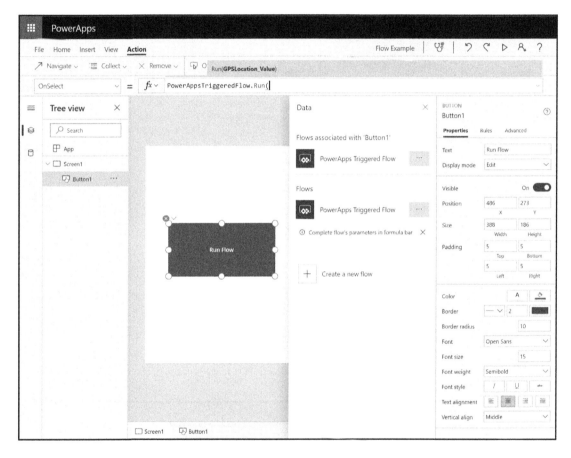

Figure 13.13: A Flow that has been successfully associated and is requesting additional parameters

This may fail if you request an unsupported data type with Microsoft Power Automate, such as an array. In this instance, the association will fail, but it won't tell you why.

Instead, consider formatting your array as a text string with PowerApps and then passing your value through as a string.

4. Once the Flow execution formula appears in the formula bar, we just need to update it to include the values that we want to pass into it. In this example, we want to provide the Flow with the GPS location. Therefore, we will use what we learned in Chapter 9, *Using GPS in PowerApps*, to pass in the current latitude and longitude of the device. For this we would use the following code:

```
PowerAppsTriggeredFlow.Run(Concatenate(Text(Location.Latitude),
",", Text(Location.Longitude)))
```

Now, when the **Run Flow** button is pressed, our PowerApps will pass the current location values for latitude and longitude and will execute the logic contained within the Flow. The result is that our Flow will run and the variable will receive the value that we have passed through in the formula, that is, the Latitude and Longitude:

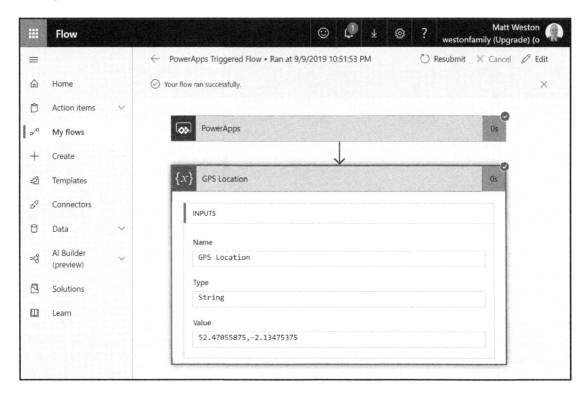

Figure 13.14: Flow result from clicking the Run Flow button in PowerApps

As well as being able to create Flows externally and then reference them from our PowerApps, we also have the ability to create a new Flow directly from PowerApps Studio, which we will do next.

Creating a Flow from within PowerApps

We have the ability to initiate the creation of a Flow from within PowerApps by going to the **Flow** blade. This blade can be accessed in exactly the same way as if we were going to associate a Flow with a control, that is, by clicking on the **Actions** menu and then selecting **Flows**. If we want to generate a new Flow, then we simply need to click the **Create a new flow** link, as shown in the following screenshot:

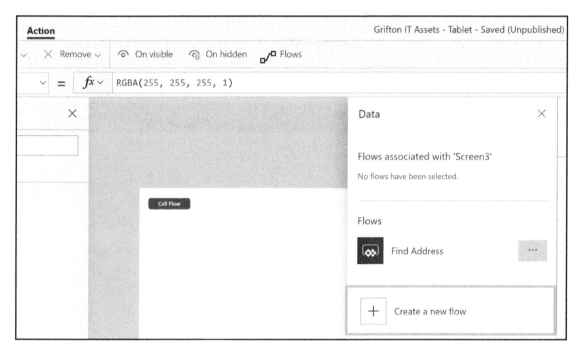

Figure 13.15: The Create a new flow link

When we select **Create a new flow**, we are taken to a list of templates within the PowerApps gallery, which are designed to run from a PowerApps trigger. Here, we have the ability to decide whether we wish to use one of the templates or create one from scratch, as we mentioned in the *Creating Flows from scratch* section .

Using Flow doesn't just have to be a one-way process. There will be times where we will require Flow to send data back to our PowerApps.

Returning data from Flow

It is conceivable that, while we are using Power Automate to perform processing that is too complex for PowerApps, we will wish to return data to PowerApps so that we can, for example, send feedback stating that something has happened.

Microsoft Power Automate has a built-in action that allows us to return data in a number of different formats, and that action is called **Respond to PowerApps**. This action is available from within Microsoft Power Automate as a part of the PowerApps connector. The easiest way to find this is to use the search box when adding an action and then searching for the name of the action, as shown in the following screenshot:

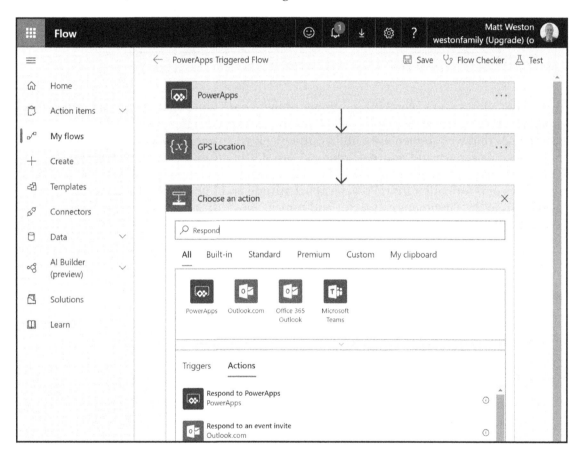

Figure 13.16: Finding the Respond to PowerApps action

This action allows you to return data in a number of different formats, as shown in the following screenshot:

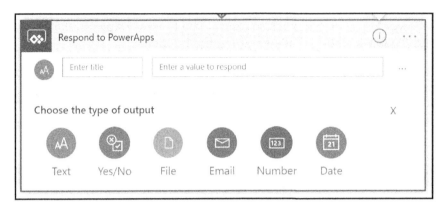

Figure 13.17: The Respond to PowerApps action options

This action allows you to combine a number of these data types so that you can return them as a single response to PowerApps, which means that we can effectively return a record to PowerApps that we can then use within our logic. If we expand our Flow so that it can interact with a service and return a value, we are starting to showcase how we can use Power Automate to its full effect. The Flow, as shown in the following screenshot, requests two pieces of information from PowerApps: **Latitude** and **Longitude**. It then requests the location from the Bing maps connector and returns the address data to PowerApps:

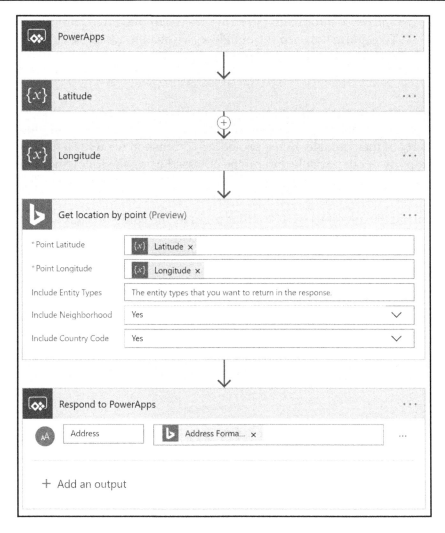

Figure 13.18: A Flow that returns address information from Bing maps to PowerApps

To capture the output from the Flow, we need to update the call to the Flow from within PowerApps. To do this, we will create a variable that will store the returned value from Flow and then output it to the screen.

To pass these two pieces of information to Flow, we've supplied two parameters: Latitude and Longitude. To capture the output from Flow, we need to wrap the call to Flow within a variable so that we are able to capture the data that is being returned:

```
Set(varLocation,FindAddress.Run(Location.Latitude, Location.Longitude))
```

In this example, the data that's being returned from Flow is called address. When we want to output this data onto the screen, we can simply reference the variable and then the desired property of that variable. In the preceding screenshot, we returned address, so this becomes a property of our variable and can be accessed using the following formula:

```
varLocation.address
```

The result of using the previous two formulas gives us the ability to click a button that will call our Flow so that we can get an address that we can then output onto the screen:

Figure 13.19: Example of the address information being output to PowerApps

In this section, we have successfully implemented a Flow, called it from within PowerApps, and then used the data that was returned by outputting it onto the screen.

Using Power Automate to process data

Power Automate can be used to perform the heavy processing that you wouldn't necessarily want to do within PowerApps. PowerApps needs to be lightweight and responsive to the end user, so you will need to pass data to Flow. You may also need to use Flow to perform actions to get data, such as calling REST APIs, which is something you can't do within PowerApps.

There are some key scenarios where Flow steps up to allow us to do some advanced processing with PowerApps. One of those key scenarios is the ability to handle files – being able to create, update, copy, and move files – depending on where we want our data to reside. A key use case is being able to take a picture that has been captured by PowerApps and save it within SharePoint, which requires some additional processing by Microsoft Power Automate. We can't just do this using the **Create file** action within the SharePoint connector since the data isn't stored correctly and as a result saves a corrupted file instead.

To store the image somewhere, we need to be able to request data in binary format. However, the only action within Microsoft Power Automate that will request data in the correct format is the **Send an Email** action. To do this, we need to follow these steps:

1. Navigate to the Power Automate portal and create a Flow using the PowerApps trigger, as described in the previous section:

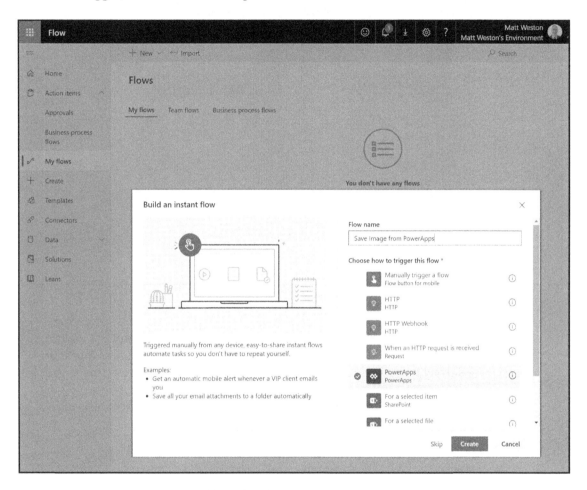

Figure 13.20 - Creating a Flow with a PowerApps trigger

2. Once the Flow canvas has loaded, we can add the **Send an Email** action, which is part of the Office 365 Outlook connector. This particular action allows us to add attachments to an email. It is this action that will request the data from PowerApps in the correct format:

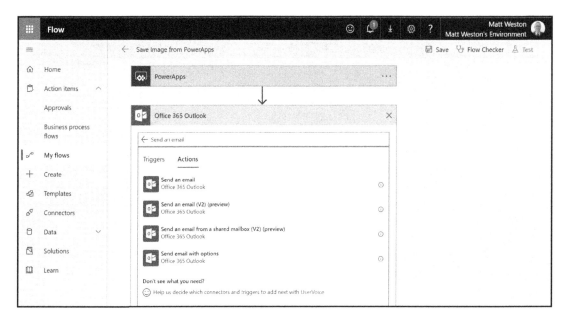

Figure 13.21 - Adding an action from the Office 365 Outlook connector

3. We need to fill in mandatory fields, that is,**To**, **Subject**, and **Body**, but we don't need to add anything of substance as we're not actually going to use this action. We are simply using it to generate the request through the PowerApps trigger:

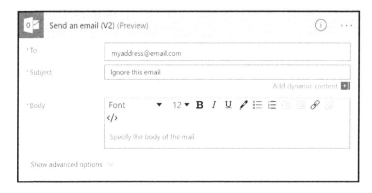

Figure 13.22 - Configuring the Send an email (V2) action

4. Then, we can click on **Show advanced options** at the bottom of the action to reveal the attachments field. We shouldn't be too concerned about the attachment's name unless we want to use it to request the file name from the app, but what we're more interested in is the attachment's content. By clicking into that field and then selecting **Ask in PowerApps** from **Dynamic content**, we will be able to request the file from PowerApps in binary format:

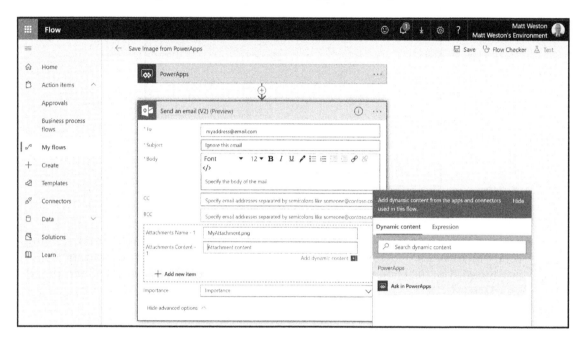

Figure 13.23 - Using the Ask in PowerApps dynamic content

5. Now that we are requesting the correct data, we should add our **Create file** action from the SharePoint connector so that we can take the binary file and save it. The ideal place to add the SharePoint action is before the **Send Email** action since we won't actually be executing it. Click on the **+** icon above the **Send Email** action and click **Add an action**. Then, select the **Create file** SharePoint action:

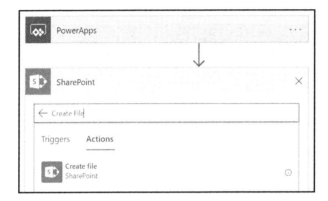

Figure 13.24 - Using the SharePoint connector

6. Once the **Create file** action appears on our canvas, we can configure it by telling it which SharePoint site to save to, the folder path, the file's name, and the file's content. The file content will be the data that we requested from the **Send Email** action:

Figure 13.25 - Configuring the Create file action

7. Now that we have configured our Flow so that it creates the file, we just need to make sure that our **Send Email** action doesn't fire. To do that, we are going to change the condition that triggers the **Send Email** action. By default, it will run if the previous action was successful. We will change this so that it runs on a timeout instead (which won't happen with the **Create file** action). We can do this by clicking on the ellipsis at the top right corner of the **Send Email** action and selecting **Configure run after**:

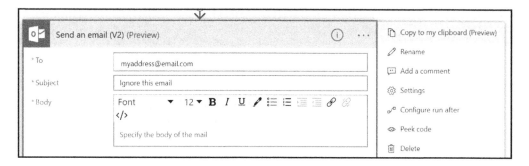

Figure 13.26 - The Settings menu for an action

8. From there, we simply need to uncheck **is successful** and check **has timed out**, followed by clicking on **Done**:

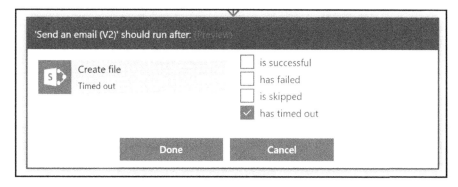

Figure 13.27 - The run after settings for the email action

Now that we have configured our Flow, we can test it by putting together a very simple PowerApp that will take a photograph using the camera control and pass it to Power Automate so that it can be processed and stored within SharePoint Online. We should create our app from scratch so that we can put it together quickly. In the following steps, we're going to be using a phone layout:

1. Using the skills that we gained in the previous chapter, add a camera control to our canvas:

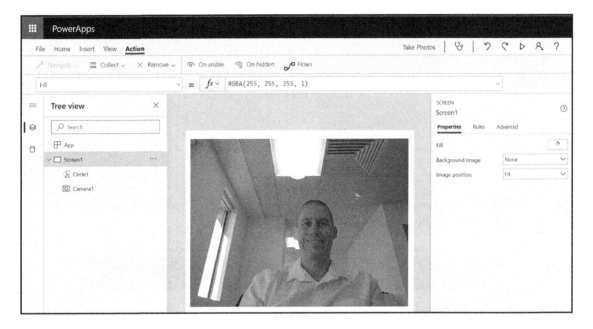

Figure 13.28 - Camera control added to the canvas

2. Select the camera control, change the property in the formula bar to **OnSelect**, and navigate to Flows by selecting the **Action** menu, followed by **Flows**. At that point, you will see the **Flow** blade appear on the right-hand side. This will contain the Flow that we created. Click on the name of your Flow to add it to the control:

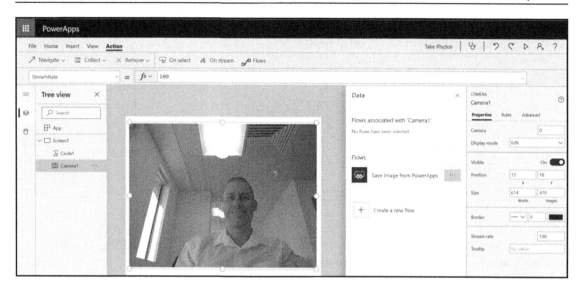

Figure 13.29 - Menu blade for adding a Flow to a control

3. The formula to execute the Flow will automatically be placed into your formula bar and will ask you to provide the parameter you need. In this example, the only parameter we need is the image file. We need to complete the formula by adding `Camera1.Photo` to it:

Figure 13.30 - The updated formula when the Flow has been added

4. Now, we can go ahead and test that PowerApps and Flow are working together. Press the play button at the top right of the screen and click the camera control to take a picture. This will be processed through Flow and saved to SharePoint.

Now, when you view your Flow, you will see that the first two actions have succeeded while the send email action has been skipped:

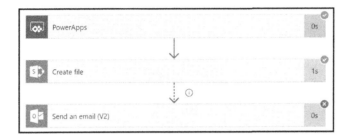

Figure 13.31 - The Flow running with status indicators in the top right of each action

When we look at the file that has been created within SharePoint, we'll see that it is the picture that we captured from the camera control in PowerApps:

Figure 13.32 - Previewing the image now stored within SharePoint

The example we have just followed was based around Microsoft Technology. We are not limited to using Microsoft-provided services, though. The integration capabilities of Flow allow us to interact and process data from a huge number of external services. There are a large number of connectors that allow you to connect to other service providers, such as Google, so that you can perform similar types of processing.

Lab 12

To complete this lab, you will need to have a Power Automate license, which can be either an Office 365/Dynamics 365 seeded license, a per-user license, or a per-app license.

Within this lab, we will use Power Automate to implement notifications when a new asset is added using our app. Using Flow, we will generate an email and send it to the person who is going to receive the asset. To do this, we will need to update the data source so that we can store the assignee and then generate the Flow.

Activity 1: Updating the data source

Within our data source, we need to create an additional field within the data table. This is going to contain the UPN of the person that the asset is going to be assigned to. Let's get started:

1. Open the `Assets.xlsx` workbook.
2. After `Asset Barcode`, insert a new column.
3. Name the column `Assignee`:

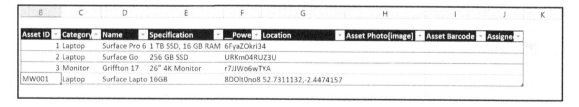

4. Save your Excel workbook and close the program.

Now that we know how to update a data source, let's create a Flow.

Activity 2: Creating a Flow

Now, we will create a Flow that will allow us to receive the object for the user who is going to be assigned the asset. Based on the user, we will find their manager and send an email notification to both to inform them that the asset has been assigned. Let's get started:

1. Navigate to the Microsoft Power Automate portal (`flow.microsoft.com`).
2. Select **My Flows** from the menu on the left-hand side.
3. From the **New** dropdown, select **Instant—from blank**.
4. Name the Flow `Asset Assignment` and select **From PowerApps** as the trigger.
5. Click **Create**:

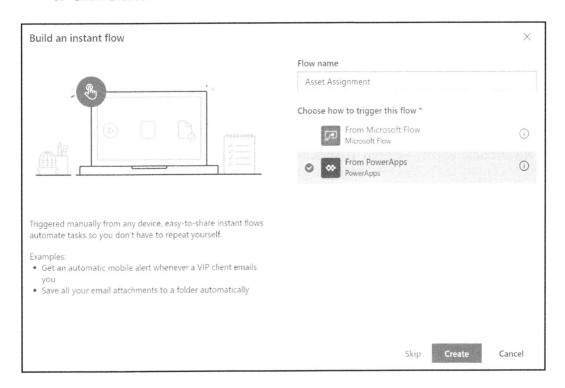

6. Flow will now open the canvas and create the PowerApps trigger.
7. Beneath the trigger, click **New step**.
8. In the **Search connectors and actions** box, enter `Initialize Variable`.
9. Select the **Initialize Variable** action.
10. Rename the action to `Assignee` by clicking the ellipsis in the corner of the action and selecting rename.

11. Configure the action as follows:
    1. **Name**: Assignee
    2. **Type**: String
    3. **Value**: Leave blank for now:

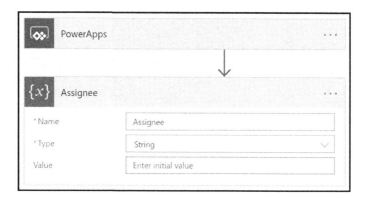

12. Save the Flow.
13. Now, complete the configuration of the Assignee action by placing your cursor in the **Value** field.
14. From **Dynamic content**, select **Ask in PowerApps** so that it places the **Dynamic content** within the value:

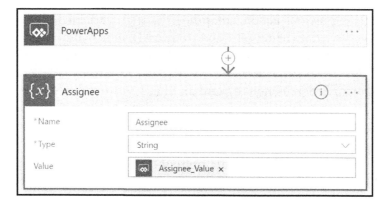

15. Repeat this process for a second variable called Asset.
16. Create another action below Asset, this time searching for the Office 365 users connector.

17. Select the **Get user profile (V2)** action to get the full profile for the assignee.

18. Within this action, click within the **User (UPN)** value and select the **Assignee** variable from **Dynamic content**:

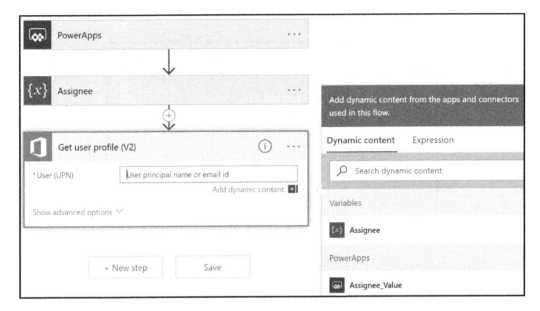

19. Add another action, again using the Office 365 users connector, but this time select the **Get manager (V2)** action.

20. Just like the previous action, enter the `Assignee` variable into the UPN field. Now, we have data being returned from AAD, which allows us to use profile information from both the assignee and their manager. Now, we need to send an email.

21. Add another action using the **Send an Email Notification (V3)** action.

22. At the bottom of the action, expand the available options by selecting **Show advanced options**.

23. Configure the action in the following way:
    - **To**: Filter the **Dynamic content** by typing `email` into the filter box. This will return two values for **Mail**: one under the **Get manager (V2)** heading and the other under the **Get user profile (V2)** heading. Select **Mail** beneath **Get user profile (V2)**:

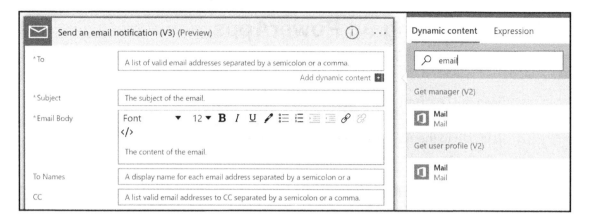

- **Subject**: Type in `An asset has been assigned to you.`
- **Email Body**: In this field, use **Dynamic content** combined with typed text to create your email. The following is an example of this, with **Dynamic content** surrounded by </>:

```
Dear <Get user profile (V2): Display Name>

An asset has been assigned to you for the duration of your
employment with Griffton. You have been assigned the
following asset:

<Variables: Asset>

Regards

IT
```

- **To Names**: Select the **Display Name** under the **Get user profile (V2)** action.
- **CC**: Select the **Mail** attribute from the **Get manager (V2)** action.
- **CC Names**: Select the **Display Name** attribute from the **Get manager (V2)** action.

In this section, we created a Flow and prepared it so that it can receive information from PowerApps. Now, we just need to prepare PowerApps so that it can send the data to Flow.

Activity 3: Wiring up PowerApps

In this activity, we will modify PowerApps so that, when the asset is updated and assigned to someone, we will send the data to Flow to process the notifications. Let's get started:

1. Open the **Griffton IT Assets** PowerApp, which we have been creating throughout this book.
2. Navigate to the **Asset Form** screen.
3. Refresh the `Assets` data source to pick up the new **Assignee** field:

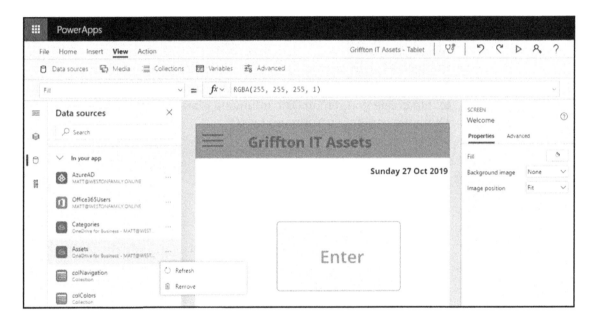

4. Open the **New Asset** screen, select **frmNewAsset**, and change the data source back to **Assets** to make it easier to update the form:

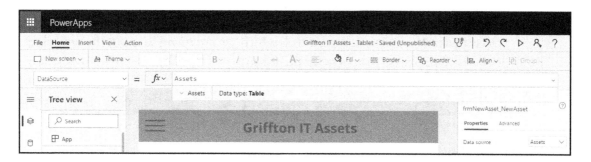

5. Add the **Assignee** field to the form by clicking on **Edit fields** and then selecting **Assignee**:

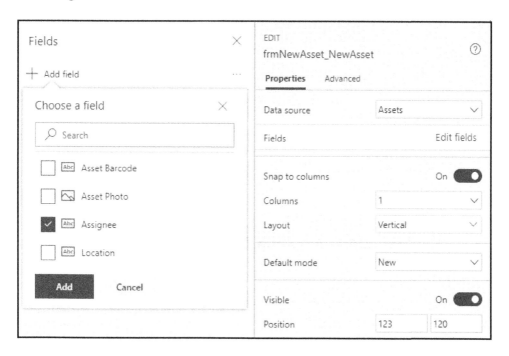

6. Ensure that you reorder the fields so that the data card for the **Save** button appears below the **Assignee** field.

7. Rename the text input control in the **Assignee** data card to `txtAssignee` so that we can easily reference it later.

8. Select the **frmNewAsset** form control, which we are using to input the new asset.

9. Select the **OnSuccess** property for the form:

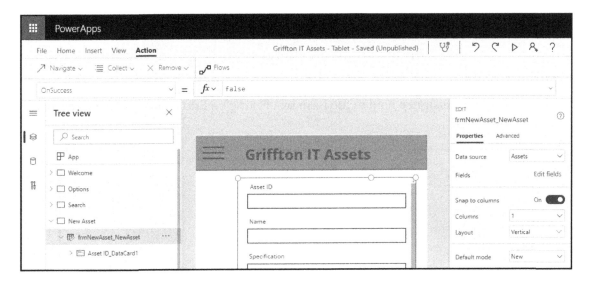

10. Click on the **Action** menu.

11. Select **Flows**:

12. You will see your Flow, that is, **Asset Assignment**, in the list. Click it:

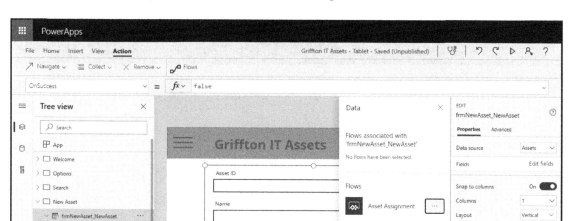

13. The run formula for the Flow will be created automatically. However, because we are using the `OnSuccess` method, we need to get the last item that was submitted to the data source. Due to this, we will use the **LastSubmit** property to get the assignee and the name of the asset:

    ```
    AssetAssignment.Run(frmNewAsset.LastSubmit.Assignee,
    frmNewAsset.LastSubmit.Name).
    ```

14. Reset the data source for `frmNewForm` so that it points back to the `colAssets` collection:

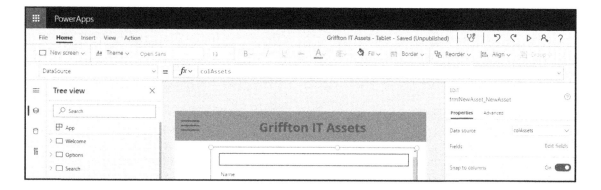

15. Before saving, don't forget to update your offline collection. This will save the **Assignee** field in the asset changes collection:

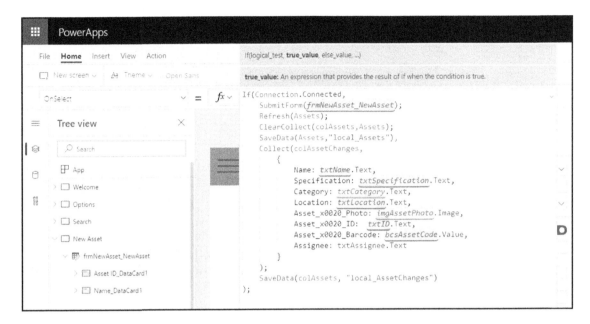

16. Save your PowerApps and test it by selecting an asset, assigning the asset by entering the email address of the person you want to assign it to, and then pressing **Save**.

Your app will now perform two actions when the **Save** button is clicked: it will write back any changes to your data source and then trigger the Flow. In the Flow run history, you will see that you now have a run, and an email will have been sent to the users you chose to receive emails.

Summary

In this chapter, we have unlocked a huge amount of potential by utilizing another part of the Power Platform. We did this by using Power Automate to provide integration services and a heavy processing platform for our PowerApps.

Power Automate can be used for personal workflow automation, business process automation, or integration between services, so it's somewhat versatile. It has the same underlying engine as Azure Logic Apps, but while Logic Apps are aimed at developers, Power Automate is aimed very much at business users. It can be accessed through the Office 365 portal.

Power Automate shares the same connectors as PowerApps, which means it also has the ability to connect to hundreds of different services. The key advantage over directly connecting with PowerApps is that we can schedule workflows, handle files, and handle long-running processes that wouldn't suit the client-facing aspect of PowerApps.

For us to utilize Flows within PowerApps, we need to use a PowerApps trigger. Flows that use this trigger can either be created from within the Flow portal and then referenced from our app, or created from the app directly.

Once we have created the trigger, we can then build out the logic using a number of actions to process the data as we see fit. Within these actions, we can request information from PowerApps. This information is presented to the app developer as parameters when they call the Flow.

Power Automate also has the ability to respond to a PowerApp by passing one or several pieces of data back for the app to consume. To achieve this, we need to wrap the Flow call within a variable declaration so that we can use it in our other controls.

In the next chapter, we will be using Azure in PowerApps to further extend the capabilities of the apps that we're developing.

Questions

1. Microsoft Power Automate is built on another Microsoft technology. What is it?
2. What is the intended user base for Microsoft Power Automate?
3. There are three types of trigger. What are they?
4. What trigger should I use to request data from PowerApps?
5. What action should I use to return data from Power Automate to PowerApps?
6. True or False: Power Automate can integrate with third-party data sources, not just Microsoft.

Further reading

Flow has an extremely good community following and has support from Microsoft support staff, Microsoft MVPs, and Flownauts (Super Users), all of whom can be contacted through the Microsoft Power Automate Community: `https://powerusers.microsoft.com/t5/` `Microsoft-Flow-Community/ct-p/FlowCommunity`.

Using Azure with PowerApps

14

So far, we have created functionalities using the various components that are available through PowerApps and then extended that by using Flow. In this chapter, we are going to look at Azure and how we can start to utilize the power of Azure, the Microsoft cloud platform, to perform actions that we wouldn't be able to perform directly through PowerApps.

Due to the nature of Azure, this chapter will feel as though it has a developer-focused feel to it as we start to explore how we can use scripts and code to build functionality for our PowerApp.

There are a huge number of services that can be utilized within Azure to add depth to our apps, although some areas are more accessible by PowerApps than others. In this chapter, we will focus on the three areas that are used the most with PowerApp development to achieve outcomes that wouldn't be possible otherwise.

In this chapter, we will cover the following topics:

- Utilizing Azure resources
- Interacting with **Azure Active Directory** (**AAD**)
- Implementing Azure Automation
- Calling Azure Functions

When we look at AAD, we will look at the user management abilities it offers and how they can be used within PowerApps. Using Azure Automation, we will extend our PowerApps functionality through the use of PowerShell. Moving on, we'll use Azure Functions through queues to describe how we can interact with and trigger Azure Functions through queues in order to provide a robust solution when it comes to interacting with serverless code running within the Microsoft cloud.

By the end of this chapter, you will have an understanding of how you can leverage aspects of Microsoft Azure directly from within your PowerApp. Specifically, we will focus on how we can leverage the key Azure technologies that have connectors available.

Technical requirements

To follow along with the topics that will be covered in this chapter, you will need access to a number of resources that are available through the Microsoft Azure portal (portal.azure.com). You can create Azure resources using a free trial, which will give you $200 of credit for 30 days. Simply visit https://azure.microsoft.com/free to start your free trial.

Utilizing Azure resources

Azure allows you to create resources that you can call to provide additional processing resources, store data, or manage areas of your tenancy, such as AAD. Much like Microsoft Power Automate, Azure can provide additional processing power to your PowerApps through a number of **Platform as a Service (PAAS)**, **Software as a Service (SAAS)**, or **Infrastructure as a Service (IAAS)** offerings. There are a large number of connectors available to Azure, some standard and others premium, which allow you to extend the functionality you have available to you within PowerApps.

There's also a growing number of connectors in preview, such as connectors that have pre-general availability and therefore can be used for testing, which means that Microsoft is increasing the number of Azure resources that you have directly available within your PowerApp. The most common resources that are employed alongside PowerApps are as follows:

- AAD
- Azure Automation
- Azure Functions

We will begin by looking at the identity service provided by Microsoft Azure known as AAD.

Integrating with Azure Active Directory

Integrating with AAD allows you to access a number of key pieces of information from the user store, as well as create bespoke ways of putting data into Azure. AAD contains a large number of attributes about users, as well as groups, and serves as the primary user management portal for Office 365. As shown in the following screenshot, AAD will consolidate all the users, regardless of whether they have been created on-premises (as long as AD Connect has been installed and configured), in Azure, or as guest accounts, into a single management screen:

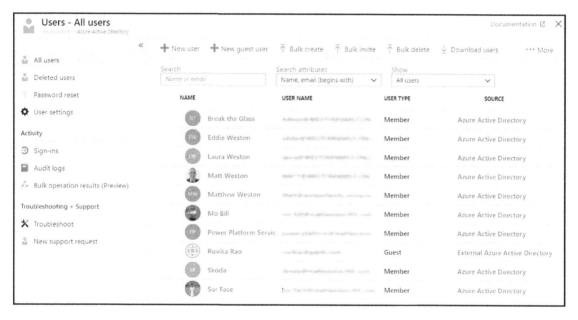

Figure 14.1: AAD users

If AAD is your key user management provider, that is, you're not using **Active Directory Domain Services** (**ADDS**), then you can build graphically rich PowerApps to manage your users. In this case, you could consider building a PowerApp to allow users to be able to create, edit, or delete users, as well as assign groups through PowerApps. If, for example, our app was using AAD groups to manage security, it is possible for us to build an element within the PowerApp to control the membership of this group.

Often, however, the first interaction we need to do is create a user using the `CreateUser` function. Here, we need to supply some basic information:

- `accountEnabled`: This is a Boolean value that determines whether the account is active or not.
- `displayName`: The name of the user as it would be seen by others; for example, Matt Weston.
- `mailNickname`: The alias for the mailbox that is created for the user.
- `passwordProfile`: The password that is assigned to the user.
- `userPrincipalName`: The identifying name that allows the user to sign in.

Each of these pieces of information can be captured from controls with PowerApps or can be typed in, as shown in the following screenshot:

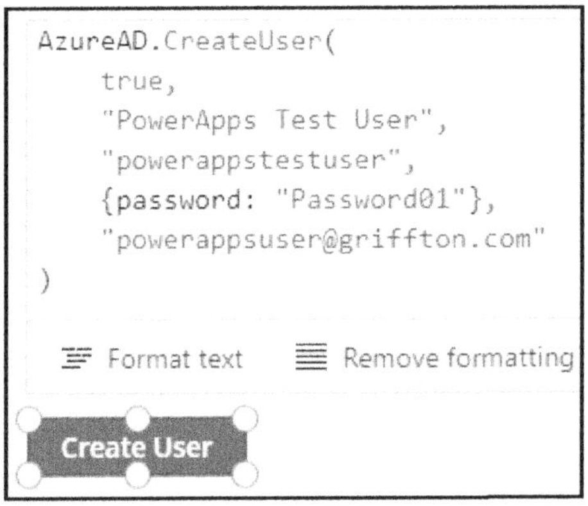

Figure 14.2: Creating a user in AAD using the CreateUser function

This formula will create a new user in AAD as a cloud user, that is, a user who has been created directly within the cloud. This will not create a user in ADDS.

As well as being able to interact with user objects in AAD, we can also interact with groups in the same way as we can with users. Here, we would create a new group, which requires the following information:

- `displayName`: The name of the group, as seen by a user.
- `description`: The description of the new group.
- `mailNickname`: The email alias assigned to the group.

- `groupTypes`: Allows the creation of an Office 365 group if we provide a string array with the word `"Unified"`. If you just want a standard security group, then use the word `"None"`.
- `securityEnabled`: A Boolean value that will identify the group as a security group that can be used across various applications.
- `mailEnabled`: A Boolean value that will identify whether the group in question is a mailing group.

Once again, all of this information can be captured from the controls within our PowerApps or coded in, as shown in the following screenshot:

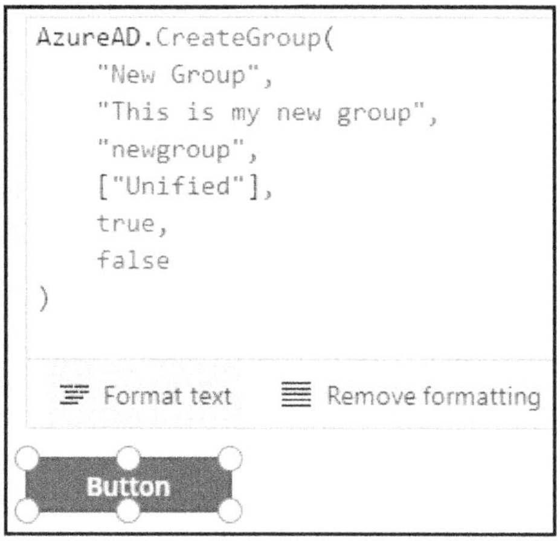

```
AzureAD.CreateGroup(
    "New Group",
    "This is my new group",
    "newgroup",
    ["Unified"],
    true,
    false
)
```

≡ Format text   ≡ Remove formatting

Button

Figure 14.3: Creating a new Office 365 group

The function in the preceding screenshot will create a new Office 365 group within AAD called `New Group`.

Where Azure really starts to add value to PowerApps is when it gives us the capability to offload some more complex tasks or process heavy automation; for example, the ability to provision new sites in SharePoint.

Implementing Azure Automation

Azure Automation is a way of being able to extend your PowerApps by implementing functionalities through PowerShell. This is commonly used when we need to perform actions that aren't directly possible by using connectors and functions with our PowerApp, such as if we want to create a new SharePoint site or a new Microsoft Teams team.

Since it is on PowerShell, Azure Automation starts to take PowerApp developers out of the realm of creating no-code/low-code solutions as it requires us to create scripts to perform our actions rather than using something graphical. Azure Automation allows a number of different scripting languages to be used to create functionality, with the main options being PowerShell and Python. In the following examples, we will be using PowerShell since it is the most common scripting language that's understood by both Office 365 admins and developers.

There are a huge number of advantages of using Azure Automation, the main one being that we can quickly and easily import any PowerShell modules from the PowerShell gallery and then manage them directly with our Azure Automation account. We also don't need a local development environment as it provides a browser-based editor where we can develop and test our scripts. Like the other services provided by Azure, we can integrate with DevOps or GitHub, which means that we can apply source control to the scripts, as well as configure continuous deployment.

Azure Automation has a massive benefit, though – it will run up to 500 minutes of compute time for free. This isn't 500 minutes per month or 500 minutes since the PowerShell was created; this is 500 minutes of free time for each execution. If you're familiar with PowerShell, then you will understand that you can execute a huge amount of PowerShell code in a 500-minute window. This makes Azure Automation an extremely cost-effective method of running scripts.

Automation allows us to call PowerShell directly from PowerApps using the Azure Automation connector. This means that we now have the ability to perform a huge number of operations beyond what we can do through the standard user interface, or without having to interact with Flow first.

To utilize Azure Automation, we need to create an Azure Automation account.

Creating an Azure Automation account

To create an Azure Automation account, we need to log in and subscribe to Microsoft Azure. This can be configured through the Azure portal (`portal.azure.com`).

The simplest way of finding Azure Automation is by using the search bar at the top of the Azure portal and selecting **Automation Accounts**:

Figure 14.4: The search bar at the top of Azure portal allows you to quickly find resources

 If you haven't got an Azure subscription, then you can create one using a free trial, which will give you 30 days to build and experiment with a huge number of Azure services. Alternatively, if you already have a subscription, you can keep your subscription open and use free services that are available to you.

When you create an automation account, you need to provide a few details to get it up and running:

- The first is a unique **Name** for your automation account.
- The **Subscription** where you are going to create the automation account.
- The **Resource group.**
- The location where the service will be hosted.
- The other option that's available is **Create Azure Run As account**, which will create a new service principal within the subscription and assign it to contributor rights. They are designed to allow you to remotely provision new assets with Azure using PowerShell using an account that has the least amount of privilege to perform the action. This is optional.

The output of providing these details is shown in the following screenshot:

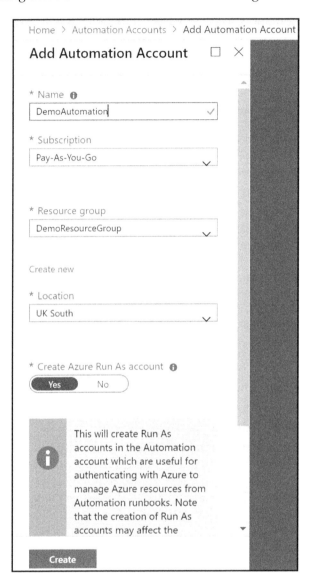

Figure 14.4: Add Automation Account blade

Now that we have created an automation account, there are some elements that we need to configure before we can start scripting so that we can work more efficiently.

Preparing your automation account for use

Just like writing PowerShell locally, we need to prepare our environment so that we can develop. For example, we need to check that we have the correct PowerShell modules installed, and that we have any credentials ready so that we can access our services. Exactly the same considerations are required when we work with Azure Automation, but we can do all of this through the Azure graphical user interface rather than doing it through scripts.

From the navigation on the left-hand menu, you will see the **Shared Resources** header, as shown in the following screenshot. Under this header, you will find three key areas, all of which you need to be aware of:

- **Modules**
- **Credentials**
- **Variables**

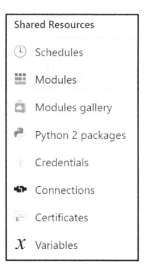

Figure 14.5: Shared Resources menu in Azure Automation

The most important of these menu options is the **Modules** menu, which allows us to install the modules that we need for our automation. Let's learn how to install modules.

Installing modules

Modules allow you to search for and import PowerShell modules directly from the PowerShell gallery (`www.powershellgallery.com`). This means that any modules that can be used with a standard PowerShell script, that is, scripts that you create on your local machine, are also available to use within Azure. For example, if we want to import the Microsoft Teams modules, we can do so by searching for and selecting it from the gallery. This is shown in the following screenshot:

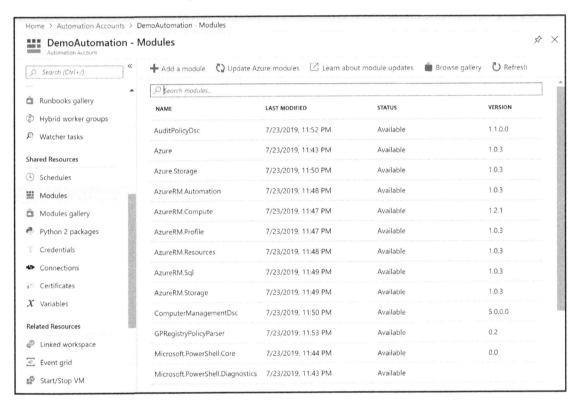

Figure 14.6: PowerShell Modules gallery in Azure Automation

Selecting and installing a module in this way is the equivalent to running the `Install-Module` commandlet from your local environment.

When updates are available for the PowerShell modules, we can also update our installed modules through the user interface, which is the equivalent of running `Update-Module`.

Once we have added all of the required modules, we can consider what credentials we need and store them securely within our automation.

Storing credentials

When connecting to Office 365 using PowerShell, we often need to provide user credentials, such as the username and password of a service account. Often, these are stored within the PowerShell scripts themselves, but this means that anyone with access to the script can see these credentials.

The automation account has a built-in credential manager, as shown in the following screenshot. This allows us to securely store usernames and passwords, which then become easily usable through a PowerShell commandlet:

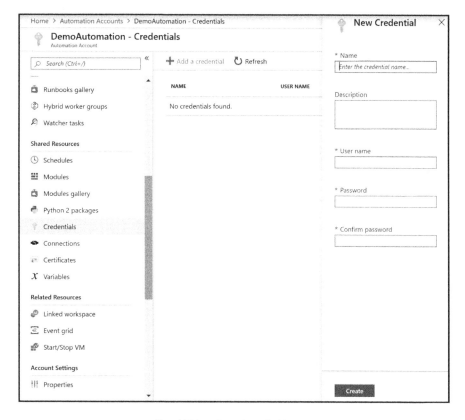

Figure 14.7: Azure Automation credential manager

When actually writing scripts, we can access our credentials using the following command within our script:

```
Get-AutomationPSCredential -Name <Name of credential>
```

This will retrieve the username and password in the correct format so that it can be used in authentication calls against a large number of services, such as when calling services within Office 365.

In the same way that we have a central register of credentials, we also have the ability to create a centrally managed list of variables.

Storing variables

In the same way that we can store credentials within the Azure Automation account for reuse, we can also store variables. These are particularly useful for creating, managing, and reusing global variables throughout our PowerShell scripts.

Just like credentials, variables are created through the automation screen in the Azure portal, as shown in the following screenshot. When creating a variable, we can define the data type and specify whether the field is encrypted or not. If we are going to store a client ID and secret, for example, we can ensure that the secret is encrypted and therefore protected from anyone going into the variables list and retrieving that information:

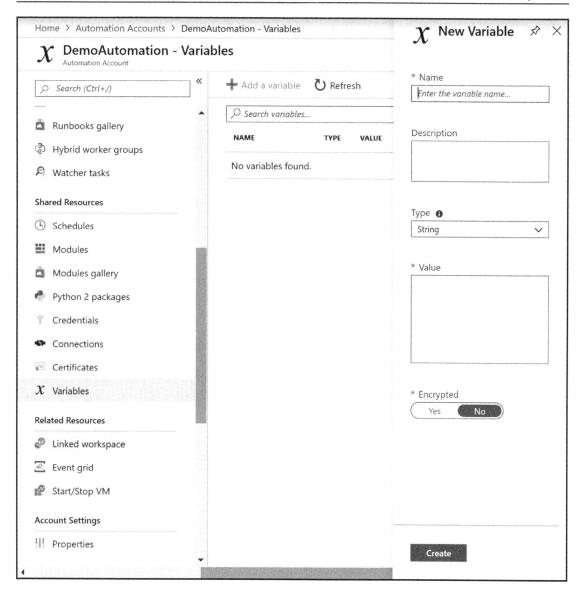

Figure 14.8: Azure Automation variables manager

When we want to use this variable within our PowerShell scripts, we can use a simple command to retrieve the value of the variable:

```
Get-AutomationVariable -Name <Name of Variable>
```

This means that the value of our variable is now usable within our automation. Variables, however, are also subject to change and can be updated from within our scripts. Unlike credentials that are read-only from scripts, variables can be written to using the following command:

```
Set-AutomationVariable -Name 'DevOps Access Token' -Value <System.Object>
```

This means that our scripts are updating variables without a user physically having to change them. Once we have created a variety of variables or credentials, we need to create our runbook.

Using runbooks

The final thing we need to do so that we can utilize Azure Automation within our PowerApp is to write a PowerShell script to perform the desired actions. There are a number of basic scripts that are created as examples for runbooks – some are graphical, some use Python, and others use PowerShell. This gives you the flexibility to write your functionality in your desired language. Given that PowerShell is used for a lot of administration tasks within O365, the following example runbook will be demonstrated in PowerShell.

To create a runbook, follow these steps:

1. Select **Runbooks** from the **Process Automation** menu on the left-hand side and select **Create a runbook**. Here, a blade appears on the right-hand side of the screen that will allow us to create the runbook by giving it a name, selecting its type, and giving it a description:

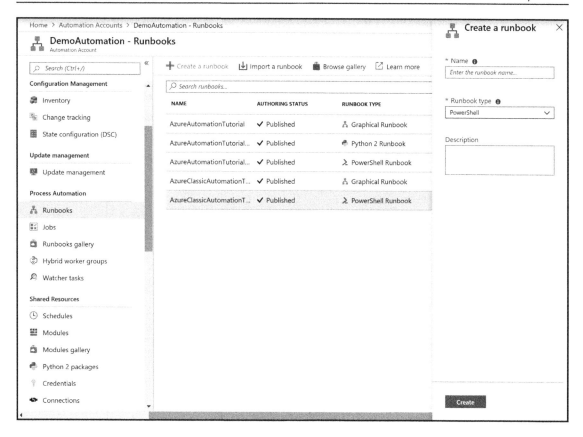

Figure 14.9: List of runbooks

2. Once the runbook has finished provisioning, we can add some lines of script to perform whatever functionality we desire by clicking on **Edit**. This will allow us to edit our script within the browser:

Figure 14.10: Basic PowerShell script in the online editor

3. Once we have written and tested the script, we need to ensure that it has been published by clicking on the **Publish** button at the top of the screen:

Figure 14.11: The Publish button in the runbook editor

Now that we have created our runbook, we can configure our PowerApp so that it calls and executes the script.

Using Azure Automation in PowerApps

Within PowerApps, we can make use of runbooks to either kick off tasks that we want to run in the background or to run a task and return a response. There are two key functions of the Azure Automation connector that we can use within our PowerApps:

- Create the job
- Get the output

To trigger this automation in Azure, we must create a job through the Azure Automation connector.

Calling CreateJob

Using the `CreateJob` function will take our inputs from PowerApps and add an automation job to the queue in Azure. This will mean that, after a few seconds, the runbook will execute the script and perform the actions that we have scripted.

Here, we need to provide some key parameters, all of which can be found on the runbook's overview screen:

- `subscriptionId`: This is the GUID that identifies the subscription we're going to create the job in.
- `resourceGroupName`: This is the string that identifies the resource group.
- `automationAccount`: A string that identifies the automation account (called **Account** on the screen).

- `runbookProperties`:
  - `runbookName`: The string that contains the title of our runbook
  - `wait`: A Boolean that tells the PowerApp whether to just initiate the automation or whether to suspend any further processing until it is complete
  - Any properties that are required by the script:

Figure 14.12: The automation job has been received and added to the local queue

So, if we put this into practice, we would need to create a formula similar to the following one, whereby we're providing the required information to queue a new automation job:

```
Set(varAutoJob,AzureAutomation.CreateJob(
  "45634c51-c503-48d7-96d1-1c47a2eed8aa",
  "DemoResourceGroup",
  "DemoAutomation",
  {
  runbookName: "Packt",
  wait: true
  }
)
)
```

The result is that the runbook will be queued in Azure and will execute the script. Here, I have wrapped everything within a variable so that we can track the information that's returned from the action since it includes important information such as the `jobId` that we need in order to retrieve the output.

Getting the job's output

Once the runbook has successfully completed the action, we can get the outputs from the script using the `GetJobOutput` function. This will take almost the same inputs that we provided when we initiated the job call:

- `subscriptionId`: This is a GUID that identifies the subscription we're going to create the job in
- `resourceGroupName`: This is the string that identifies the resource group
- `automationAccount`: A string that identifies the automation account (called **Account** on the screen)
- `jobId`: This is the job ID that was returned from the call when we created the job and can be accessed by calling `varAutoJob.properties.jobId` (in my example)

When we want to use the output of the automation job within our PowerApp, we would use the following formula and wrap it within a set variable function to allow the app to capture the output:

```
Set(
 varAutoJobOutput,
 AzureAutomation.GetJobOutput(
 "45634c51-c503-48d7-96d1-1c47a2eed8aa",
 "DemoResourceGroup",
 "DemoAutomation",
 varAutoJob.properties.jobId
 )
)
```

Now, we can use any outputs from a runbook, for example, the URL of a newly generated SharePoint site within our app.

An alternative method when it comes to extending our PowerApp using Azure is to use Azure Functions.

Using Azure Functions

Azure Functions are a way of creating small amounts of isolated code that run when a specific event is triggered. They differ from Azure Automation in the way that the amount of time a function should run for is less than 10 minutes, and if you require longer run times, then the code should be split across multiple functions.

Azure Functions do, however, allow you to be much more flexible in terms of your development approach since you can use all the common development languages that are available, including C#, Node.js, and PowerShell. You can also use a number of different **integrated development environments (IDEs)** to create Azure Functions, such as Visual Studio Code or VS Code.

There are a large number of events that can be used to trigger the function, with the common ones including calls to a webhook or creating an item within an Azure queue. Both of these triggers could be used from within PowerApps, although the webhook trigger would need Flow to act as the broker between the app and the Azure Function as it relies on making an HTTP call and providing header and body content in order to start the execution. This means that we can explore alternative methods of triggering Azure Functions, such as by using a queue. We will cover this in the next section.

Using a queue

As an alternative to using webhooks, a more PowerApps-friendly way of triggering an Azure Function is using the Azure queue connector since this simply relies on passing a body of JSON containing the required data to the queue. Azure queues effectively act as storage accounts for messages so that they can be created and then processed by a number of other Azure resources. In this scenario, they are being picked up and processed by functions.

To create a queue, you simply need to create a storage account through the Azure portal and then complete the form to generate a new account. Like we've done previously, you'll need to provide a subscription and resource group that you want the storage account to be created within:

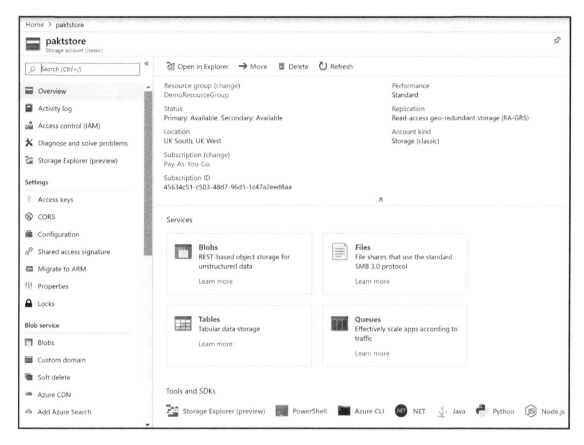

Figure 14.13: Azure storage account configuration screen

Once your storage account has been created, you'll need to create a new queue to receive your PowerApps requests. This is achieved by selecting **Queues** from the storage account and selecting **Add new**:

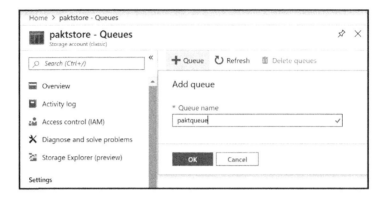

Figure 14.14: Creating a new queue

Now that we have a queue, we can use the Azure queues connector from PowerApps to be able to create a message and place that into the relevant queue for an Azure Function to pick it up and process. This requires using the `AzureQueues.PutMessage` function. For this, we simply need the name of the Azure queue and the message that we want to place in the queue:

```
AzureQueues.PutMessage("packtqueue","My Info")
```

This will place the value **My Info** into the queue, which can then be picked up and processed by the Azure Function. This is shown in the following screenshot:

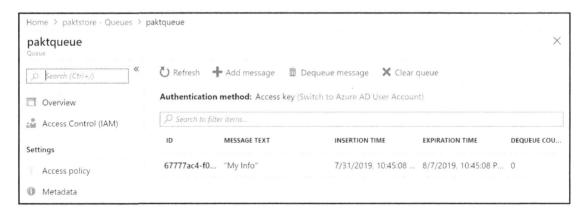

Figure 14.15: A message that has been placed into an Azure queue

Now that we have a queue, we need to create some logic to take the information from the queue and then process it. For that, we are going to create a function.

Creating an Azure Function

To create an Azure Function, we need to be logged in to the Azure portal (`portal.azure.com`). Once we're there, we can create a function by following some basic steps:

1. The first thing that we need to do is create a new Function App by navigating to **Create a resource** and then searching for "function". Officially, it is called a Function App since it is a serverless app that's hosted within the Microsoft cloud:

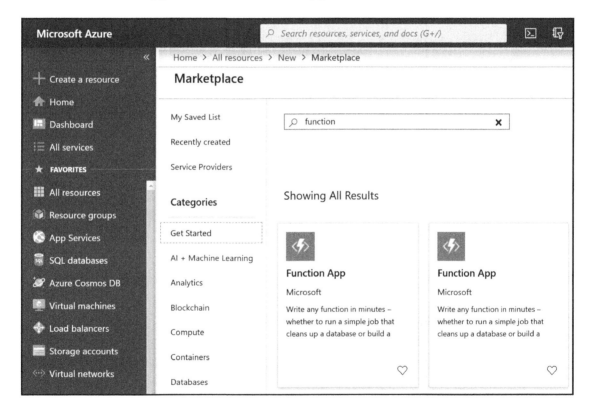

Figure 14.16: Search results when searching for a Function App

2. Once we are faced with the creation screen, we can click **Create** and fill in the required details for the creation of the Azure Function. These details include the following:

- **App name**: This is the name that is given to the web app that's created within Azure and is where the code resides.

- **Subscription**: The payment subscription that this Function App belongs to.

- **Resource Group**: This allows us to create and use a storage queue. We have the ability to either create a new storage account or use an existing storage account:

Figure 14.17: The function creation blade

3. Once the Function App has finished provisioning, we can start to configure it so that we can host our logic by clicking on **Go to resource**:

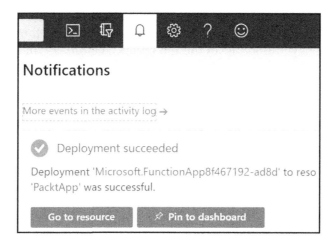

Figure 14.18: Successful deployment has confirmed

4. Once we get to the Function App screen, we are able to create functions by clicking the + next to functions. This will present us with some options that we can use to edit our function. Here, we have the ability to select our chosen editor, whether that's Visual Studio, VS Code, or the in-browser editor. For the following steps, I have selected to use the browser:

Figure 14.19: Function Apps options

5. Then, we have the ability to select how we would like the trigger to be scaffolded. For example, this could be based on a webhook or a trigger. Alternatively, you can click **More templates** to view more. Selecting this option will present you with a full range of templates that you can use to create your Function App. Here, we will be using the Azure Queue Storage trigger template. If you have never used one of these templates before, it will automatically install any dependencies for you:

Figure 14.20: Creating a function from the Azure Queue Storage trigger template

 By default, all Azure Functions are now created using version 2 of the Azure runtime, meaning that they will be created with .NET or JavaScript by default. If you wish to create one using PowerShell, please take a look at the following blog article: blog.mattweston365.com/2018/10/dude-wheres-my-powershell-azure-function.html.

Now that we have created the Function App, it will listen to the queue and look for any new items that have been placed on it. Now, we can write logic that can be placed in the queue, which would then be processed by our function.

Lab 13

In this lab, we will practice the skills that we discussed in this chapter by utilizing the AAD connector. We will replace our previous app security with an AAD security group, and then create an admin screen so that we can add and remove users as required. For this to be successful, your account will need write access to AAD within your tenancy.

We will begin by creating the security group.

Activity 1: Creating the security group

First of all, we will create a security group called `App Administrators`. Let's get started:

1. Navigate to the Azure portal (`portal.azure.com`):

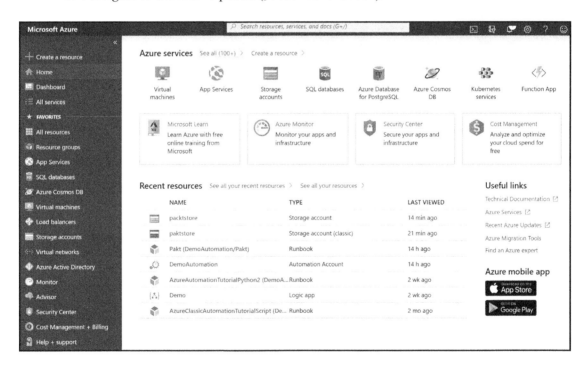

2. From the menu on the left-hand side, select **Azure Active Directory** to display the AAD overview:

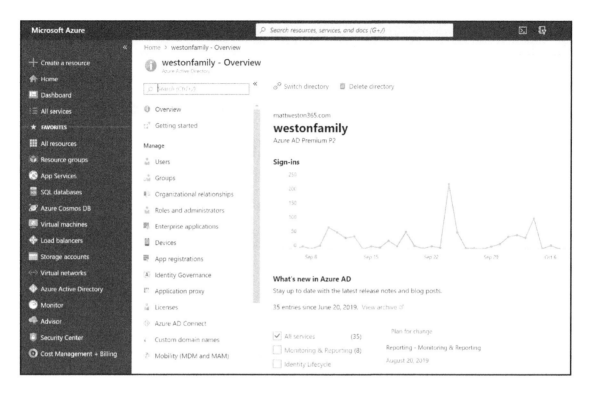

3. In the **Azure Active Directory** menu, select **Groups** and select **+ New group** to open the group creation screen:

4. Fill in the relevant information by naming the group **App Administrators** and ensuring that the group type is **Security**:

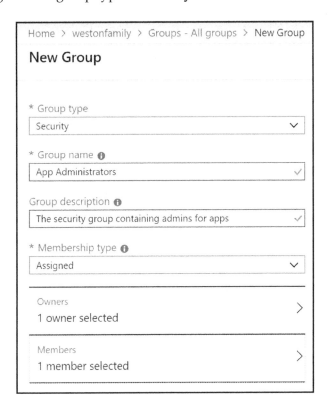

5. Ensure that you assign yourself to the **Owners** and **Members** for the group by clicking on the respective options on the screen and typing in your name.
6. Once created, click on the group and make a note of the object ID that is displayed. We will need this when we use PowerApps.

Now that we have prepared our security group in Active Directory, let's use it in our app.

Activity 2: Displaying the group users

Now, we will build upon the functionality within our Griffton IT Assets app by allowing the security group user to be edited from within our app. Let's get started:

1. Open the app that we have been building in edit mode.
2. Insert a new screen and rename it `Users`. This is where we will manage the membership of our group.
3. Copy and paste the header controls and the navigation controls from one of the previous screens. Change the screen name to `Admin Group Management`:

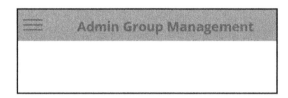

4. Click on the **View** menu and select **Data Sources**. Then, create a new connection to AAD:

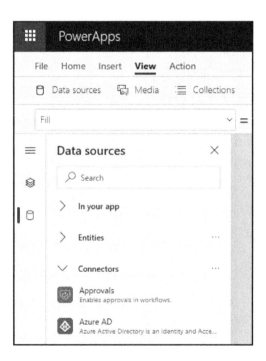

5. The AAD connection isn't a managed data source, so if we want to refresh the data, we need to have it within a collection. Therefore, we will populate a collection from AAD when the screen becomes visible. To do this, place the following formula into the **OnVisible** property (you will need the group ID from the preceding section at this point):

```
ClearCollect(colUsers,AzureAD.GetGroupMembers("<Your group ID
here>").value)
```

6. Once the collection has been created, place a **Blank vertical** gallery control on the page and name it `galSecurityUsers`. Select **Items** and enter the following formula to connect the gallery to the AAD members group:

```
colUsers
```

7. Set the following properties on the gallery. The width is based on a 15px margin to the left and right of the screen, as well as to the right of the gallery:
   - **X**: `15`
   - **Y**: `120`
   - **Width**: `(App.Width - 45) / 2`
   - **Height**: `625`

8. Place a label within the gallery and set the **Text** property to the following in order to display the user's name: `ThisItem.displayName`.

9. Repeat *step 7* for the mail property.

10. Lay out your gallery as you desire:

Now that we have added a way of displaying users within the security group, we need to add a way of adding or removing users within the group.

Activity 3: Adding add and remove functionality

Now, we will use the formulas provided by the Azure AD connector to add and remove users to and from this group. Since this isn't a data source that lends itself to form control, we will need to build our own form to select and add a user. Let's get started:

1. Place a rectangle icon onto the screen and name it `rectAddFormBG`.
2. Set the following properties for the rectangle:
   - **X**: `galSecurityUsers.X + galSecurityUsers.Width + 30`
   - **Y**: `galSecurityUsers.Y`
   - **Width**: `galSecurityUsers_Users.Width-15`
   - **Height**: `glaSecurityUsers.X / 2`
   - **Fill**: `ColorFade(LookUp(colColors,Name="Primary").Color, 0.7)`

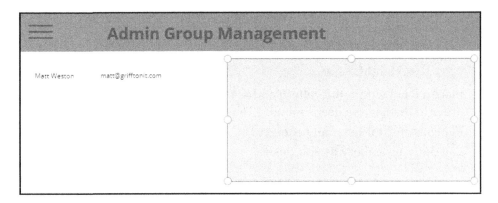

3. Insert a label called `lblNewUser`, a combo box called `cmbNewUser`, and a button called `btnAddUser` onto the screen and position them inside the rectangle that we created in the previous step.
4. Change the text of the label to `Add New User` and apply any styling you want to your label:

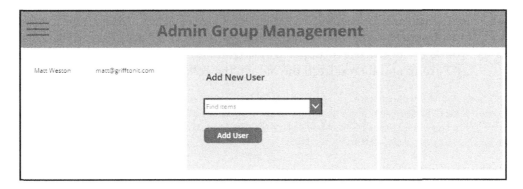

5. Click on the **View** menu, select **Data Sources**, and create a connection to Office 365 users. This will give us the ability to feed a list of users to our combo box. First, we need to enable it to allow searching by toggling the relevant field in the **Properties** pane:

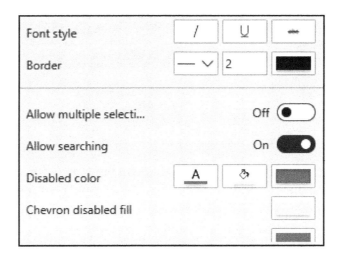

6. Now, we will connect the combo box to the Office 365 users connector and use it to search, filter, and select users in Office 365. Set the following properties for the combo box:
   1. **Items**: `Office365Users.SearchUser({searchTerm: cmbNewUser.SearchText}).DisplayName`
   2. **SearchFields**: `["DisplayName"]`

7. Now we will add a formula to the button to take the user that has been selected from our combo box control and add them to the AAD group. Add the following formula to the **OnSelect** property of `btnAddUser`, which will add the user to the AAD group and then refresh the data in the collection:

```
AzureAD.AddUserToGroup("aae98899-36f3-4fdb-9032-
c2f9865a684d",cmbNewUser.Selected.Id);
ClearCollect(colUsers,AzureAD.GetGroupMembers("aae98899-36f3-4fdb-9
032-c2f9865a684d").value)
```

This can be seen in the following screenshot:

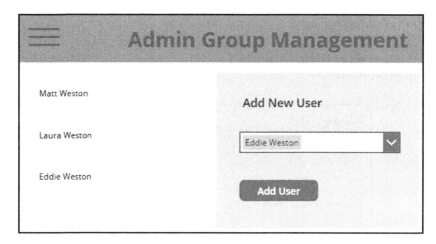

Now, we have added functionality to our app that will integrate with Azure resources – specifically AAD – and interact with those services. Now, save your app and test that it's working.

Summary

In this chapter, we have looked at some of the elements that currently exist within Microsoft Azure that provide a lot of benefits to the creators of PowerApps. There are a number of connectors that exist within PowerApps, some standard and some premium, that allow us to exploit various areas of Azure.

The first area that we looked at was AAD, where we can interact with and manage user objects within the user profile manager. This is quite useful when we want to create interactions with users objects, such as the ability to add or remove users from a security group within a PowerApp, which is extremely useful when combined with security.

The biggest area of exploration was Azure Automation, which allows us to execute and get responses from PowerShell scripts directly from our PowerApp. This type of Azure interaction is extremely popular within PowerApps development as it doesn't require huge amounts of development experience – it just requires that we have the skills to develop scripts, which can be learned quite quickly. These scripts are often used to perform actions that neither PowerApps nor Flow can achieve on its own, such as the creation of SharePoint sites or Teams.

The third area that we explored was Azure Functions, which allow developers to create functionality using a larger range of programming languages, including C# and Node.js. Azure Functions contain small amounts of functionality that typically takes less than 10 minutes to execute. In particular, we focused on the use of the connectors that are available through PowerApps by looking at how we can push a message to a queue in Azure, which is then processed by the Azure Function.

Regardless of which way we choose to extend our apps, through automation or Azure Functions, we have the ability to reach out to other services so that we can start taking our PowerApps to the next level.

In the next chapter, we will be looking at another type of PowerApp: model-driven apps.

Questions

1. What two Azure services that were mentioned in this chapter can we use to host custom code?
2. What URL do we use to access Microsoft Azure?
3. What native connector is available to PowerApps that allows us to interact with Azure Functions?
4. Which service provides us with an amount of free processing time so that we can run scripts?
5. If we want to write functionality using Node.js, what service would we use?

Further reading

Refer to *Hands-On Azure for Developers*, by Kamil Mrzygłód: `https://www.packtpub.com/gb/virtualization-and-cloud/hands-azure-developers` for further knowledge on Azure.

Section 4: Working with Model-Driven Apps

4

In this section, we are going to change our development approach to apps and switch from canvas apps to model-driven apps. We will now be focusing much more on the versatile data source known as the **Common Data Service (CDS)** and how that can be used to develop apps that are dedicated to a data structure.

In the first chapter of this section, we will look at the CDS in order to understand what it is, how it can be used, and ultimately how it drives this different type of app.

The second chapter will then build on the CDS and walk through the common building blocks related to model-driven apps.

This section has the following chapters:

Introducing Model-Driven Apps

15

Within the previous chapters of this book, we have used several data sources that are external to the Power Platform. We are now going to explore **Common Data Service (CDS)** (`https://docs.microsoft.com/en-us/powerapps/maker/common-data-service/data-platform-intro`), a data source that underpins PowerApps and Power Automate and provides a robust, yet simple, method for storing data in a way that feels very similar to creating tables within a database.

We have also focused primarily on canvas apps as we've progressed through this book; however, now, we will start to introduce model-driven apps, which have a much different look, feel, and editing experience to what we have so far been used to. The emphasis switches from the design aspect to the data, meaning that much more work takes place around the data structures before the actual app build begins.

Within this chapter, we will cover the following topics:

- Understanding CDS
- Understanding the **Common Data Model (CDM)**
- Modeling data
- Understanding and building a basic model-driven app

In this chapter, we will look at why to use the CDS and how it is structured. We will then start to create our own entities within the CDS to prepare for the creation of an app. We will also learn the basics of a model-driven app and how it is different from a canvas app.

By the end of this chapter, you will have an understanding of the CDS, what it is used for, and how you can start to use it to architect your model-driven apps.

Technical requirements

This chapter is working with premium components of the Power Platform; therefore, you will either need to be working in a community plan or have a PowerApps Plan 1 license assigned to you.

Understanding the CDS

The CDS is a data source that is available to the Power Platform and that allows you to store data in a structure that shares a lot of similarities to a database. The data is structured in entities that use fields to hold and structure the data very much like a database table that you expect to see in something as simple as a Microsoft Access database.

The CDS enables users to share data across several different applications within Office 365 including PowerApps, Microsoft Power Automate, and Power BI. Unlike other data sources, to use the CDS, we do not need to provide specific connection information as the underlying database is automatically connected to the environment where the app exists.

The CDS allows you to build relationships between entities. Most developers within Office 365 would default to using lookup columns between SharePoint lists, whereas the CDS allows us to define and manage relationships between the different entities in the same way as we would define relationships in databases. This may seem quite daunting, but one of the key features of the CDS is that it can be built through the web portal rather than having to rely on another application.

It should be noted that, to use the CDS, we need to have access to the full capabilities of PowerApps to allow us to create the database for the environment. This means that we need to have either a per app or a per user license assigned.

Creating the CDS database

Databases are associated with an environment, which we will investigate more in `Chapter 17`, *Exploring Environments within Our Tenancy*, and we are limited to creating one database per environment. I can either create the database from within the PowerApps portal or through the PowerApps **Admin center**. In the following example, we are going to do this through the PowerApps portal:

1. As a user, the easiest way to achieve this is to navigate to `make.powerapps.com` and then select **Entities** from the **Data** menu. This will then present you with a screen allowing you to create a database:

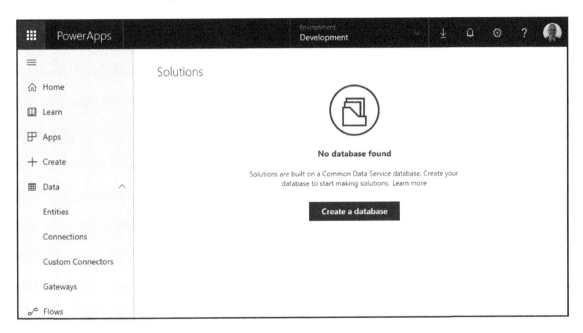

Figure 15.1: Create a database screen

2. As a part of the database creation process, you will be asked to set some local details, in particular, the language and the currency. You must select the correct currency and language at this point. Once the database has been created, you will no longer be able to change it. In this example, I've set my currency to **GBP** and the language as **English**. Also, make sure to check the **Include sample apps and data** checkbox, as shown in *Figure 15.2: New database blade* (these apps can be deleted later):

Figure 15.2: New database blade

The key thing to also be aware of is the warning that is shown in the gray warning box. This states that, by agreeing to use the database, you are allowing Microsoft to collect data on the entities to improve the CDM. It does point out, however, that Microsoft is only collecting information on the models that you create, not the actual data within the entities themselves. Microsoft has a strict policy on accessing content throughout their cloud services—only accessing it with explicit permission from the tenant owners. This also applies to the content within your databases.

3. Once you click **Create my database**, the database will then begin to build, including sample apps if you selected that option during creating. After a few minutes, you will be presented with the **Solutions** gallery, as shown in the following screenshot:

Figure 15.3: Example model-driven apps that are created with the database

Once the database has been created, we can then start to look at how we can create our data models ready for use within apps. To achieve this, we must first of all understand the CDM, and how we can apply that to our apps.

Understanding the CDM

The CDM is a standard collection of commonly used data collections and activities across the Microsoft business and productivity applications. We can compare them to common database schemas such as users, addresses, and more. The CDM, just like a database, is made up of several key elements such as entities, attributes, and relationships. Relationships are particularly important for reducing the amount of data duplication and being able to reference data from one entity to another.

Entities, as we mentioned earlier, are ways of classifying data and providing metadata about that data, essentially building up the model that our data will follow. To do this, we need to access the PowerApps portal and select **Entities** again from the **Data** menu on the left side of the screen.

First, let's start by introducing entities.

Introducing entities

When you first access the **Entities** screen, you will notice that the database has already been populated with several examples. These examples, as illustrated in *Figure 15.4: Entities created as part of the CDM*, are based on the common entities that have been created throughout the CDS and have been identified by Microsoft as a common pattern:

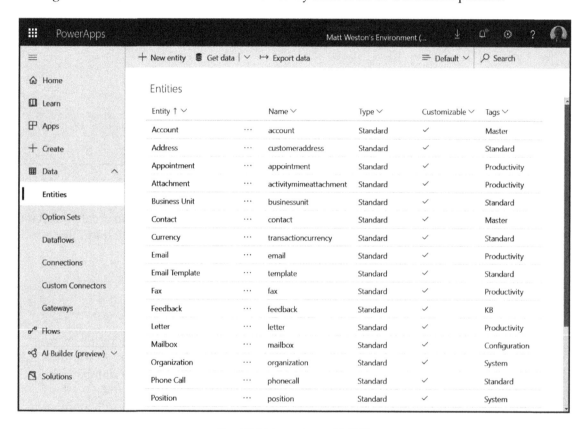

Figure 15.4: Entities created as part of the CDM

 To create entities, users need to have the relevant permissions assigned to them. A full description of those roles can be found at `https://docs.microsoft.com/en-us/power-platform/admin/database-security`.

The list of entities can be quite difficult to browse, especially when you start building your own entities within the list; therefore, you should be aware of two pieces of functionality that have been included to assist you:

- The first is **Search**, which appears in the top-right corner of the screen. This will allow you to search throughout the list of templates for a specific keyword. This keyword can appear in any of the columns that are being displayed.

> Consider using this as a way to filter the list as there are no native filters to use on this screen.

- The second is the view selector, which by default is **All**, but this allows us to select several different views for us to find our entities more easily. As an example, we can change the view from **List** to **Group** so that we can view each of the entities by type:

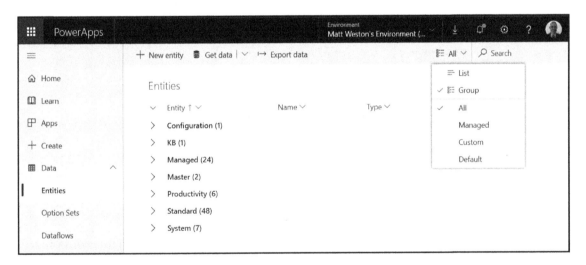

Figure 15.5: Entities being displayed in groups based on the tag

I can click into one of the entities and explore the structure further.

Exploring an entity

When we navigate into an entity, we start to unlock all of the functionality that surrounds it so that we are not just looking at the fields, but we are looking at the relationships, views, forms, and other key operational areas that will help us to build our model-driven app. An entity helps to pull together all of the key components of the data model, which then feeds into the model-driven app creation process, which we will see more of in `Chapter 16`, *Creating Model-Driven Apps*.

To look at the workings of an entity, we can look at something that we can all relate to—a **User** entity as it contains the usual fields that you would expect to find about a person:

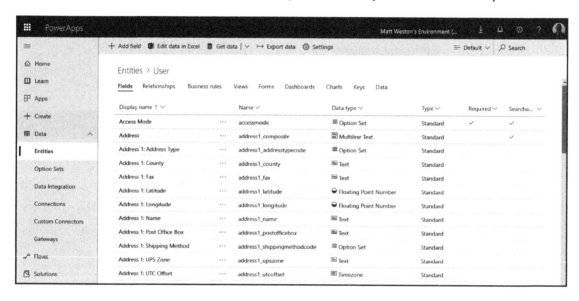

Figure 15.6: The structure of an entity when we navigate to User

Once we have navigated into the entity, you will notice that the screen contains a lot of information. First of all, it contains several navigation links that allow us to investigate the key areas of the entity, as shown in *Figure 15.7: The Entity navigation links that help to move in and out of the screens*:

Figure 15.7: The Entity navigation links that help to move in and out of the screens

Over the next few pages, we will look at each of the following areas:

- **Fields**: **Fields** are the individual pieces of data for each record. For example, for each user, with associated data types, and whether they are required or searchable.

 The full list of data types available in the CDS can be found at `https://docs.microsoft.com/en-us/powerapps/maker/common-data-service/types-of-fields`.

- **Relationships**: **Relationships** allow you to link entities together, in the same way as you can relate tables within SQL databases, and help you to enforce referential integrity. You can apply the same relationship rules as with databases, for example, many-to-one, one-to-many, and many-to-many.
- **Business rules**: **Business rules** allow you to apply logic and validation to the field without having to write code, through a browser-based editor.
- **Views**: **Views** allow you to create predefined filters on the records within the entity, which makes the queries more efficient when we use the CDS as a data source within model-driven PowerApps.
- **Forms:** In the same way in which we can create views of the data for model-driven apps, we can also define forms for inputting or editing the data. There will always be a main form associated with the entity; however, we can define additional forms with different formats such as a form formatted as a data card.
- **Dashboards**: **Dashboards** allow you to create preconfigured graphical representations of the data using multiple controls.
- **Charts**: In a similar way that dashboards allow you to use multiple graphical representations of your data, this is a single chart that can then be used within a dashboard.
- **Data**: This link allows you to view the contents of your entity, that is, look at the data stored within it. The views that you have defined are usable from the top-right corner of the screen, allowing you to change the data and the columns being displayed according to your rules.

 You can create any additional **Fields**, **Forms**, **Dashboards**, and more by clicking on **+** at the top of the screen.

All of the areas that we have just described at a high level combine to build our data model. We should now look at exactly how we do that by modeling our data.

Modeling data

The modeling of our data is the first aspect of creating a model-driven app. It is imperative that your data structures and relationships are all defined as much as possible. There are many out-of-the-box entities that we can use within our apps; however, they become more useful when we start to create our own, as every organization is different. Modeling data in this scenario really means deciding what the high-level data types are, and then identifying the data that we need to know about the type. This method of thinking can then be applied to the creation process.

To walk through the creation process, we will take books as an example. A book has a title, author, editor, published date, and ISBN.

Creating an entity

The first thing we need to create when modeling our data is an entity. This is so that we can build the definition of our data and create the rules and artifacts that relate to it. To create a new entity, we need to navigate to our **Entities** list and then click **+ New Entity** at the top of the screen:

Figure 15.8: Create a New entity button

Clicking on this button reveals the **New Entity** blade on the right-hand side of the screen. We need to have a few details ready:

- **Display name**: This is the singular name of the item we are creating the model for, so, in our example, this will be Book.
- **Plural display name**: This is the collective name for more than one of your entity, and notice that it has been populated automatically with the **Display name** with an *s* appended to it. Feel free to change this if it is not correct grammatically (for example, if your **Display name** is Goose, then your plural name would be Geese).

- **Name**: This becomes the internal name for the entity; it will have a unique prefix, followed by the **Display name**. This field is used when we refer to the field programmatically.
- **Primary Field**: This is the main identifier for your record and will be shown to users when they need to select a record from the list. Ideally, this should be unique, so, in our example, I will enter ISBN.

There are also several additional settings that you can explore, such as setting a description, setting the entity type, and updating settings (such as duplicate detection). Once you have finished with your configuration, click **Create**:

Figure 15.9: New entity blade

 If you wish to use a custom prefix within your entities, they should be created from the **Solutions** screen, on the left-hand menu; otherwise, they will be created with the default prefix: https://powerusers.microsoft.com/t5/Common-Data-Service-for-Apps/Define-Prefix-on-Entity/td-p/313733.

When your entity has first been created, it will show you a screen that contains the field that you defined in the creation blade. If you change the filter in the top bar from **Default** to **All**, you will notice that there are a large number of fields that have automatically been created for you, for example, a unique identifier called **Book**, creation, and modified fields, and more:

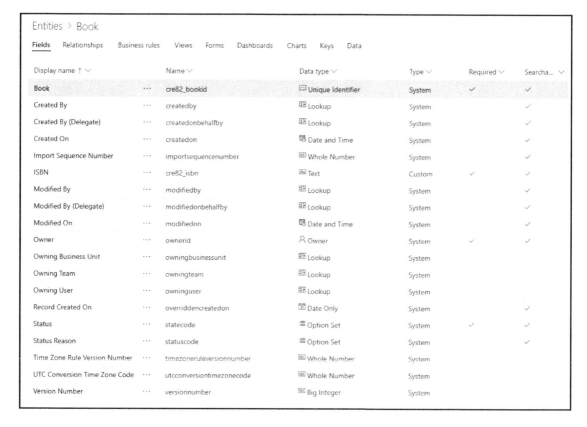

Figure 15.10: Entities list showing our new entity called Book

We have created an entity; we now need to create additional fields.

Creating Fields

While we are on the **Fields** link within our entity, we can add additional fields by clicking **+ Add field** in the toolbar at the top of the screen, as shown in *Figure 15.11: The Add field button located on the entity screen*. Once again, this will open a blade on the right-hand side of the screen, this time called **Field properties**:

Figure 15.11: The Add field button located on the entity screen

Once the blade has appeared, we again fill in the fields that are presented to us. The **Display name** is the friendly name, which is presented to the user, while the **Name** field is the internal name.

The **Name** of your field must be unique across your environment, and it cannot be changed once created.

As a part of the field creation, I can set the **Data type** that controls how they are stored within the database and how they are formatted when the data is being output by our apps. The data types contained within this list are the common types of data that you use across all applications, including the ability to create lookup columns that can reference other entities to provide selectable data:

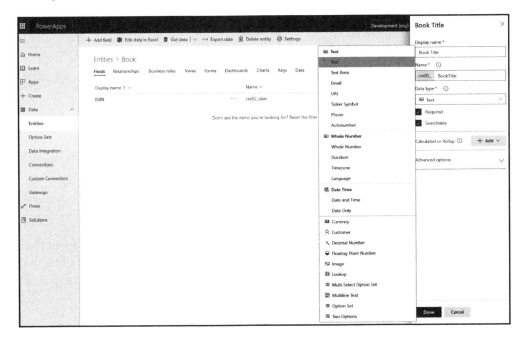

Figure 15.12: Field creation blade being completed

Ensure that you are aware of the length of the data that is going to be entered into each field as there are limitations on some fields (for example, a **Text** field can store up to 4,000 characters).

We can follow this exact same process for `Book Title` and `Published Date`, adding them as fields to the entity. Remember that you need to save your changes to the entity before trying to use the fields as they are not automatically committed to the CDS.

For `Author`, we will get that information from the `User` entity (which we explored earlier in the *Exploring an entity* section) to create a relationship.

Creating entity relationships

A relationship is a way of connecting two entities together, just like relationships work within databases. As we start to build our data model, we can use relationships to ensure that our data is normalized, that is, it is only stored once and then referenced by other entities. A key principle of good information management is *one version of the truth*, using relationships allows you to enforce.

To create the relationship, we should first click the **Relationships** link in the navigation bar and then select **+ Add relationship**:

Figure 15.13: The Add relationship button

When we first select the relationship, we should consider how the two entities are related.

The types of relationships are as follows:

- **One-to-many/many-to-one**: This type of relationship creates a join from the record of one entity to many records in another. For example, `Users` (`Authors`) may write many `Books`; therefore, the relationship will be one-to-many from `Users` to `Books`.

- **Many-to-many**: This type of relationship creates a join where many records in one entity can be related to many records in another. This relationship behaves slightly differently, as it does not result in a lookup field being created, instead, a hidden link table is created and maintained by the CDS.

In this example, we will assume that a single author writes a book. Therefore, we are going to create a relationship from the `Book` entity to `User` (`Author`), where many books could have a single author and an author could have many books. Since we are creating a relationship from books to users, we would select the *many-to-one* relationship. This means that many books could have a single author. If we were creating a relationship from `User` to `Book`, we would be using *one-to-many*.

When the blade appears, we first of all need to specify which entity we are creating a relationship for; in this case, we are linking to `User`. Notice that the **Primary** box automatically generates a display name and field name for our related field, which would default to `User` in this case. However, we want this to be called `Author`, so I can go ahead and rename the **Display name** to `Author`:

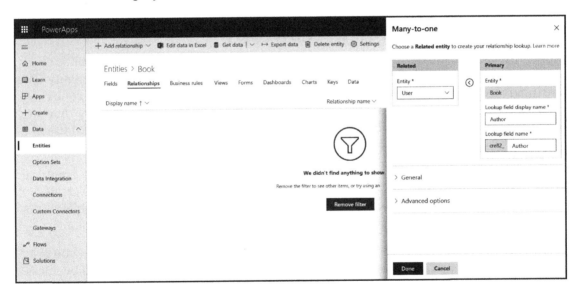

Figure 15.14: Create entity blade

The other key aspect of the relationship that you should consider is the type of behavior that can be found under the **Advanced options**. This will define what will happen if something happens to a record in the related entity. For example, you could set the behavior to **Referential, Restrict Delete**, which means that the parent record cannot be deleted while a child record exists (that is, an author cannot be deleted if a book exists). There are various versions of this type of behavior, or you can select **Custom**, which then allows you to define exactly what happens in each scenario such as deletions, assignments, sharing, and more.

 Always consider the *what-if* scenario; for example, what would I do if someone deletes a parent record, as this will have an impact on the data stored within your entity?

So far, we have looked at how to create entities and model our data; however, we also can build model-driven apps that are based on the CDS.

Building a model-driven app

Model-driven apps are created through the PowerApps portal and share some similarities with canvas apps, such as not being required to write code to create your functionality. The key difference, however, is that while canvas apps allow you to have almost full control over the look, feel, and layout of your screens, model-driven apps are much more rigid in terms of the layout and is mostly determined by the components that you place on the screen.

Model-driven apps are more commonly used in back-office apps, as they are less graphical and engaging than canvas apps. Both types of app, however, can be combined to create a good end-to-end solution. Canvas apps provide a richer user experience and mobile capability, whereas model-driven apps can be used for the management of the data.

The approach to building a model-driven app is also much more rigid than when you are creating a canvas app. The most important thing, to start with, is the modeling of business data within the CDS, and this is the reason that the first part of this chapter goes into detail about how to create entities, fields, and relationships.

The second element is to create business processes, which refers to creating logic and validation rules around the entities to ensure that you are getting the correct data and correct behaviors when data is entered.

Thirdly, we build the app by selecting the components that we want to display on the page. We will look at how we can build an app from scratch in the next chapter; however, there are templates that we can use to explore model-driven apps.

If we revisit the templates page in the PowerApps portal, there are several template apps available for us to create such as **Fundraiser** or innovation challenge. If we create one of these apps, we can immediately gain an appreciation for the different feel of the interface. Just like a canvas app, we also can click on play in the top-right corner of the screen to start using the app within the designer:

Figure 15.15: The design screen for a model-driven app

This will then render all of the components that you have put on the screen and will allow you to click through the different dashboards, as follows:

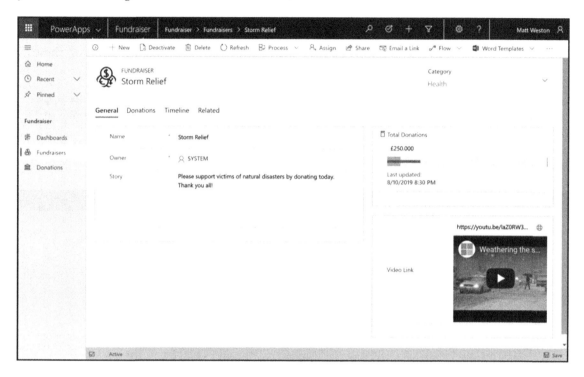

Figure 15.16: The model-driven app running within the browser

We have now explored the basic concepts of how we can create a model-driven app, and we will build on this within Chapter 16, *Creating Model-Driven Apps*.

Lab 14

Within this lab, we are going to create our database and create our basic entities so that we can build an app upon it in the next chapter. Within this lab, we are going to build an app that will allow us to store and assign cars to members of staff.

Let's start by creating the database first.

Activity 1: Creating the database

This is an optional step; if you already have a database within your environment, then you won't need to go through the creation steps:

1. Log in to the Office 365 portal by navigating to `portal.office.com`.
2. Click on the app launcher and select **PowerApps** (if it is not on the app launcher, then select **All apps**):

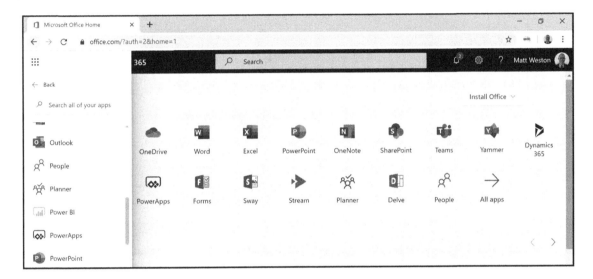

3. From the left-hand navigation, expand the **Data** menu and select **Entities**:

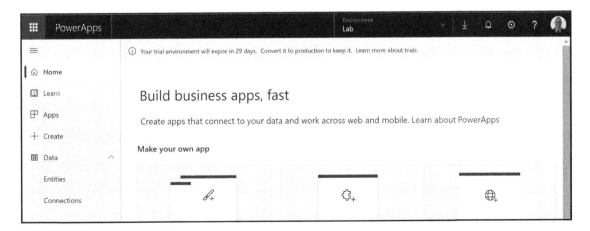

4. If the database has not been created, click the **Create a database** button in the center of the screen:

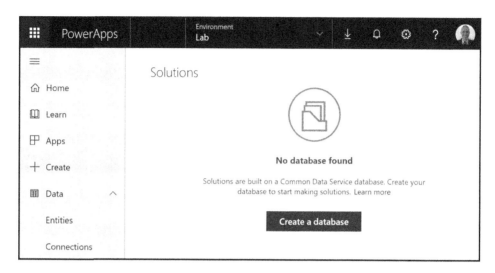

5. On the create database blade, select your **Currency** and **Language**. Leave **Include sample apps and data** checked, and then click **Create my database**:

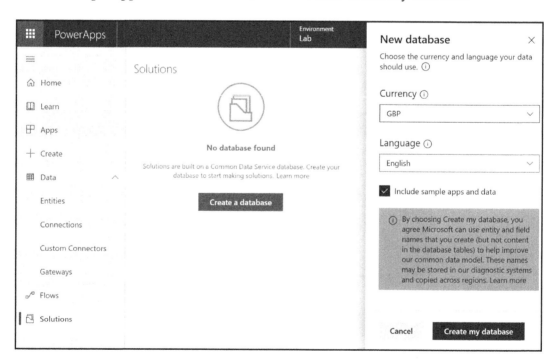

After a few seconds, your database will have been created and we are now ready to start modeling our data.

Activity 2: Modeling data

In this part of the lab, we are going to create the entities that we are going to use within our model-driven app. The structure will be as follows:

- Car Manufacturer:
    - Manufacturer
    - Date Established
    - History
- Car Model:
    - Model
    - Description
- Car Variant:
    - Variant Name
    - Engine Size
    - Transmission
    - Doors

Now, let's follow these steps to model our data:

1. Navigate to the PowerApps portal.
2. From the left navigation, select **Entities**:

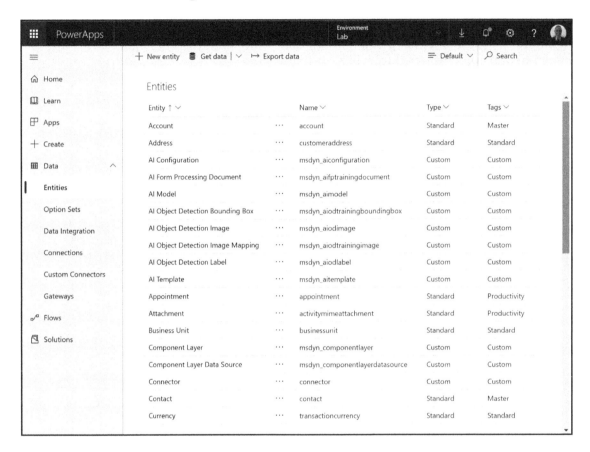

3. On the **Entities** screen, click **+ New entity**.
4. Create the Car Manufacturer entity with the following configuration:
   - **Display name**: Car Manufacturer
   - **Plural display name**: Car Manufacturers
   - **Name**: Leave as default
   - **Primary Field** - **Display name**: Manufacturer
   - **Primary Field** - **Name**: Leave as default
5. Click **Create**:

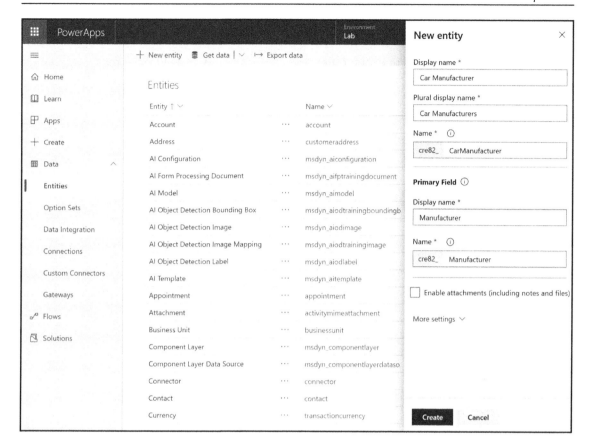

6. Once your entity has been provisioned, you will automatically be taken to your entity. Notice that the entity will display our **Manufacturer** field:

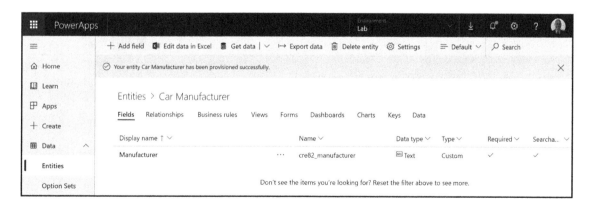

7. Now, add a new field by clicking on the **+ Add field** button at the top of the screen.

8. Create a new field with the following configuration and click **Done**:
    - **Display name**: Date Established
    - **Name**: Leave as default
    - **Data type**: **Date Only**
    - **Required**: Checked
    - **Behavior**: **Date only**:

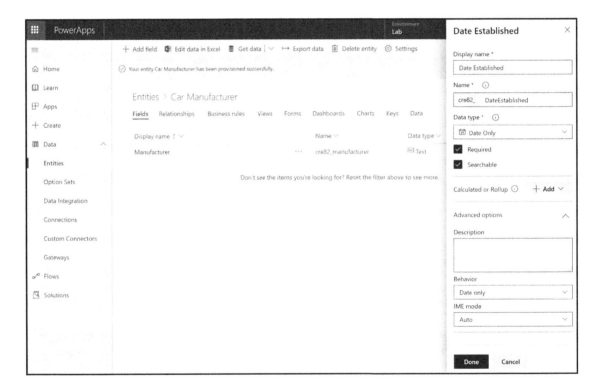

9. Create another field with the following configuration, as seen in the following screenshot:
    - **Display name**: History
    - **Name**: Leave as default
    - **Data type**: **Multiline Text**:

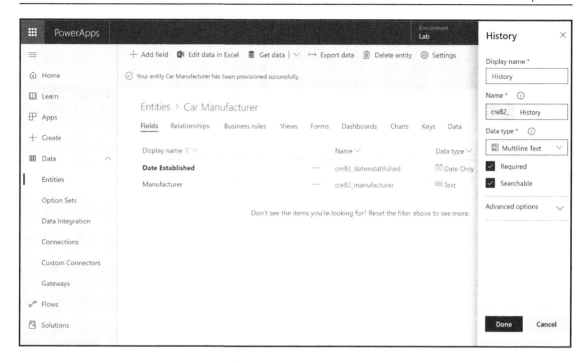

10. Now that we have created our fields, click **Done** in the bottom-right corner of the screen and you'll get the list of entities:

11. Navigate back to the **Entities** screen by clicking on **Entities** in the left navigation so that we can create a new entity called **Model**. Create this entity with the fields that were defined at the start of the lab:

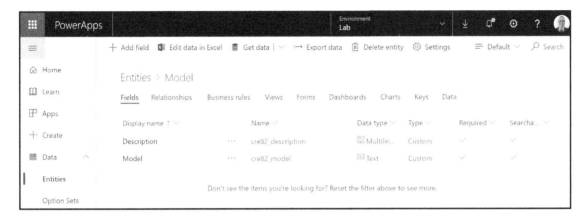

12. Within the **Model** entity, select the **Relationships** link:

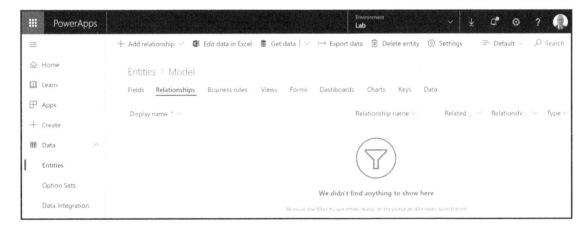

13. Select **+ Add relationship** from the top of the screen and select **Many-to-one**.
14. The **Primary** field will already be populated; however, you need to select **Car Manufacturer** from the drop-down list under **Related**:

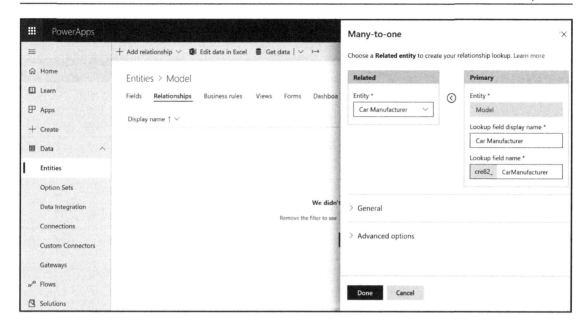

15. We now have a relationship established between **Car Manufacturer** and **Model**.
16. Repeat the process for the **Variant** entity:

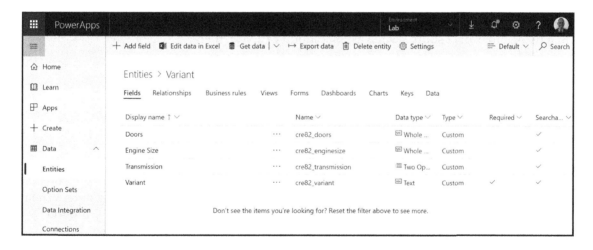

17. Create a many-to-one relationship from **Variant** to **Model**:

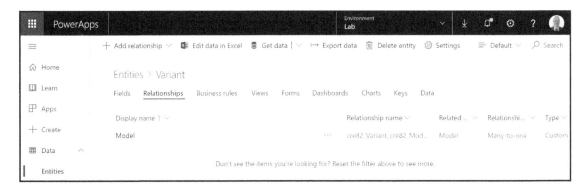

We have now modeled our data ready to create an app in the next chapter.

Summary

In this chapter, we introduced the CDS—a premium data storage element that underpins all aspects of the Power Platform. Being completely cloud-based and having the same feel as simple database solutions such as Microsoft Access, the CDS provides an excellent choice for storing data. If you are looking to structure your data in a more controlled way rather than using other data sources such as SharePoint or Excel, then the use of the CDS is the preferred way.

The databases generated by the CDS are directly linked to the environment and therefore has a limit of only one database per environment. Due to the integration within the environment, however, there are no requirements for database names or credentials to connect to the database.

We learned how data within the CDS is held within entities, which is the equivalent of a table within a database. Within those entities, we can define fields with a large range of data types available to us to ensure that we are storing and correctly presenting data. When we create fields, the name, which is the programmatic name, must be unique within the environment and cannot be changed once it has been committed to the database. The **Display name**, however, can be changed.

We also saw how fields are used to create relationships with other entities in the same way as with databases, defining relationships such as one-to-many or many-to-many. These relationships allow you to define behaviors, so that if an action such as a deletion occurs on one side of the relationship, then you can define what happens on the other. Entities also allow us to define other elements that become extremely useful within model-driven apps, such as logic and validations, forms, dashboards, and charts.

We can use the CDS within canvas apps, which we looked at earlier in this book; however, the database really lends itself more to model-driven apps, which allow us to create apps directly from the entities and rules that we define. There are several templates available to use that allow us to create apps based on the built-in entities, and in the next chapter, we will look at building our own app.

In the next chapter, we will be creating model-driven apps from data.

Questions

1. What types of apps can use the CDS as a data source?
2. What do we need to create before being able to use the CDS?
3. What are the primary data structures within the CDS called?
4. What types of relationships can be created between entities?
5. True or false: A model-driven app can be created with SharePoint as a data source?

Further reading

Common Data Service: `https://docs.microsoft.com/en-us/powerapps/maker/common-data-service/data-platform-intro`.

16
Creating Model-Driven Apps

In the previous chapter, we learned that model-driven apps are designed (to an extent) to share the same type of development principles as canvas apps whereby you can create apps that are simple or complex in nature without the need to write code.

This chapter will help you understand how and when to use model-driven apps. The whole approach to model-driven apps is different from that of canvas apps in that we need to define more of our functionality around the data, and define more of it upfront before we actually start to build. Therefore, we will need to be aware of what these building blocks are and how we can use them. Finally, when we have our foundations in place and the building blocks at the ready, we can start to combine them all together to create our app.

In this chapter, we will look at how we can create our second type of app—a model-driven app. Model-driven apps haven't been a part of the Power Platform as long as canvas apps; however, since they have arrived, there has been a growing sense of excitement about them within the PowerApps community.

In this chapter, we will look at the following topics:

- What is a model-driven app?
- Introducing the building blocks of model-driven apps
- Creating a model-driven app from scratch
- Using your model-driven app

The key thing to remember is that model-driven apps will always conform to your data, so it is extremely important to ensure that your data structures are correct and that you have all of the building blocks in place before you try to construct the app itself.

By the end of this chapter, you will have an understanding of what it means to create a model-driven app and the key differences in the development approach, as well as its implementation.

Technical requirements

This chapter is working with premium components of the Power Platform; therefore, you will either need to be working in a community plan or have a PowerApps Plan 1 license assigned to you.

Introducing Views, Forms, and Dashboards

In the previous chapter, we really focused on creating the data elements of our entities. Now, we will look at the other features that will start to feed into our model-driven app—**Views**, **Forms**, and **Dashboards**.

We should always keep in mind the differences in approach between creating a model-driven app and creating a canvas app. With model-driven apps, you ideally need to consider what your Views and other components are going to be before you really get into the build phase of your app. You can come back later to revisit these components; however, you will need to create at least one of each element to be able to add some functionality to your app.

In Chapter 15, *Introducing Model-Driven Apps*, when we talked about modeling data, we looked at the links that were available across the top of the entity. Now we will investigate some more of these links, as well as what they do.

First, let's start with Views.

Creating Views

As we discussed in `Chapter 15`, *Introducing Model-Driven Apps*, in the *Exploring an entity* section, Views allow us to create predefined column selections and filters on our data. Views should always be created for the common ways that the user queries the data—for example, if the users often look for data that has been created with a specific value.

To create a view, go through the following steps:

1. We simply need to select the **Views** link from the link bar and select **+ Add view**, which will then prompt you to give the View a name:

Figure 16.1: + Add view button

2. When the View creator screen opens, you will notice that it looks quite similar to the main PowerApps Studio that we used for our canvas apps. Because of a number of recent updates applied to the model-driven apps, the editing experience has now been changed from looking and feeling like Dynamics to being more in line with the rest of PowerApps. In *Figure 16.2: View creation screen*, you will see the View creator window, which is broken up into three distinct sections:
    *   **Fields**: These show the fields available to the entity.
    *   **View**: This shows the view as it will appear, displaying the columns that have been selected.

- **Properties**: The **Properties** pane appears on the far right of the window, with the title **New Accounts** in the following screenshot, and shows the configuration options for the View. This area gives you the option to add a **Name** and **Description** for the View, and allows you to configure how the data is sorted and filtered.

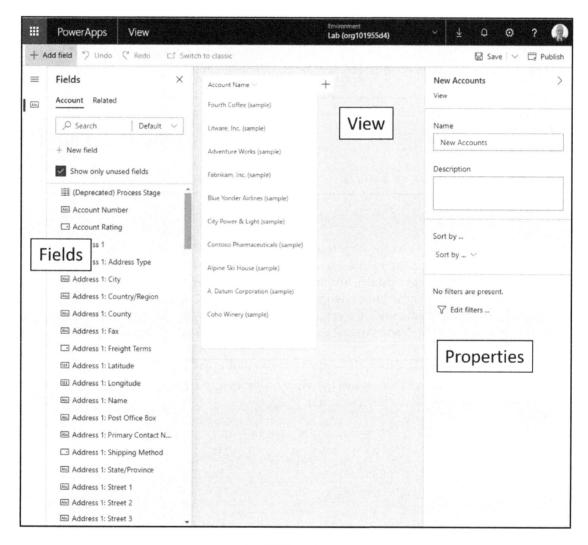

Figure 16.2: View creation screen

The left-hand column contains all of the fields that are available within your entity and allows you to drag and drop them into the center of the screen, which is where your View is being constructed.

4. To add a field, hover over it within the field list, click the ellipsis, and then click **+ Add to view**. You will then see the column in the central area:

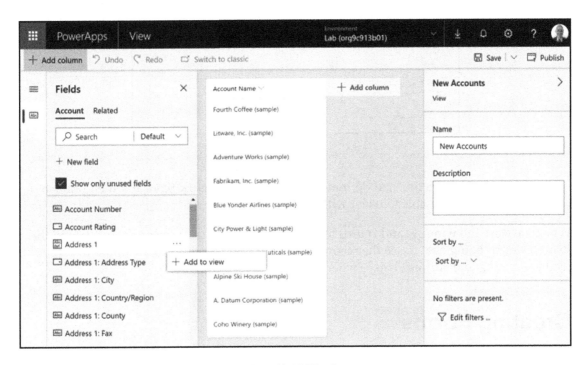

Figure 16.3: Add field to view

5. The final area is the **Properties** blade on the right-hand side, which is where we can define some rules around what data is being shown by applying filters to the columns. We can also specify the order in which the data is displayed by defining the **Sort by...** criteria. When you are defining your filters, you simply select your field and the criteria that you would like to apply—for example, records that have been created in the last 7 days:

Figure 16.4: Filter creation

6. Once we have finished defining our View, we can click **Save** and then publish it in order to be able to use it within our app.

When we close the window and return to our entity, we will then see our new View in the list. As well as being able to see the records, we need to be able to provide more detail, as well as creating and editing. This is where we start to look at Forms.

Creating Forms

Forms allow us to primarily add and edit data in our entities; however, they also provide us with more detail when clicking through from our Views. By selecting **+ Add form** at the top of the Forms screen, you will again be presented with a PowerApps-style editor that will allow us to create a Form.

Just like the View editor, the Forms editor uses the same interface as the PowerApps Studio, with the fields and components displayed on the left-hand side, the canvas in the center, and the properties available on the right. Before we start looking at the fields, we will first look at the **+ Add Component** option, which will allow us to select our layout as well as add some additional controls onto the page.

Your form will always have a layout applied to it; however, with the new editing interface, you can start modifying the overall layout by selecting a number of preset column configurations. The following screenshot shows all the options to select from to help you render your data in different ways:

Figure 16.5: Component selection list

On the right-hand side of your screen, you have the ability to change some of the basic properties related to the control, layout, or data field that you have placed on the screen, as shown in *Figure 16.6: Properties blade example*. Some of the potential options that you could see here are related to the responsiveness of the app when being viewed on a mobile phone—for example, you may wish to hide larger fields when viewing the app on a smaller screen. Let's have a look at the **Properties** blade example:

Figure 16.6: Properties blade example

Once you have added your fields into the layout that you wish to use for your form, you can publish your form by clicking the **Publish** button in the top-right corner of the form editor screen, as shown in *Figure 16.7: Save and Publish buttons on the form editor screen*. The form will then become visible within the Forms list of the entity:

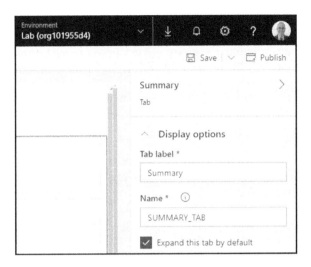

Figure 16.7: Save and Publish buttons on the form editor screen

The final element of the entity, which we can build before we start to build our model-driven app, are Dashboards.

Creating Dashboards and Charts

Dashboards allow you to create visual representations of the data stored within your entity so that you are not just looking at rows and rows of data. Consider the proverb: *A picture says a thousand words*. Depending on the audience of your app, you may wish to bring your data and charts together in order to build a more interactive interface for users. Before we can create our Dashboard, however, we need to create a Chart.

Creating charts

Charts have their own link on the entity navigation bar, and when selected, it will show you a list of any Charts that have already been created.

We can add our own Chart by clicking the **Add a new chart** button at the top of the screen. While a lot of the model-driven app development experience has now been converted to the PowerApps user experience, there are a few elements and areas that still look and feel very much like Dynamics. At the time of writing, Charts is one of them.

Even though the user experience is slightly older, the method of creating a Chart is somewhat simple, in that you really just need to supply it with some basic information and the designer will do the rest.

 You will need to tell the Chart creator screen which View of the data the Chart is going to use, so ensure that you have your Views configured before you try to build your Chart.

The best thing to do here is simply complete the form, and provide the View that is going to supply your Chart with the data, the name of the Chart, and the type of Chart you are going to use. This doesn't have the same depth of customization that you may be used to if you have used Power BI for creating Dashboards, but it will allow you to create some basic Chart types, such as bar charts and pie charts. The following screenshot shows the Chart editor screen:

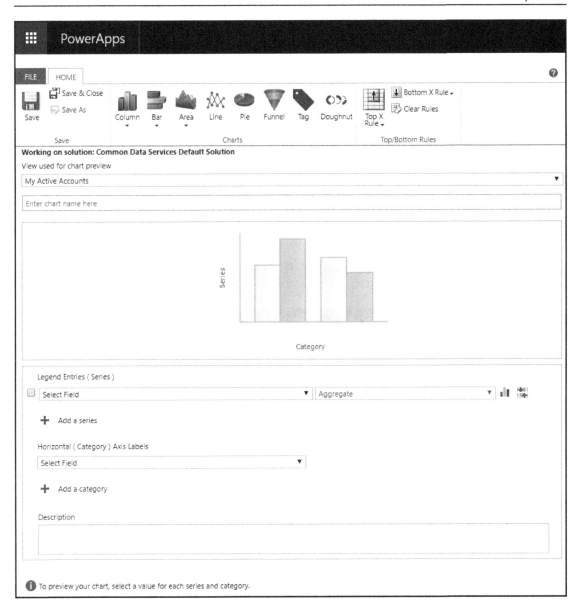

Figure 16.8: Chart editor screen

Once you have provided the form builder with enough information, it will render a preview of your Chart in the center of the screen. When you are happy with it, click **Save & Close** to close the editor.

Now that we have created a Chart, we need to include it within a dashboard.

Creating Dashboards

Similar to Charts, Dashboards still use the classic Dynamics experience when they are being built. They are accessed from the **Dashboards** link in the entity link bar and can be created by clicking **Add dashboard**. You have a number of options with Dashboards in terms of the layouts; however, these options are quite limited simply because of the number of columns that you can have displayed.

Once you have made your selection, you will be presented with the Dashboard editor, as shown in the following screenshot:

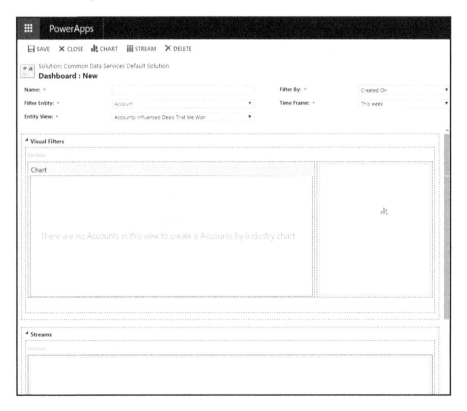

Figure 16.9: Dashboard editor screen

The editor for the Dashboard is, again, quite simple in that you just need to enter the details into the form and the editor will take care of the rest. When you select the charts you wish to display, you will be presented with a list of charts that have been created within this entity, so ensure that you have your charts in place before you try to edit your Dashboard. Once you have provided all of your data, you can then save it, close it, and return to the entity.

Now that we have all of our building blocks in place, we can go ahead and create a model-driven app.

Creating a model-driven app from scratch

The process of creating a model-driven app starts off in the same way as the process of creating a canvas app: we first navigate to the PowerApps portal. The option that we need is next to the canvas app on the app selection screen, and is titled model-driven app. When we create a new model-driven app, the editing experience starts to change immediately. There is no mention of whether we are developing it for a mobile or tablet compared to what we did previously. Instead, we now need to shift our mindset into creating just a single app that is responsive to both being viewed in browsers and on mobile devices.

We can create a model-driven app in the following way:

1. The initial creation of the model-driven app shares some similarities with the creation of canvas apps. Such similarities include being able to define what the name of the app is and the tile that represents it. The app will be given a unique name that, by default, will be derived from what you enter into the **Name** field. You can see the **Create a New App** window in the following screenshot:

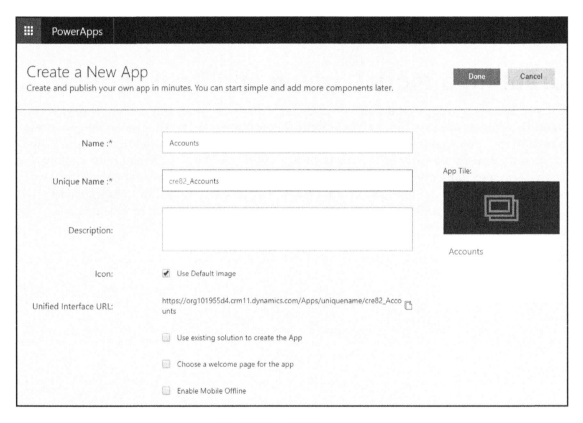

Figure 16.10: New model-driven app screen

2. Once we hit **Done** on the **Create a New App** screen, we are presented with the app designer, which again is fundamentally different from the canvas apps. The designer screen, rather than being graphical like canvas apps, is built by placing components on the screen. The components are located on the right-hand side of the screen. You can select the entities, Dashboards, and Forms that were created during the data-preparation stage.

As a reminder, the recommended process for creating your model-driven app is as follows:

1. Model your data
2. Define the business processes
3. Create the app

The following screenshot shows the first window after you open the app:

Figure 16.11: Model-driven app designer

As you can see in the preceding screenshot, the first time you open the app, you will see an error saying **Configuration Missing**.

3. If we click on the edit icon next to the Site Map, you will notice that we have an area that has already been created. This area has a group and subarea on the page. The site map is effectively building up our navigation within our model-driven app.

4. By selecting one of the components on the screen, the **Properties** blade on the right-hand side of the screen will display the configuration items that we are able to change. By clicking on the subarea, for example, we are able to change the component type by specifying whether it is a dashboard, entity, URL, and so on. We can also specify the entities that the component uses, which can be seen in *Figure 16.12: Sitemap designer*:

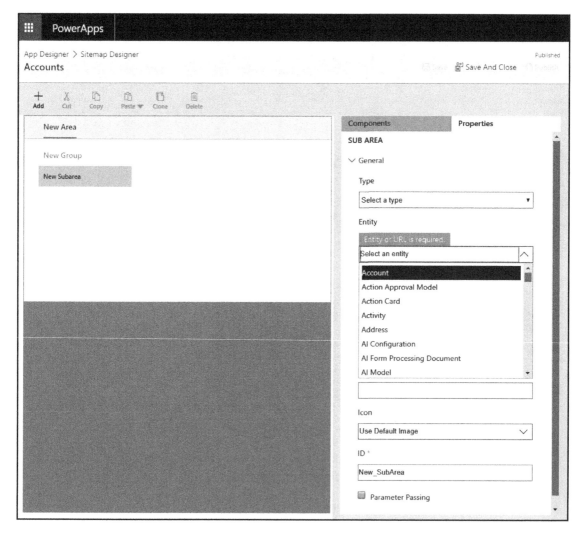

Figure 16.12: Sitemap designer

Once we have specified which entity the area is going to use for its data source, we can then return to the main app designer by clicking on **App Designer** in the breadcrumb to start configuring some of the basic screens that will appear within the app.

5. After returning to the app designer, the entity view will now display the entity selected from the site map, and break down into **Forms**, **Views**, **Charts**, and **Dashboards**. Each of these selections works in exactly the same way: you click on the drop-down and it will present you with a list of options on the right-hand side of the screen. These are all classified as entity assets, which can be seen in *Figure 16.13: Entity assets*:

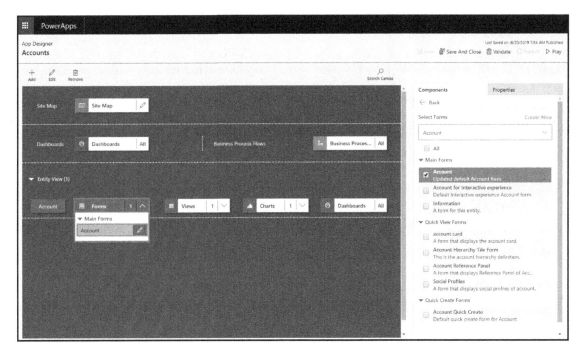

Figure 16.13: Entity assets

The **Forms**, **Views**, **Charts**, and **Dashboards** are all configured as a part of the entity. So again, this highlights that the data preparation and modeling needs to be completed before you actually start building the app.

6. Once we have selected the assets we want to include within the app, we can then save the app by clicking the **Save** button in the top-right corner of the screen. One other big difference you will notice at this point is that the **Play** button is not active: this only becomes active once you have published the app.

With our app created and ready, let's learn how to use it.

Using your model-driven app

First, we should publish the app, and then we can click **Play** to launch it. This will allow us to interact with the app within the browser in the same way that we can with canvas apps.

Once you have launched your app, you will be faced with your working model-driven app. This is where it becomes apparent to users that we are extremely limited in terms of what we can do with the look and feel of the app. This lack of design freedom really means that model-driven apps are better suited to back-office functions. As we have seen our app from the design perspective, we will now run the app so that we can see the user interface when it is actually being used:

1. The first thing I am going to do is click the **Run** button in the top-right corner of my model-driven app designer window so that I can preview the fully working app.

2. In *Figure 16.14: The preview of my app*, we can see that the fully rendered app is somewhat different from what we saw in the app designer. Each of the key areas that we have created, such as **Dashboards**, **Charts**, and **Forms**, are all available for us to start using:

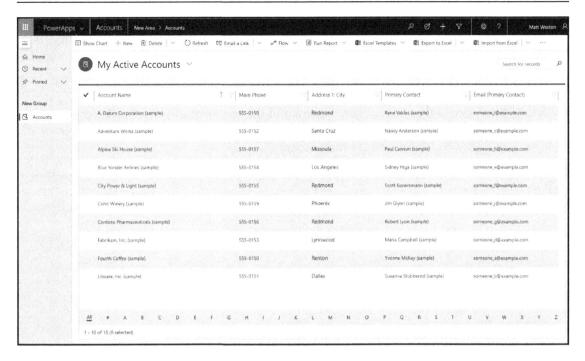

Figure 16.14: The preview of my app

3. When we create an area and a subarea, these will be displayed in the navigation area on the left-hand side of the screen. If we added multiple areas and subareas, then these would help us to build our left-hand navigation menu:

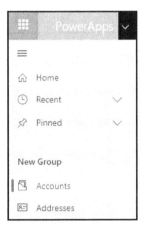

Figure 16.15: Subarea rendering within the app

4. When we click on one of the navigation items, we will then see the display in the center of the screen change, presenting the data that is contained within the entity.

5. After clicking on **Accounts**, we will then be presented with the data that is retrieved by the selected View.

6. The view of the data, which is shown in the center of the app, can be changed by using the drop-down arrow to the right of the view title, which can be seen in *Figure 16.16: Data view within the app*:

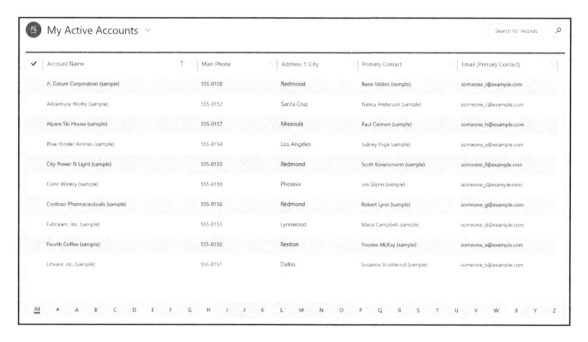

Figure 16.16: Data view within the app

Across the top of our screen, as shown in *Figure 16.17: App toolbar*, we have our data toolbar, which allows us to create new data, trigger Flows, or export to and import from Excel. This is always available at the top of our model-driven app; it is not something that we can control:

Figure 16.17: App toolbar

Using the **Show Chart** functionality will open up a new part of the page that will display a graphical representation of the data that is being displayed and then allow you to generate your own charts on the fly. The chart area behaves very much like you would expect it to if you have any experience with Power BI, where we can click on the chart to drill through to further data.

7. When we click on the chart, we will be asked for the field (for example, **drill down by**) and the type of chart. In our case, we could select **State** and then a column chart to see the geographic breakdown of the data. The resulting output can be seen in the following screenshot:

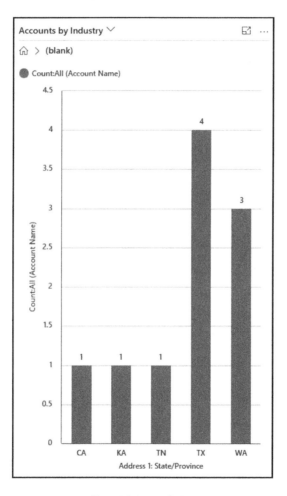

Figure 16.18: Example of a chart

8. As well as being able to see the overall list of data, which is stored within the entity, we can click on one of the records and then see the data on a form. Using the form, you can edit and interact with the data or create new data entries:

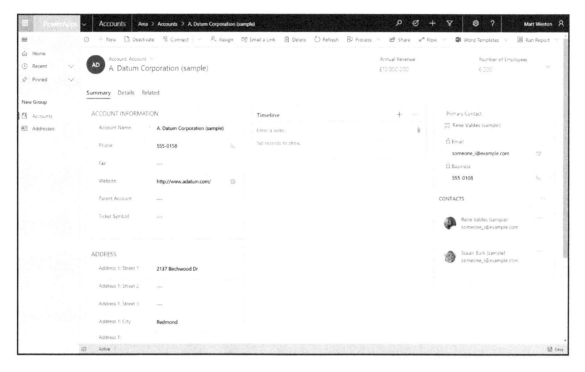

Figure 16.19: Rendering of a form within the app

Generally, the feel of model-driven apps is always quite similar, although there are some differences to the layouts that can be applied depending on the app requirements.

Lab 15

In this lab, we will build upon the entities that we created in `Chapter 15`, *Introducing Model-Driven Apps*, and use those entities to begin building a model-driven app. In this lab, we will create Views of the data and use those Views within a model-driven app. By creating the entity, PowerApps has already created a number of Forms for us to use.

Activity 1: Creating Views

In this section, we will practice creating Views on the data that we have stored within our entity:

1. Open the PowerApps portal by navigating to `make.powerapps.com`.
2. Expand **Data** on the left-hand menu.
3. Select **Entities** to bring up our entities list:

4. Select **Model** from the list of entities.
5. Select **Views** from the entity navigation and click **+ Add view**:

6. Name the View `Ford Cars` and click **Create**:

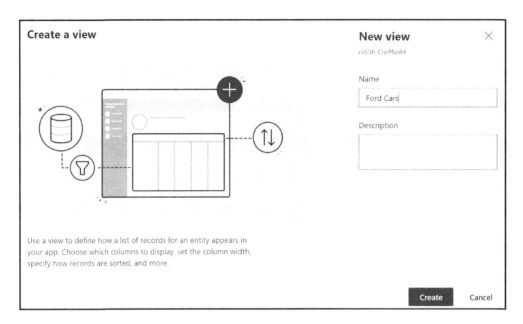

7. When the View editor appears, hover your mouse over the **Description** field, select the ellipsis, and click **+ Add to view**, which will then add the field to the area in the middle:

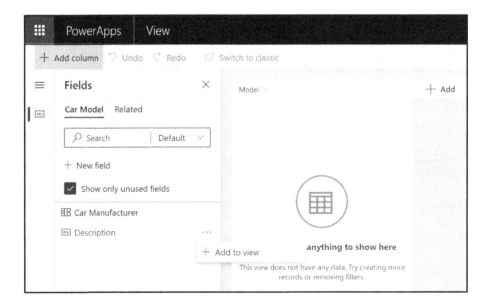

8. Select **Edit filters** on the right-hand side and click **+ Add** followed by **Add row** to create a new filter:

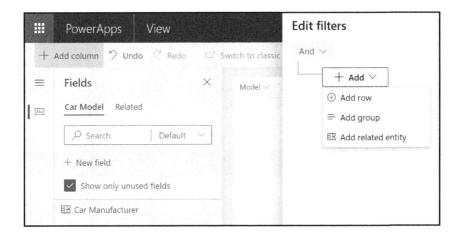

9. Configure the filter to select the cars where the manufacturer is equal to **Ford**:

10. Repeat *step 6* to *step 9* for the following:

- Tesla
- Skoda

We will now start to build our app.

Activity 2: Building the model-driven app

Having built our data model, we now need to start to build the app to allow us to surface the data and interact with it:

1. Navigate back to the PowerApps portal.
2. On the left-hand menu, click **+ Create** to return us to the app creation screen.
3. Select **model-driven app** from blank and then click **Create**.
4. Name your app `Cars` and click **Done**. The following screenshot shows the **Create a New App** window:

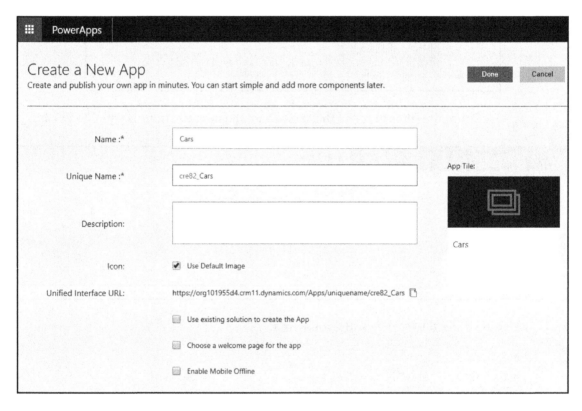

5. When the app designer loads, you will notice that the site map reports that the configuration is missing. Click on the edit icon next to **Site Map**:

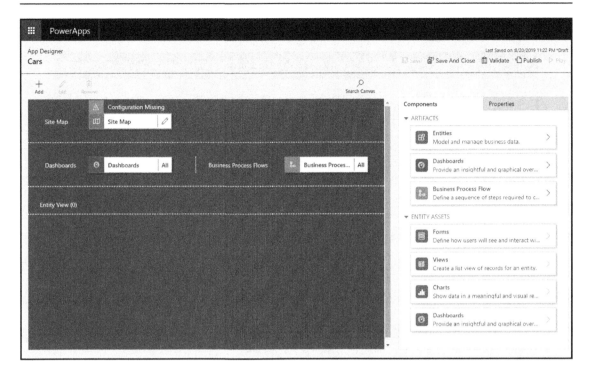

6. When the site map designer loads, click on the **New Area** header and rename
   it Car Details:

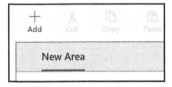

7. Click on **New Group** below **Car Details** and change the title to Cars.
   It should look like this before you make the change:

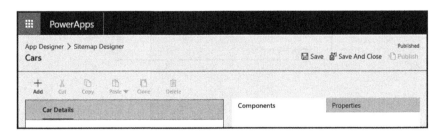

It should look like this after you make the change:

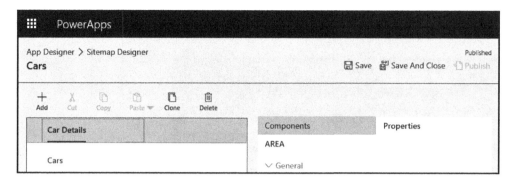

8. Click on the **+ Add** button, select **SUB AREA**, and apply the following configuration:

- **Type**: Entity
- **Entity**: Car Manufacturer

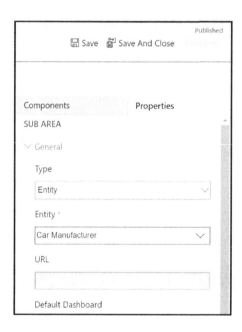

9. Repeat *step 7* for the `Model` and `Variant` entities:

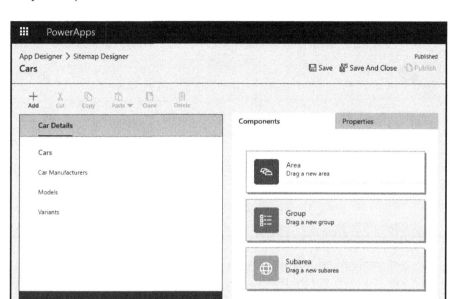

10. Click **Save And Close**. Note that all three entities now appear in the entity View within the app designer.
11. Save your app by clicking **Save**.
12. Publish your app by clicking **Publish**.
13. View your app by clicking **Play**.

We now have the basic model-driven app up and running, so we can now start to interact with our data by creating, editing, and deleting records:

1. Navigate to the manufacturer and select **+ New**. Add the `Ford` manufacturer:

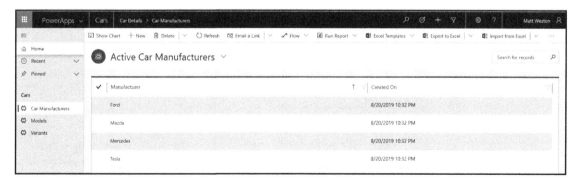

2. Once you have created it, click on **Ford** from the data View:

3. Since we create relationships within our entities, we have a **Related** tab that allows us to enter related models into the model entity. Click on the **Related** tab and select **Models** from the context menu that opens:

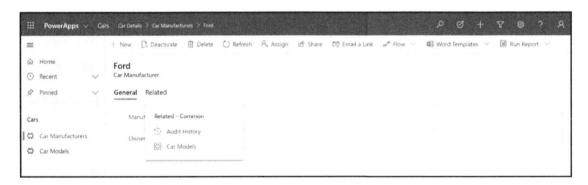

4. Click **+ Add** to add a new model and enter `Fiesta` as the model:

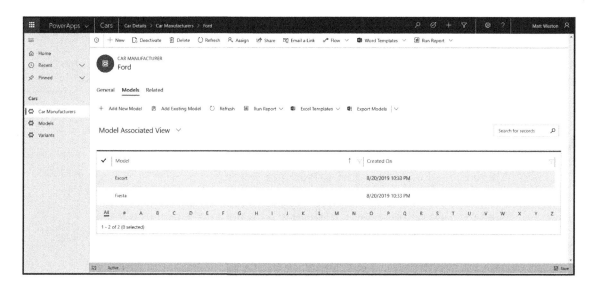

You are now starting to see the behavior of the app being driven by the behaviors created within the entities, and you will see the same behavior with the variants when clicking through the model.

We now have an operational model-driven app that we can use as a foundation for testing the other aspects of model-driven apps.

Summary

Throughout this chapter, we have looked at what it means to build a model-driven app. This helps us to understand the importance of getting the data structure right before we really start to build a working app.

The data that we are working with is stored in entities, and those entities have a number of areas that we can use to prebuild components ready for use within our apps. These components are Views, Forms, Charts, and Dashboards. Views allow us to create predefined queries against the list data, Forms allow us to create the input and edit forms for the data, and Charts on Dashboards allow us to provide defined outputs that can be used in a model-driven app—for example, by providing forms to allow the creation of users in the users' entity.

Before you commit yourself to building a model-driven app, you should remember that the only data source that it can connect to is the CDS. As a developer, you should also be aware that you don't have the same freedom of design as you do with canvas apps as you are very much driven by the components that you have built within the entity.

The final aspect of PowerApps that we are going to look at in the next chapter is related to the management of PowerApps through the use of environments.

Questions

1. Where is the data for a model-driven app stored?
2. What are the four key components created within a model-driven app?
3. What can I do within a View to display a predefined subset of data?
4. What is the recommended three-step process for creating a model-driven app?
5. What control allows users to interact with data?

5
Section 5: Governing PowerApps

In this final section, we will look at the administrative side of PowerApps and how we can add levels of governance. We will focus on key areas such as the creation and use of environments as well as how you can apply some protection to your business data through the use of data loss policies.

This section includes the following chapter:

- Chapter 17, *Exploring Environments within Our Tenancy*

Exploring Environments within Our Tenancy **17**

In the previous chapters, we concentrated on the *creation* element of PowerApps, creating both canvas and model-driven apps. This chapter will help you understand what lies beneath these apps and how we can use environments to provide additional controls and protection for your organization.

When you start to grow your use of the Power Platform within your organization, it is important to consider the use of environments to help segregate your apps and apply different user roles to them. It is vital that you understand when to use them, how to use them, and what their benefits are.

Environments, in the context of PowerApps, have two key functions. The first is to allow separate apps into different permission groups—for example, the finance department may have an environment where only finance users are allowed to use the apps. Secondly, environments can be used to provide additional safeguards for your data using **data loss prevention (DLP)**.

In this chapter, we will look at the following topics:

- Introducing environments
- Viewing and creating environments
- Applying security to an environment
- Introducing DLP

By the end of this chapter, you will have a better understanding of how to create and secure environments for different users, and you will also be able to configure DLP policies to determine how various connectors within your environment can be used.

Technical requirements

The techniques and areas covered in this chapter require a PowerApps per-user plan assigned to you, to be used within your environment.

Introducing environments

In its most simple form, an environment is an area that contains and allows you to share business data, apps, and flows. They fulfill an important role in the security and separation of apps, especially where apps may have different intended audiences.

By default, every tenancy will have one environment created that is the default environment, where all apps and flows are created.

 A tenancy is the organizational instance of Office 365 that serves all of the various applications.

All users who are licensed to use PowerApps and flows automatically get maker access to this environment, which means that they can immediately start building, creating, and sharing connections. However, there are circumstances where you should consider creating additional environments, such as when you want to control who has permissions to create new apps.

 The creation of new environments requires you to have a per-user license assigned.

As we already have an environment created, let's look at how we can view it.

Viewing your environments

By default, every tenancy has one environment that everyone in the organization can create resources in and that allows all connectors. So, let's first of all look at how we find the list of environments.

When I navigate to the PowerApps **Admin center**, I have an **Environments** navigation option on the left-hand menu. This will allow us to see and search for any environments that are associated with our tenancy. It also provides some key information about the type, such as the name, the type of environment, who it was created by and when, and which region is hosting the service. The following screenshot shows the **Environments** window:

Figure 17.1: A list of environments within a tenancy

You can click on each of these environments to drill through to see more information, such as whether you can see the security that has been set on that environment and what resources have been created within it.

If we are an organization that is starting to work more with PowerApps, then we should consider building more environments.

Creating environments

Creating additional environments allows you to create new containers to hold all of your logic. However, you first need to have the relevant licensing in place. As stated in the last section, you will require a per-user license assigned to create the new environment.

There are two types of environment that you can create:

- **Trial**: These environments last for 30 days and allow you to access the full feature set of connectors available in PowerApps, including access to the CDS. They can be converted to production by an administrator (if necessary).
- **Production**: These environments are bound by the rules of your licensing—that is, if you have PowerApps for Office 365, then you will be limited by which connectors you can access from that plan.

You can only have one trial environment per user.

Creating additional environments is a great way of separating development, test, and production apps to ensure that your users are not sharing apps that don't meet your organizational standards. Let's look at the steps that we need to go through to create an environment:

1. To create a new environment, you need to navigate to the PowerApps **Admin center** and click **New environment**, which is located in the top-right corner of the screen.
2. A dialog will ask you to provide some basic information that will allow you to set up your environment:

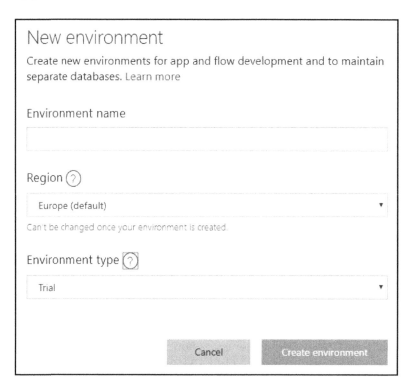

Figure 17.2: The new environment dialogue box

- **Environment name**: This is the display name that is given to your environment and will be visible in the environment selector on the Office 365 suite bar. You are limited to 65 characters within this field, so a concise name should always be given to your environments.
- **Region**: This is the regional location that your database and any resources will be served from. It should be noted that not all sub regional data centers are currently available; however, the regional data centers, such as Europe, Asia, and the United States are available.
- **Environment type**: This is the type of environment that you wish to create, and is bound by your licensing and the types of environment that you already have provisioned.

Ensure that you are selecting the correct region for your environment as it cannot be changed once it has been created.

At the point of creating your new environment, you will be asked if you want to create the database that serves the CDS, which we discussed in `Chapter 14`, *Using Azure with PowerApps*. You can either create it now or skip this step and create it later.

Quite commonly, environments are used to separate development, test, and production tiers, with tighter controls applied to the production environment compared with the development environment. Once we have an environment created, we can assign permissions to allow specific users to have more control over one environment than they do over others, thereby improving the overall security.

Setting security on the environment

Setting security on your environment involves two very different processes, depending on whether you opted to create the database or not.

Working with security with no database

When we are working with an environment that isn't using a database, the security model is extremely simple. Users are categorized as either **Environment Admins** or **Environment Makers**.

Environment Admins have the ability to perform all actions across the environment, including the creation of DLP policies, which we will look at in the *Introducing Data Loss Prevention* section. A user can be an Environment Admin without being a Global Admin, and so they will only get admin access to their specific environments.

Environment Makers are users who can create new resources—that is, Apps and Flows—within the environment and are listed as Environment Admins.

Figure 17.3: Setting permissions on an environment

To set permissions on an environment without a database, perform the following steps:

1. First of all, navigate to the PowerApps **Admin center** and select the environment that you would like set permissions on.
2. Select the **Security** tab to display the roles that are available to you—namely **Environment Admin** and **Environment Maker**.
3. In the **Enter names** box, you can start to type the name of a user within your tenancy. After you have typed approximately three characters, the picker will appear, allowing you to pick the user or group that you want to give permissions to, as shown in the following screenshot:

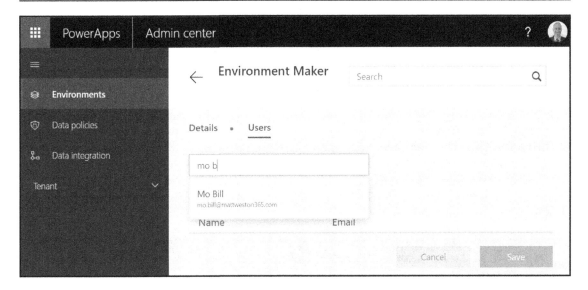

4. Once you have added the relevant users, you can click **Save**. After a short period, you will see a message across the top of the screen informing you that you have successfully saved your permissions:

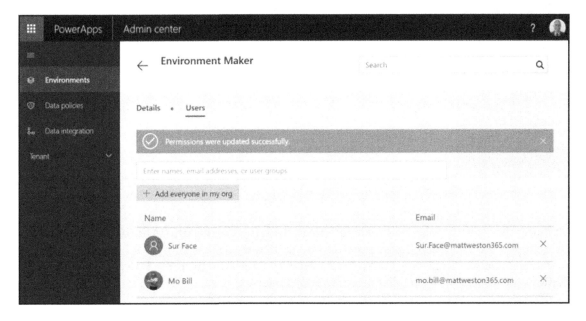

Now that we have looked at setting security without a database, we should look at how to do this with an environment that contains a database.

Working with security within a database

When we have a database within an environment, the permissions are managed through Dynamics 365 rather than by remaining in the PowerApps **Admin center**. Being driven by Dynamics, there are additional levels of security that you could assign, giving you greater granularity and control.

To assign security roles, we need to select the desired environment and then select the **Security** tab. This will then present us with a two-step process to allow us to add users and assign them a role. *Step 1* asks you to define who the user is, and this is done by entering the user's email address. Once the user has been added (which can take a few minutes), you can then assign them a security role by clicking on the **Assign security roles** button, as shown in the following screenshot:

Figure 17.4: The security screen in PowerApps when there is a database

Opening the security roles will take you away from the PowerApps **Admin center** and will present you with a screen that is provided by Dynamics 365, as shown in *Figure 17.5: The user screen provided by Dynamics*. Any users that you added within the PowerApps **Admin center** will automatically be displayed as active users:

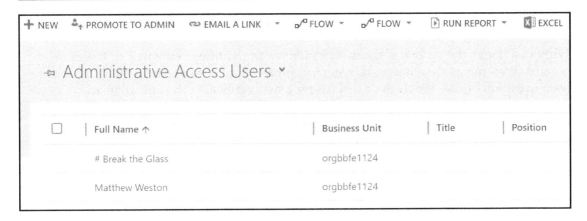

Figure 17.5: The user screen provided by Dynamics

From here, you can promote users to administrators or assign specific roles, such as Environment Maker, CDS User, or Delegate, which will specify what the assigned users can do. The roles can be seen in *Figure 17.6: Assigning roles to a user*, which shows that a single user can be assigned multiple roles.

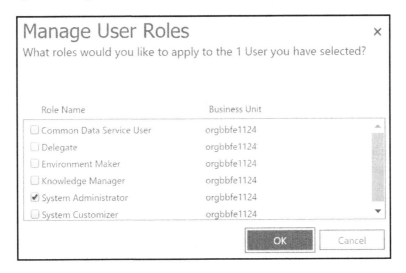

Figure 17.6: Assigning roles to a user

Once you have defined what users can do within a given environment, you should then consider what additional security measures you are going to apply to help you protect your data.

Introducing data loss prevention

Without a doubt, data is one of the most valuable commodities in the world. Therefore, organizations must take all necessary steps to protect their data to ensure that it cannot be used to exploit or damage them or their users. Data is critical to the operation and, therefore, the success of an organization. Because of this, the PowerApps **Admin center** gives you the ability to employ protective measures.

Employing protective measures means that we define which connectors may access and share your organization's data. The policies we define relate to both PowerApps and Flow and define which connectors can be used together. For example, we can stop the use of SharePoint data being used for external connectors, such as Twitter. It also ensures that business data is being handled in a consistent manner across the whole organization.

 All Microsoft DLP tools should be considered useful tools for security. Using them won't guarantee that you will never have a breach.

While we talk about DLP, the capabilities of DLP within the Power Platform are far less than that of the wider Office 365 environment. To truly employ DLP and protect your data, you should consider applying DLP policies from the security and compliance center to your data, as well as using data policies within PowerApps to determine the usage of connectors.

Creating data loss prevention policies

Policies are the rules that define what combinations of connectors we can use within an environment. Compared with policy creation in other areas of Office 365, creation is very simple, as you can see from the following steps:

1. Navigate to the PowerApps **Admin center** and select **Data policies** from the left-hand menu, as shown in the following screenshot:

Figure 17.7: DLP screen

2. To create a new policy, simply click on the **New policy** button in the top-right corner of the screen. You will then have the option to select which environments your policy is going to belong to, as shown in *Figure 17.8: Selecting the environment setting for the DLP policy*. As a tenant administrator, you can choose to apply your policy to all environments. If you're an Environment Admin, then you can select which environments to apply your policy to:

Figure 17.8: Selecting the environment setting for the DLP Policy

3. The next step is to define which groups of connectors can be used together by categorizing them as **Business data only** and **No business data allowed**, as shown in *Figure 17.9: SharePoint and OneDrive for Business assigned as Business data only*:

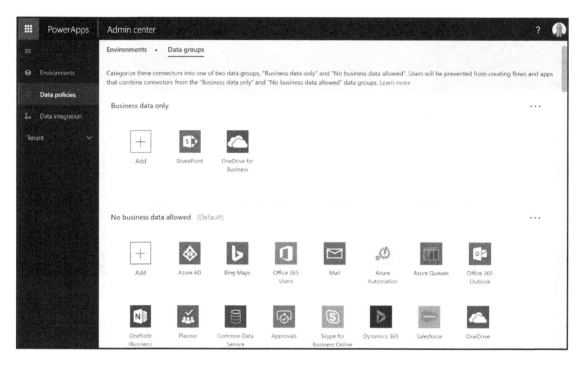

Figure 17.9: SharePoint and OneDrive for Business assigned as Business data only

4. By clicking on the **Add** button in either bucket, you can select which category a connector is assigned to. If the connectors are in the same bucket, then they will be able to communicate with each other, so I can separate all my public connectors from the ones that should be purely internal.

 When you add your connector to one group, it will automatically be removed from the other.

Once I have defined whether my connectors are business data or not, I can then save my policy so that it appears in my policy list, as shown in the following screenshot:

Figure 17.10: The DLP screen updated with policies

 Whenever you set a DLP policy, you should communicate with your users to explain the impact of it.

Once saved, the data policy becomes active in the relevant environment, and so applies to all users who are using Apps and Flows. If anyone then tries to create an App or a Flow that mixes the connectors, you will see an error message displayed that informs you that your actions contradict the DLP policy for that environment. In *Figure 17.11: DLP error message*, you will see the error that occurred when connections were made to SharePoint (business data) and to Twitter (nonbusiness data):

Figure 17.11: DLP error message

Once your DLP policies have been created, they should then be reviewed on a regular basis to ensure that any new connectors that are added to PowerApps are correctly classified as either business data or nonbusiness data.

Lab 16

Within this lab, we are going to create a new environment in the PowerApps **Admin center**. You don't need to have completed any previous lab; this is purely administrative in nature.

 Please ensure that you have administrator rights in order to follow these steps.

Activity 1: Creating an environment

The first thing we are going to do is create an environment by going through the following steps:

1. Log into the Office 365 portal (`portal.office.com`).
2. In the **Apps** list, select **Admin**:

3. In the menu on the left side of the screen, select **All admin centers** (if this is not visible, select **Show All**):

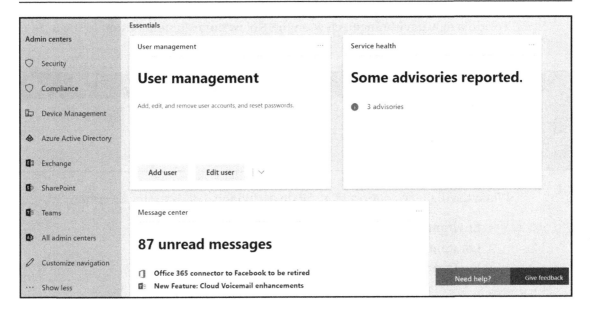

4. When the list of admin centers appears, select **PowerApps**:

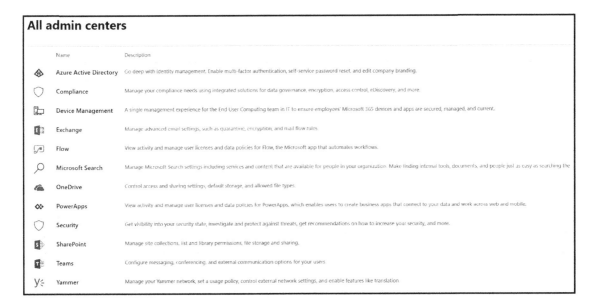

5. To add a new environment, click on the **+ New environment** button in the top-right corner:

6. When the dialog box appears, provide it with the details for the environment:

- **Environment name**: For example, `Matt's Environment`.
- **Location**: Select your regional data center.
- **Environment type**: Select **Trial**.

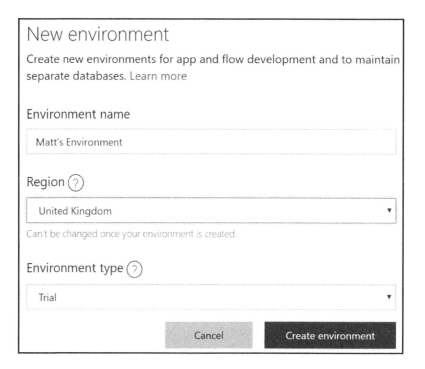

7. Click **Create environment**.

8. When prompted to create a database, which will appear once you have created the environment, click **Skip**:

9. You will then be returned to your environment list, and you will be able to see your newly created environment in the list.

10. Now that you have created an environment, click on it to view the settings. Note the location of the **Convert** button, the option to create a database, and the **Security** tab where we will now assign roles to users:

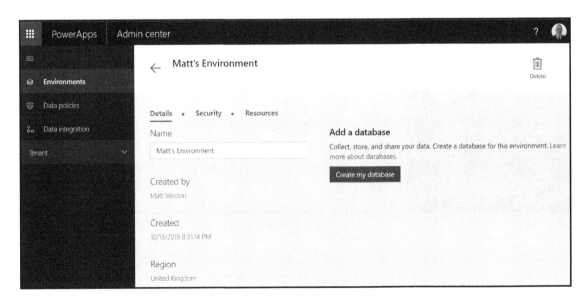

11. Click on the **Security** tab. Note that the two levels of user are available: **Environment Admin** and **Environment Maker**:

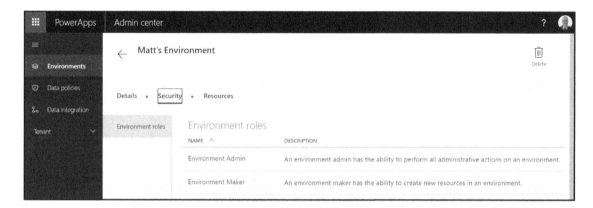

12. **Environment Admin** will contain you, as the person who created the **Environment Admin**, so let's add an Environment Maker by clicking on the **Environment Maker** link. Note that, at the moment, this is empty:

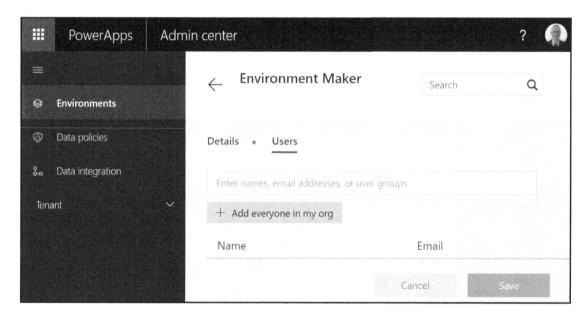

13. Start typing the name of another user into the names, email addresses, and user groups box, and click on them once they have been found. They will then appear in the users list:

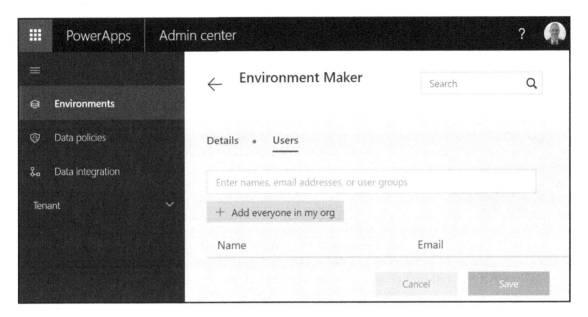

14. This user will now be able to create resources within this new environment and will see it listed in their environment list:

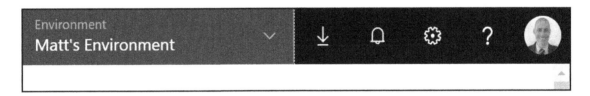

Now that we have created a new environment, we want to put some controls around what the users of that environment can do in order to protect our data. We will now add a DLP policy to it.

Activity 2: Setting a DLP policy

In this activity, we will apply a basic DLP policy to our new environment so that you can see the effects on the Apps created. Let's set this up by going through the following steps:

1. Navigate to the PowerApps **Admin center**, as we did in *Activity 1: Creating an environment*.
2. Select **Data policies** from the left-hand menu.
3. To create a new policy, click the **+ New policy** button in the top-right corner of the screen:

4. The first configuration item is the environment that we are going to apply the policy to. Select **Apply to ONLY selected environments** and choose the environment that was created in *Activity 1: Creating an environment*:

5. Click **Continue** to move on to the next configuration screen.

6. On the **Data groups** screen, we will declare our **Business data only** as **SharePoint** and **OneDrive for Business**. Click **Add** beneath the **Business data only** header:

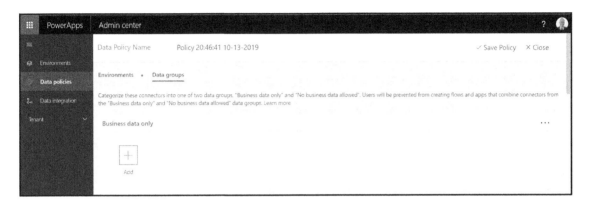

7. When the **Add connectors** dialog appears, use the search box to search for the **SharePoint** connector:

8. Select the connector, and then search for **OneDrive for Business**. Select the connector, and then click **Add connectors**:

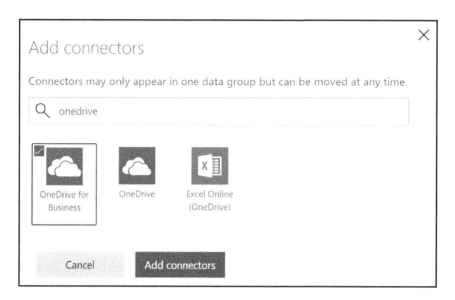

9. The connectors will now be listed under business data.

Allow up to 24 hours for the policy to apply, but then test it by creating an app that first of all uses a SharePoint connector and then add a connector to a nonbusiness data source. You should see an error message informing you that you are contradicting a data loss policy.

Summary

In this chapter, we have looked at environments, with a key focus on what environments are and how they are created, as well as how they can be used to apply security and DLP policies. Environments are a key piece of technology, particularly in organizations that need to compartmentalize Apps and Flows or limit sharing. They also serve as a good way of being able to separate development, test, and production Apps and Flows, allowing only specific users to create assets in each environment, depending on their role.

We looked at the two key types of environment that can be created from within the PowerApps **Admin center**—developer and production. Developer environments last for 30 days and give access to the full range of functionality available to PowerApps, with each user being able to create their own developer environment. The developer environments are the perfect temporary area to allow users to trial functionality within PowerApps without any risk to live apps. Production environments will remain within your tenancy until deleted and are subject to any limitations of the PowerApps licenses. Environments are a useful way of being able to provide development, test, and live tiers without having to resort to creating separate tenancies.

We saw how environments allow us to configure DLP policies that govern which connectors can be used together. There are two categories: business data and nonbusiness data. If a connector appears in one category, then the actions cannot be used alongside a connector in the other category—for example, you may not use SharePoint and Twitter connectors together.

All of these elements—environments, security, and DLP—are all designed to help you provide as much protection for your environment as possible. You can—and it is recommended that you should—consider all of these within any governance plans that you have in place for Office 365.

Questions

1. How many environments do you have created within your tenancy by default?
2. What are the types of environment that can be created?
3. What needs to be done to an environment for you to be able to use the CDS?
4. How long does a developer environment last for?
5. What are the two categories of data when creating a DLP?

Assessments

Chapter 1

1. What are the two types of app that can be built?
   Canvas apps and model-driven apps
2. What is the name of the underlying database?
   Common data service (CDS)
3. What is used to bridge PowerApps and Flows to other systems?
   Connectors
4. What technology can be used to access on-premise data sources?
   Data gateway
5. Which type of app allows you full control over the layout of your components?
   Canvas app
6. What can be used to control the potential values of a data field?
   Option sets
7. Who do I need to share with to make my app an "org app"?
   Everyone
8. If I want to use the data gateway, which license do I need to buy?
   A per-app or per-user plan
9. Which submenu would I use to insert a pen input control?
   Insert
10. What are the two views that I can use in the screens list?
    Tree and thumbnail
11. Which menu would I select to create a connection to a Flow?
    Actions menu
12. Where would I go to check my data sources?
    View menu
13. What would I use to create conditional logic for a control?
    Rules

Chapter 2

1. What are the two types of canvas that can be created within PowerApps?
   Mobile and tablet
2. Which canvas will allow you to define custom dimensions?
   Tablet app
3. Which app setting would you go to in order to change the icon?
   App name + icon
4. Which set of features should you test on a regular basis to ensure your app will continue to work?
   Preview features
5. Which option can I use to set my app to rotate along with the device?
   Mobile app
6. What is the largest number of items I can return from a nondelegable query?
   2,000

Chapter 3

1. Which user experience does SharePoint need to use in order to allow autogeneration of an app?
   The modern experience
2. Which canvas is the app generated on?
   Phone canvas
3. What do I need to do in order to allow users to use my new form?
   Publish my app
4. What is the key addition to the screen picker on the left-hand side of the screen?
   SharePointIntegration
5. True or false: Managed metadata fields are fully supported by PowerApps.
   False
6. If I wanted to change the form that is used by SharePoint for editing, where would I go?
   List Settings followed by Form Settings

Chapter 4

1. What information do I need to provide to the SharePoint web part in order to render the PowerApp?
App URL or App ID

2. How is an app identified as being the current version that users are actively using?
It has Live tagged against it in the version list

3. Can I add a sample app to a Microsoft Teams channel?
Yes

4. Is the PowerApps app available for Android?
Yes

5. What would I do to create the illusion of having the app installed locally on the device?
Pin it to Home

6. True or false: A PowerApp can be installed on a Classic SharePoint page.
False, it can only be installed on a modern page

7. If I have three versions of an app—1.0, 2.0, 3.0 (live)—then what happens if I restore version 2.0?
It will become version 4.0

Chapter 5

1. Which control allows you to capture either a number or a string of text?
Text input

2. What is the maximum value for the Rating control?
200

3. Why would you use a drop-down control over a list control?
A drop-down control uses much less real estate on the screen

4. What is the main difference between a combo box and a dropdown?
A dropdown has a scrolling list of values, whereas a combo box allows you to search

5. What do I use to build up visual effects within my PowerApp?
Icons and shapes

6. What two values can a checkbox take?
   True or False
7. Which control could I use to capture a signature from a user?
   Pen input

Chapter 6

1. In the date format dd mm yy, what does mm return?
   The month
2. What does the logical operator && mean?
   And
3. If I had multiple outcomes from a single condition, what would be the best function to use?
   Switch
4. What would I use to validate a string against a known pattern?
   Regular expressions
5. Cos, sin, and tan are examples of what type of function?
   Trigonometry
6. What would precede any comment that I am going to put into my formula?
   Two forward slashes (//)
7. What are the two results that can be returned from an IF statement?
   True or False
8. What type of variable would I use if it was only going to be used on one screen or manually passed to another?
   Contextual

Chapter 7

1. What two formulas available within PowerApps can I use to populate a collection with data?
   `Collect()` **and** `ClearCollect()`
2. Which control provides the quickest method of creating an edit form for an item of data?
   Form control

3. Which control allows me to define a flexible repeating design for each record or data?
   Gallery control

4. Which formula would I use to update a record in a data source or collection?
   `Patch()`

5. Which formula would you use to submit a form control back to the data source?
   `SubmitForm()`

Chapter 8

1. There are two types of built-in connector. What are they?
   Standard and Premium

2. True or false: Custom connectors can be created from a URL.
   True

3. True or false: I can use an Excel Workbook stored on a filesystem as a data source.
   True

4. True or false: Azure AD can be used as an authentication method when defining a custom connector.
   True

5. What is the name of the free tool that can be used to test an API?
   Postman

Chapter 9

1. Why should a signal be captured rather than used directly in a formula?
   So that it doesn't impact the battery of the device

2. What three pieces of data will the location formula retrieve?
   Latitude, longitude, altitude

3. How is direction expressed when using Compass?
   Degrees

4. What function can I use to disable GPS?
   `Disable(Location)`

5. Why would you not leave location services on permanently?
   Excessive battery drain and poor performance

Chapter 10

1. True or false: I can upload a `.jfif` image into my PowerApp.
   False
2. Which control would I use to be able to upload an image into an app?
   Add picture control
3. If I wanted to use the `Camera1.Photo` formula, which control would I interact with?
   Camera control
4. If I wanted to use another control to interact with the camera, which camera property should I change?
   Stream rate
5. What format is a captured image stored in?
   Base64 string
6. True or false: Text within a QR code can be retrieved and used within an app.
   True

Chapter 11

1. What is the name of the global store of users within Office 365?
   Azure Active Directory
2. True or false: The security of the data is maintained purely through the PowerApp.
   False
3. True or false: When using SharePoint as a data source, the user needs to have full control rights to the underlying SharePoint site.
   False. You only need to grant the permission required for the interaction that is contributed to the list rather than full control
4. Access lists can be added to the app and stored in what type of data storage?
   Collections

Chapter 12

1. What function would I use to check whether an app is connected to the internet?
   `Connection.Connected`
2. True or false: My PowerApp can detect whether the app is using a metered connection.
   True
3. Which function is used to save the data from PowerApps to the local device?
   `SaveData`
4. Which function is used to load the data from the local device?
   `LoadData`
5. True or false: A data file from one PowerApp can be used in another on the same device.
   False
6. True or false: Devices have an unlimited amount of space available to them to store local data.
   False

Chapter 13

1. Microsoft Power Automate is built on another Microsoft technology. What is it?
   Azure Logic Apps
2. What is the intended user audience for Microsoft Power Automate?
   Business users
3. There are three types of trigger. What are they?
   Manual, automated, scheduled
4. What trigger would I use to request data from PowerApps?
   PowerApps trigger
5. What action would I use to return data from Power Automate to PowerApps?
   Respond to PowerApps
6. True or false: Power Automate can integrate with third-party data sources, not just Microsoft.
   True

Chapter 14

1. What two Azure services, mentioned in this chapter, can we use to host custom code?
   Azure Automation and Azure Functions
2. What URL do you use to access Microsoft Azure?
   `portal.azure.com`
3. What native connector is available to PowerApps to allow us to interact with Azure Functions?
   Azure Queues
4. Which service provides you with an amount of free processing time to run scripts?
   Azure Automation
5. If I wanted to write functionality using Node.js, what service would I use?
   Azure Functions

Chapter 15

1. What types of app can use the common data service as a data source?
   Canvas apps and model-driven apps
2. What do we need to create before being able to use the common data service?
   A database
3. What are the primary data structures within the common data service called?
   Entities
4. What types of relationship can be created between entities?
   One-to-one, one-to-many, many-to-one
5. True or false: A model-driven app can be created with SharePoint as a data source?
   False

Chapter 16

1. Where is data for a model-driven app stored?
   Common data service
2. What are the four key components created within a model-driven app?
   Forms, Views, Dashboards, and Charts
3. What can I do within a View to display a predefined subset of data?
   Add a filter
4. What is the recommended three-step process for creating a model-driven app?
   Model your data, define the business process, create the app
5. What control allows users to interact with the data?
   Forms

Chapter 17

1. How many environments do you have created within your tenancy by default?
   One
2. What are the types of environment that can be created?
   Production and developer
3. What needs to be done to an environment to be able to use the common data service?
   A database needs to be created
4. How long does a developer environment last for?
   30 days
5. What are the two categories of data when creating a data loss prevention policy?
   Business data and nonbusiness data

Other Books You May Enjoy

If you enjoyed this book, you may be interested in these other books by Packt:

Microsoft Dynamics 365 Business Central Cookbook
Michael Glue

ISBN: 978-1-78995-854-6

- Build and deploy Business Central applications
- Use the cloud or local sandbox for application development
- Customize and extend your base Business Central application
- Create external applications that connect to Business Central
- Create automated tests and debug your applications
- Connect to external web services from Business Central

Programming Microsoft Dynamics 365 Business Central - Sixth Edition
Mark Brummel, David Studebaker, Et al

ISBN: 978-1-78913-779-8

- Programming using the AL language in the Visual Studio Code development environment
- Explore functional design and development using AL
- How to build interactive pages and learn how to extract data for users
- How to use best practices to design and develop modifications for new functionality integrated with the standard Business Central software
- Become familiar with deploying the broad range of components available in a Business Central system
- Create robust, viable systems to address specific business requirements

Leave a review - let other readers know what you think

Please share your thoughts on this book with others by leaving a review on the site that you bought it from. If you purchased the book from Amazon, please leave us an honest review on this book's Amazon page. This is vital so that other potential readers can see and use your unbiased opinion to make purchasing decisions, we can understand what our customers think about our products, and our authors can see your feedback on the title that they have worked with Packt to create. It will only take a few minutes of your time, but is valuable to other potential customers, our authors, and Packt. Thank you!

Index

Made in the USA
Columbia, SC
14 May 2021